"Tibbs combines her considerable professional engagement with Western Christian thought and theology with her personal background and experience to present a fresh approach to Orthodox Christianity. Tibbs does not limit herself to simply explaining differences in doctrine and practice between Orthodoxy, Catholicism, and Protestantism. She provides effective examples and real-life stories that illustrate how Orthodoxy has maintained an entirely distinct character and history, which cannot be understood within the framework of the typical Catholic-Protestant dichotomy and debates. She presents Orthodoxy and its most important claim—of a direct and unbroken continuity with the ancient, historical Church—not as a relic of the past but as a vibrant faith community with its own beliefs, practices, mode of thought, and way of life."

—**Eugenia Scarvelis Constantinou**, Franciscan School of Theology, University of San Diego

"Because this book was 'born' in classes attended mainly by evangelical Protestant theological students at Fuller Theological Seminary, Tibbs's *A Basic Guide to Eastern Orthodox Theology* wonderfully shifts from being an introduction to and apologetic for Eastern Orthodoxy to being a comparative study in dialogue with Western Christianity. Her engaging text reveals a fluency with both Orthodox theological sources—the extensive footnotes will lead readers deeper into many topics—and Protestant and Roman Catholic sources."

—**Anton C. Vrame**, Holy Cross Greek Orthodox School of Theology

"Tibbs's years of teaching evangelical students have enabled her to write a basic but effective introduction to the beliefs and practices of the Eastern Orthodox Church and its relationship with the Protestant and Catholic traditions."

—**Bradley Nassif**, North Park University

A BASIC GUIDE
to Eastern Orthodox
THEOLOGY

A BASIC GUIDE
to Eastern Orthodox
THEOLOGY

Introducing Beliefs and Practices

EVE TIBBS

Foreword by
His All Holiness
Ecumenical Patriarch Bartholomew

Baker Academic
a division of Baker Publishing Group
Grand Rapids, Michigan

Published by Baker Academic
a division of Baker Publishing Group
PO Box 6287, Grand Rapids, MI 49516-6287
www.bakeracademic.com

Printed in the United States of America

Library of Congress Cataloging-in-Publication Data
Names: Tibbs, Eve, 1955– author.
Title: A basic guide to Eastern Orthodox theology : introducing beliefs and practices / Eve Tibbs.
Description: Grand Rapids, Michigan : Baker Academic, a division of Baker Publishing Group, [2021] | Includes bibliographical references and index.
Identifiers: LCCN 2020053973 (print) | LCCN 2020053974 (ebook) | ISBN 9781540962805 (paperback) | ISBN 9781540964342 (casebound) | ISBN 9781493430918 (ebook)
Subjects: LCSH: Orthodox Eastern Church—Doctrines. | Orthodox Eastern Church—Customs and practices.
Classification: LCC BX320.3 .T53 2021 (print) | LCC BX320.3 (ebook) | DDC 230.07/319—dc23
LC record available at https://lccn.loc.gov/2020053973
LC ebook record available at https://lccn.loc.gov/2020053974

24 25 26 27   7 6 5

For Steve, with love

Contents

Foreword by His All Holiness Ecumenical Patriarch Bartholomew   xiii

Preface   xv
The Origins of This Book   xv
The Intended Audience for This Book   xvi
How This Book Should Be Read   xvi

Acknowledgments   xvii

Introduction   1
Assumptions and Terminology   2
The Approach   3
Change?   4

1. The Orthodox Christian Worldview   7
"Returning" to the Unknown Ancient Church?   7
The Orthodox Church in the Christian World   9
East Is East and West Is West   13
The Primacy of Worship   17
Come and See!   20
"Doing Theology" in Orthodox Christianity   22

2. The Church   29
Joined Together in the Church   29
What Is the Church? Where Is the Church?   30
The Orthodox Church Today   34
What Is "This Rock"?   35
One, Holy, Catholic, and Apostolic   37

3. Communion and Revelation   41

What Holds the Orthodox Church Together?   41

Communion and Conciliarity   42

Holy Tradition   46

The *Eikōn*   51

Holy Scripture   52

Holy Icons   57

4. Ministry and Leadership   61

The Royal Vocation of All People   62

First among Equals   65

Three Orders of Clergy   67

Ordination of Women   69

Apostolic Succession   71

5. Christology   77

The Word of God Is a Person   77

Who Is Jesus?   78

Early Challenges to Christology   80

The Rule of Truth   83

Error and Heresy   85

Christology and the Ecumenical Councils   88

Singing Theology   96

6. Who Are We? What Are We to Do?   99

Created for Communion   99

Tragedy in the Garden   103

Being Saved   112

Theosis   113

All Creation Rejoices   115

Humanity, We Have a Problem   117

The Cross and Resurrection   120

7. The Holy Trinity   125

The Revealed Trinity   127

Trinitarian *Taxis*   129

The Cappadocian "Settlement": One Essence and Three
Persons   130

The Holy Spirit   132

The Church as an Icon of the Trinity   137

8. Orthodox Worship   141
Liturgy   141
An Earthly Heaven   146
Relevant and Ancient   150
The Holy Mysteries   152

Epilogue   165

Appendix: Excerpts from Selected Apostolic and Patristic Writings   167
Excerpts from the *Epistle of St. Ignatius to the Philadelphians*   167
Excerpts from the *Epistle of St. Ignatius to the Smyrnaeans*   168
Excerpts from *Against Heresies* 3.3 by St. Irenaeus, Bishop of Lyons   170
Full Text of *The Didache: The Lord's Teaching through the Twelve Apostles to the Nations*   171

Glossary of Orthodox Terms   179

Index   191

Foreword

Grace and peace from God to the esteemed readership of this publication, beloved brethren and children in the Christ Jesus, our Lord.

"Jesus Christ is the same yesterday, today, and forever."
(Hebrews 13:8)

As He is the same yesterday, today, and forever, so too is His Holy Body, the One, Holy, Catholic, and Apostolic Church. Often in bumper stickers displayed by some Orthodox Christians in the United States appears the phrase, "The Orthodox Church: Founded in 33 A.D." This claim may appear oversimplistic and hyperbolic, but it still reflects the reality that those local churches that today call themselves "Orthodox" have a strong awareness about their close ties and their uninterrupted continuity with the origins and beginnings of Christianity in the ancient Eastern Christian centers in Middle East, Asia, and Northern Africa.

However, despite the fact that the Orthodox Christian Faith is today practiced in every corner of the world, with more than 250 million adherents worldwide, its rich history, beliefs, practices, and spirituality remain largely unfamiliar to many in the West. Even in regions where Orthodox Christians are relatively numerous, Orthodox Christianity, which has played an integral role in the development of civilization as we know it today, still is perceived as an exotic and picturesque remnant from an alien past.

If the Orthodox Church were approached only from the perspective of its history and institutions, it could indeed appear foreign and fragmented to an outsider. For this reason, we take great pleasure in recommending this publication, titled *A Basic Guide to Eastern Orthodox Theology: Introducing Beliefs and Practices*, because it does not follow the abovementioned approach, but, instead, its perception is molded by the author's experience of the Orthodox sacramental life, its life of worship. The very word "orthodoxy" means both holding the right beliefs and also right worship and practice, the proper way of giving glory (δόξα) to God, the communication of the basic truths of the Christian faith in ways that go beyond mere words and are readily accessible to everyone.

In congratulating the author of this textbook, Dr. Paraskevè (Eve) Tibbs, we warmly encourage the readers not only to come to a deeper understanding of the Orthodox Christian Faith, but to acquire a greater appreciation of the role which Eastern Christianity has played, and continues to play, in the West. May our High Priest Jesus Christ bless the readers, and provide them with a newfound awareness of Orthodox theology that will help them to discover—or rediscover—its *living* tradition.

At the Ecumenical Patriarchate, Winter 2021
Your fervent supplicant before God,

✠ **Bartholomew**
*Archbishop of Constantinople-New Rome
and Ecumenical Patriarch*

Preface

The Origins of This Book

This book developed out of the course entitled Introduction to Eastern Orthodox Theology, which I developed at Fuller Theological Seminary in Pasadena,
California. Most students who enroll in this course are evangelical Protestants
with great diversity in their personal ecclesial traditions. Typically, very few
have any previous knowledge about the Orthodox Church, so my approach
is to begin generally with the Orthodox Church in history and in the contemporary Christian world before identifying the most obvious distinguishing
features of its theology. This is the approach I have also taken in this book.
After broadly situating Orthodox Christianity within the thought-world of
the Apostles and global Christianity, I introduce other characteristic themes
and attributes of Eastern Orthodoxy, such as the importance of the Church
and of worship, of conciliarity, and the essential nature of communion. I
subsequently introduce some of the central dogmas of the Faith, especially
regarding Christ and the Trinity. Finally, there is an intentional transition from
doctrine to the practice of the Faith in chapter 8, with an introduction to the
liturgical worship of the Orthodox Church and a brief discussion about its
sacramental life.

My experience from having taught systematic theology in an evangelical
seminary for many years has also made me aware of a perception that Eastern
Orthodoxy is something like an exotic sect of Roman Catholicism, due to
obvious commonalities such as saints, priests, sacraments, and a high view
of Mary. Therefore, I also strive to distinguish Eastern Orthodox theology
from Western theology, both Protestant and Latin Roman Catholic theology.
While Eastern Orthodox Christianity has much in common with both of these

Western forms on essential Christian beliefs, there are nonetheless many differences that separate the two in both theology and practice. I have also tried to approach differences descriptively, setting out theological developments in an objective way. While the differences that have developed throughout history are real, I would never want to offend any Christian believer reading this book, and I sincerely hope and pray that I have not done so.

The ecclesial context of my own experience as a Greek Orthodox Christian has also colored the pages of the book. For example, many of the English translations of ancient Christian hymns and prayers that I have included in this book are those most familiar to me as a chanter and choir director in a Greek Orthodox parish.

The Intended Audience for This Book

"Basic" is used in this book's title not because the content is simplistic but because it intentionally remains at the level of summary—a true introductory guide to Eastern Orthodox theology. The intended audience for this book includes Christians who may or may not be Orthodox, and who may or may not have a prior theological background. It is also appropriate for use as a course textbook. Discussion questions at the end of each chapter can be helpful for discussions or writing assignments, and the glossary defines common Orthodox terms that may be unfamiliar to some readers.

How This Book Should Be Read

Both the introduction and chapter 1, "The Orthodox Christian Worldview," should be read by anyone for whom this book is their first venture into Eastern Orthodox theology. Many of the concepts presented early in the book are basic enough for introductory theological studies. The level of theological detail gradually increases in succeeding chapters. For example, the chapters on Christology and the Holy Trinity focus on the technical language used by the Church Fathers to articulate important dogmas of the Christian Faith. Although it is helpful to read the chapters in order, they are nevertheless somewhat self-contained. In many cases I refer back to the chapter where a concept was introduced, or forward to where a concept will be discussed in greater detail.

Acknowledgments

I am profoundly grateful to God and humbled by many blessings, among which is the love of family and friends, the instruction of wise pastors and teachers, and the honor of working on such a project as this. I wish to express my deepest gratitude to His All Holiness the Ecumenical Patriarch Bartholomew, a faithful guardian of the Apostolic Christian Faith, for the great blessing of his authorship of the foreword to this work. I also thank God for the unfailing encouragement of my bishop, His Eminence, Metropolitan Gerasimos (Michaleas), presiding hierarch of the Greek Orthodox Metropolis of San Francisco, a compassionate and visionary hierarch and an ardent champion of Christian education.

It was Father George Stephanides of blessed memory who first encouraged me to begin teaching adult Christian education classes, and I remain appreciative for his guidance and trust. I am especially grateful to my pastor, Father Steven Tsichlis, one of the most knowledgeable Orthodox Christian teachers today, from whom I have learned much. Father Steven encourages lay leaders to develop the diverse and unique gifts of the Holy Spirit, and I would certainly not be writing this book had Father Steven not encouraged me to pursue a graduate education in theology.

I also wish to express my gratitude to Rev. Dr. Veli-Matti Kärkkäinen and Rev. Dr. Anton Vrame for their encouragement at the outset of this project. I am indebted to Robert Hosack at Baker Academic for championing this topic and for his patient guidance along the way. Abundant thanks to Maria Conley and Nicholas Bundra for their eagle-eyed review of the manuscript and for their valuable suggestions, and to Tim West and the many amazing professionals at Baker Academic, whose insights and careful attention to detail have been exceedingly helpful in refining this manuscript and navigating the publishing process.

Of the many blessings of which I am certainly unworthy, I continue to thank God for my wise, kind, and generous husband, Steve; for our daughters: Jennifer, Presvytera Mary, and Andrea; for their husbands: Jason, Father Angelo, and Derick; and for the great gift of being "Yiayia" to James, Jonathan, Andreas, Stephen, Evfemia, Nicholas, Eleni, and Emilia.

Glory to God for all things!

Paraskevè (Eve) Tibbs
July 26, 2020
Feast of the Great Martyr St. Paraskevè of Rome

Introduction

This book is an academic approach to Orthodox Christian theology, and yet—paradoxically—Orthodox Christian theology can never be merely academic. The word "orthodox" (Greek: *orthodoxia*) can be translated both as "proper opinion or belief" and as "proper glory or worship." *Ortho* means "straight" or "upright," and *doxa* can mean either "belief" or "glory." Without minimizing the importance of correct belief, the Orthodox Church focuses more on the second meaning: "proper glory," which more broadly encompasses faithfulness in both worship and belief.

In the Orthodox Christian worldview, as in the early Church, theology (Greek: *theologia*) is not principally an academic endeavor but the contemplation of the experience of God. Although information about God can be studied from a teacher or a book, a relationship with God comes through direct contact in prayer and worship. Nevertheless, since human beings have been created by God with the ability for rational thought, we may assume that our rational abilities, as with every divine gift, may be used to bring us closer to the Creator. This book, therefore, was written to contribute to the task of seeking greater knowledge about God, especially through the **doctrines** and **dogmas** that arose in the first millennium of Christian history and continue to be upheld, preached, and lived out in the Orthodox Church today.[1]

This is not a book about personal spirituality, nor is it a catechism. It will not tell you what you should believe or how you should act, but it will certainly convey a sampling of what most Orthodox Christians believe and have believed over the past two-thousand-plus years. The "Eastern," or Orthodox, Christian view of the created world and our place in it is often very different from the typical "Western" Christian understanding, whether Protestant, Pentecostal, or Roman Catholic. Therefore, I will occasionally situate Orthodox

---

1. Terms defined in the glossary are set in boldface when they first appear in the book.

Christianity in contemporary thought. The comparison or contrast with other views can often amplify the unique characteristics of Eastern Orthodoxy that might otherwise be difficult to convey in a book and in isolation from Orthodoxy's lived context.

Assumptions and Terminology

In any academic textbook in a specialized field of study, terminology is the basic tool of communication. In this book, precision about terminology is even more important since the Eastern Orthodox view of things is often different from that of the Western Christian world, even when the same or similar terms are used. For example, the Orthodox repeatedly confess belief in the "One, Holy, **Catholic**, and Apostolic Church." Those four terms, which scholars often refer to as the "marks" of the Church, had a particular meaning in the early fourth century when they were inserted into the Nicene **Creed**, and they have the same meaning for Orthodox Christians today. Pentecostal Christian scholars also use the same "marks" to express their understanding of the Church, but with very different conceptions of where that one Church is and what it does. This means that even basic terms such as "Orthodox," "Catholic," "Apostolic," and so forth will need to be clarified or defined throughout this book. The glossary should also be helpful in this regard.

What is the difference, one might ask, between doctrine and dogma? These terms are often used somewhat interchangeably. I tend to use "doctrine" to refer to the teaching of a person or a group, and "dogma" to refer to doctrine that has the "official" status of guiding and shaping the beliefs of a specific faith tradition. For example, it is not only a teaching but incontrovertible dogma in the Orthodox Church that Jesus **Christ** is God **incarnate**—fully divine and fully human. A term with lower status in the Orthodox world is **theologoumenon**. The word shares the same root as "theology" but has a different technical meaning. A theologoumenon is a pious belief or individual opinion that may or may not be true and cannot be substantiated. A simple example would be the details about Christ's Second Coming. The Orthodox Church believes that Jesus will come again to judge the living and the dead (2 Tim. 4:1). Christ's Second Coming is dogma, since this is what the Lord Himself promised His Church. However, the Orthodox Church considers speculations about the end times to be theologoumena that cannot be part of any authoritative teaching of the Church, since the details cannot be verified in this present life.

The Approach

Many of the discussions in this book might be likened to a tour bus repeatedly circling around four areas of interest: Scripture, history, people, and concepts. "Scripture" includes the witness recorded in the Old and New Testaments. "History" includes the events and ideas in history that affected Christian thought and life, beginning with the primitive Apostolic Church and continuing through the Church's flourishing during the **Byzantine** era and into the present. "People" includes Apostolic, **Patristic**, and contemporary commentators. "Concepts" includes the definition of terminologies as well as an overview of major themes, doctrines, and dogmas of the Orthodox Faith.

Our task as students of theology is to seek to answer how, what, why, and who questions. For example, how did a certain dogma come to be? How did the Orthodox Church determine once and for all that it was proper to say that Jesus Christ shares the same essence as God the Father? Or, what is the belief taught by the Church and why is it to be believed? Why is it so important to acknowledge the Christian God as **Trinity** even though the word "Trinity" cannot be found anywhere in the Bible? And because theology for the Orthodox is always personal (but not individualistic), we must consider questions like these: Who is God? Who is Jesus? Who are we and what are we to do? Many of the most basic "how," "what," "why," and especially "who" questions of Eastern Orthodox theology will be addressed in this book, sometimes in dialogue with answers from a Western Christian perspective.

It is crucial to recognize that the development of human theological language over the ages does not mean that Christian theology is "man-made." As I hope to show in this book, the Holy Spirit has guided the one undivided Church through many challenges to a **conciliar** view of truth, not only in its theological doctrines and dogmas but also in all of its forms of expression, including Scripture, worship, ministry, iconography, and even its building architecture and administrative forms of governance. The theology that arose in response to challenges in the early Church was not merely an exercise in academic debate. The thought-world of the early Church was initially formed by an experience of the risen Lord in worship. Even today, Orthodox theology arises out of the lived experiences of God, not from scholastic concepts. This present book is a book about ideas, however, so at best it can be only a facsimile of actual Eastern Orthodox Christianity. I will nevertheless occasionally offer some insights into the Orthodox Church's praxis within the context of its thought.

The basic dogmas of the undivided Church of the first millennium are affirmed by most Christians today, yet few know about the often-dramatic battles fought by the Church—sometimes over hundreds of years—in order to arrive at unified expressions of the Apostolic Christian Faith. The Orthodox Church has protected the conciliar dogmas of the undivided Church in their original forms, despite the inbreaking of external challenges that have included **Gnosticism**, **Arianism**, and dozens of other heresies, and despite a history that has included vicious persecutions and **martyrdoms** and political oppression that continues into the present day.[2] The Orthodox Church has also managed to withstand the contemporary challenges of pluralism and postmodernism. This book, therefore, offers a high-level sketch of how the essential dogmas of Christianity originated from the common experience of God by the "grassroots" faithful, how these teachings were defended by the conciliar witness of the Holy Spirit through the seven **Ecumenical Councils**,[3] and how the Apostolic teachings continue to be faithfully observed in the Orthodox Church today.

Change?

There is a category of jokes that begin, "How many [fill in the blank] does it take to change a light bulb?" For example, "How many psychologists does it take to change a light bulb?" (Answer: "Only one, but the light bulb must really want to change.") Here's another: "How many sound technicians does it take to change a light bulb?" (Answer: "One-two, one-two, testing, one-two.") The Orthodox version of the joke is "How many Orthodox does it take to change a light bulb?" The satirical answer: "Change . . . ?" (Do the Orthodox ever change anything?)

There is certainly some truth to this humorous example, in that some things intentionally do not change in the Orthodox Church. St. John of Damascus (676–749) wrote, "We do not remove the ancient boundaries set in place by our fathers."[4] One Baptist preacher who visited an Orthodox church

2. The past one hundred years have witnessed the elimination of many Eastern Christians by the Turkish government's Armenian Genocide (1915), the anti-Christian campaign of the former Soviet Union (1917–1991), and—more recently in the twenty-first century—the mass murder of Eastern Christians by the militant Islamic State group (ISIS). It is estimated that over 25 million Christian martyrs have died in anti-Christian campaigns during the past century, more than in all previous centuries combined. See James M. Nelson, *Psychology, Religion, and Spirituality* (New York: Springer, 2009), 427. Less dramatic but still noteworthy is President Erdogan of Turkey's declaration on July 10, 2020, that the ancient Orthodox Christian cathedral Hagia Sophia (Holy Wisdom) in Istanbul, built by the Byzantine emperor Justinian in the sixth century, will be converted into a Muslim mosque again.

3. Nicaea I (AD 325), Constantinople I (381), Ephesus (431), Chalcedon (451), Constantinople II (553), Constantinople III (680–681), and Nicaea II (787).

4. St. John of Damascus, *On the Holy Icons* 2.12, in *Three Treatises on the Divine Images*, ed. and trans. Andrew Louth (Crestwood, NY: St. Vladimir's Seminary Press, 2003), 69.

during the **Divine Liturgy** even called it "the most in-your-face, retrograde old stuff you could imagine."[5] As I will show in this book, the Orthodox Church has never been afraid of change per se—but it has been, and will continue to be, suspicious of changes that are promoted by an individual or a few if they are not in agreement with the shared experience of God by the entire Church. Orthodox theology offers the rest of the Christian world a unique opportunity to understand how the Church through history has balanced staunch dogmatic conservatism and the always-new and life-giving witness of the Holy Spirit across all ages and through a multitude of diverse cultures.

It is the stability of thought in Orthodox theology that has generated the greatest interest from my Protestant students, primarily because of their often-new realization that there still exists a "predenominational" and Apostolic Christian worldview that is largely unaffected by the polemical debates of the Reformation. In fact, many of the doctrines and dogmas of Eastern Orthodoxy can certainly be embraced by those outside the Orthodox Church, such as its trinitarian theology and its conciliar approach to leadership and administration. As we will also see in the course of this book, the Orthodox will always try *not* to speak for God, especially in consideration of whom God will bring into **communion** in His eternal **Kingdom**. Therefore, while the Orthodox Church claims to be the historically continuous New Testament Church without addition or subtraction, it makes no judgment about the salvation of anyone outside its **sacramental** borders.

In the preface to *The Household of God: Lectures on the Nature of the Church*, the twentieth-century Protestant churchman Lesslie Newbigin speaks of three ways to be engrafted into Christ. First, we are incorporated into Christ by hearing and believing the **Gospel**. Second, we are incorporated into Christ by sacramental participation in the life of the historically continuous Church. Third, we are incorporated into Christ by receiving and abiding in the Holy Spirit. Newbigin points out that that Protestant, Roman Catholic, and Pentecostal traditions, respectively, have exhibited priority on one of these three ways and to some degree have minimized or neglected the importance of the other two ways. Newbigin's point is that the Church needs to be all three simultaneously and in balance. He concludes, "I am quite sure that the recovery of the wholeness of the Church must depend heavily upon what the

5. Dwight Allan Moody, "Memo from a Church Consultant: Survival Guide," *Christian Century*, November 6–19, 2002, 10. Reprinted in Moody, *The Other Side of Oddville* (Macon, GA: Mercer University Press, 2006), 164–65. See chap. 8, "Orthodox Worship," for more about Rev. Moody's visit to an Orthodox Divine Liturgy.

Orthodox have to teach us."[6] This is not to say that the Orthodox do not also learn and receive in other ways from other Christians. My own training speaks to this fact. Reciprocally, it is my hope that this humble, basic guide to Eastern Orthodox theology reflects and offers something of the balance that Newbigin had in mind for the whole of Christianity.

6. Lesslie Newbigin, *The Household of God: Lectures on the Nature of the Church* (London: SCM, 1957), 10.

1

The Orthodox
Christian Worldview

"Returning" to the Unknown Ancient Church?

In 1987, about two thousand North American Protestant Christians were received into the Orthodox Church en masse in Los Angeles, California. They were welcomed "home" by Metropolitan Philip Saliba to the Apostolic Church of Saints Peter and Paul. This was the culmination of many years of searching for the New Testament Church by regional leaders within the Campus Crusade for Christ organization. One of these campus ministry leaders, Peter Gillquist, reflected on the "big picture" questions that he and other campus leaders had been asking about the early Church during their quest: "Whatever happened to that Church we read about on the pages of the New Testament? Was it still around? If so, where? We wanted to be a part of it."[1]

Along the way, and as a result of their research into ancient texts, they had realized (much to their surprise) that the early Church was both liturgical and hierarchical. They had even tried to reconstruct what they believed to be the theological expression and worship life of the earliest Christians, using some of the ancient texts. "Our motivation was to be . . . a twentieth century expression of the first century Church."[2] The amazing part of this story is that they were unaware that the New Testament Church they were trying to reconstruct still

---

1. Peter E. Gillquist, *Becoming Orthodox: A Journey to the Ancient Christian Faith* (Brentwood, TN: Wolgemuth & Hyatt, 1989), 31.
2. Gillquist, *Becoming Orthodox*, 29.

existed, and in very much the same form that it had in the earliest centuries.[3] Readers of this book may also be unfamiliar with the Orthodox Church, or at least may not have heard much about its theology or practices.

Even at the World Council of Churches, where one might expect to have found a broader understanding of global Christianity, the Eastern Orthodox Church simply did not fit into the council's decidedly Western categories. For example, Fr. Alexander Schmemann (1921–1983), former dean of St. Vladimir's Orthodox Seminary in New York and one of the most respected Orthodox teachers of the twentieth century, was a delegate at the very first assembly of the World Council of Churches in Amsterdam in 1948. Fr. Schmemann described going through the typical registration process, during which he encountered an ecumenical dignitary who, in a very friendly fashion, informed him that the Orthodox delegates would be seated to the extreme right of the hall together with all the representatives of the "high churches,"[4] such as Swedish Lutherans, Old Catholics, and Polish Nationals. Fr. Schmemann explained that while he certainly had nothing against those excellent people, he wondered how that decision had been made. The answer was that it simply reflected the "ecclesiological makeup" of the conference, categorized by the dichotomy of the "horizontal" and "vertical" ideas of the Church, and that Eastern Orthodoxy was certainly more "horizontal," wasn't it? Fr. Schmemann remarked that in all his studies he had never heard of such a distinction between horizontal and vertical, but—had the choice been up to him—he might have selected a seat at the extreme left, with those whose emphasis on the dynamic life of the Holy Spirit the Orthodox share.[5] His experience underlined a fairly common misconception that because the Orthodox Church is liturgical, it must also be formal and static.

Protestant author James Payton, in *Light from the Christian East*, has stated the Orthodox way of doing theology quite nicely:

> Within Orthodoxy, study leads to wonder and, thus, to meditation; those who engage in such mystical contemplation come to know the one of whom the Christian faith speaks, and yet—paradoxically—the one whom it cannot adequately express. The knowledge of God that issues from such encounter is

3. "The truth is, none of us had ever to our knowledge been inside an Orthodox Church. Most of us did not know it existed. For that reason, I am chagrined to report that we decided to try to start it over again!" Gillquist, *Becoming Orthodox*, 58.

4. Though "high church" was originally used to describe the Protestant Anglican tradition, some Westerners use the term to refer to Eastern Orthodoxy, even though it does not accurately reflect the **pneumatological** character of Orthodox Christianity.

5. Alexander Schmemann, *Church, World, Mission* (Crestwood, NY: St. Vladimir's Seminary Press, 1979), 193–201.

rooted in the revelatory data, to be sure, but the fruit it bears certainly tastes different than what hangs on the vine of an academic study of doctrine.[6]

All theology in Orthodox Christianity derives from knowledge of God, which is the fruit of direct encounter with the Holy Spirit. This means that Eastern Orthodox theology does not fit well into the typical scholarly categories of the Christian West. And yet the fundamentally different worldview of Orthodox Christianity is appealing to some precisely because of this difference.

Influential Church historian Jaroslav Pelikan, an ordained Lutheran pastor and Sterling Professor of History at Yale, shocked the Protestant world when he was received into the Orthodox Church with his wife in 1998. He indicated to his family that he was not so much converting as returning to the Orthodox Christian Faith, "peeling back the layers of my own belief to reveal the Orthodoxy that was always there."[7] A prolific author of more than thirty books, Pelikan reportedly commented that while others read their way into a conversion, he wrote his way into the Orthodox Church.[8]

When Hank Hanegraaff, the popular evangelical radio and internet "Bible Answer Man," was received into the Orthodox Church with his wife and two adult children on Palm Sunday in 2017, the internet exploded with questioning. Some Protestant bloggers were certain that Hanegraaff had left the Christian Faith for something akin to the Roman Catholic Church (the target of the Protestant Reformation) and warned Hanegraaff's radio listeners that their salvation was now in jeopardy. This horror at a well-known Protestant joining the two-thousand-year-old "traditional" and "liturgical" Orthodox Church was clearly the outgrowth of a view of Christian history with roots in the sixteenth century, compounded by ignorance of the theological differences between the Orthodox Church and Roman Catholicism. It may be beneficial, therefore, to begin with a brief summary of the history of the Orthodox Christian Faith and the Church's place in world Christianity.

The Orthodox Church in the Christian World

The Orthodox Church considers itself to be the Apostolic Christian Church because it has existed continuously since **Pentecost** with an unbroken visible

6. James Payton, *Light from the Christian East: An Introduction to the Orthodox Tradition* (Downers Grove, IL: IVP Academic, 2007), 63.

7. "Dr. Jaroslav Pelikan Falls Asleep in the Lord," St. Vladimir's Orthodox Seminary, accessed July 1, 2020, https://www.svots.edu/content/dr-jaroslav-pelikan-falls-asleep-lord.

8. Jan Schumacher, "Jaroslav Pelikan," in *Key Theological Thinkers: From Modern to Postmodern*, ed. Svein Rise and Staale Johannes Kristiansen (Abingdon, UK: Routledge, 2016), 495.

and historical connection to the faith communities founded by the twelve Apostles and the Apostle Paul. It is also "Apostolic" because apostolicity, for the Orthodox, means preserving the fullness of the Apostolic **Tradition**. In other words, not only does the Orthodox Church have an uninterrupted connection to the Church of the Apostles in time, but it also has maintained the same faith and worship as the Apostles.

Until 1054, the Apostolic Church was undivided. There were five main centers, called "Sees," in that one, undivided Church. Together, Jerusalem, Alexandria, Antioch, and Constantinople (Byzantium) in the Greek-speaking Eastern Roman Empire, and Rome in the Latin-speaking West, were referred to as the "Pentarchy" of the ancient Christian world. There was great diversity from place to place, and there was not always agreement on everything, but the Church remained unified nevertheless.

One little Latin word, *Filioque* ("and the Son"), was the spark that would later become a blaze. Some churches in the Roman provinces had added this word as a change to the Creed, which had been agreed upon by the undivided Church. The four Eastern Sees disagreed with the theology behind this move, but objected mainly because changes in dogma required agreement by the whole Church under the guidance of the Holy Spirit. (The *Filioque* controversy is discussed in greater detail in chap. 7.) Other disagreements arose concerning Rome's introduction of a celibate priesthood and the type of bread to be used in the **Eucharist**. However, most scholars point to the *Filioque* controversy as the issue that led to the notion of papal supremacy and became "the straw that broke the camel's back."

On a particular Sunday in July 1054, during the Divine Liturgy, Cardinal Humbert of Rome placed a papal edict of excommunication on the **altar** of the Hagia Sophia cathedral in Constantinople. This action marked the formal divide between East and West, which has been named "the Great **Schism**." After 1054, the **bishop** of Rome became the head, or pope, of the new Roman Catholic Church, while the bishops in the Eastern Sees of the Christian world continued in communion with one another as spiritual leaders of the faithful in the Orthodox churches. These four ancient Eastern Sees are still intact as centers of Orthodox Christianity today.

Major shifts in the Latin-speaking Christian West began to occur about five hundred years after the Great Schism. A Roman Catholic Augustinian **monk** named Martin Luther gained notoriety by posting ninety-five points for reform he believed were needed in the Roman Catholic Church. By that time in the sixteenth century, several practices and ideas had been added to Roman Catholicism that had no counterparts in the Eastern Christian world. One such novel teaching was that Roman Catholics should contribute their own merits to Christ's merit (such as by attending Mass and buying "indulgences")[9] to lessen the time they might spend in purgatory after death.[10] Luther passionately opposed the concept of indulgences, but nothing like the ideas of Christ's merit, indulgences, or purgatory had taken root in the Orthodox Church.

Luther also complained about the Roman Catholic practice of not allowing regular laypeople to receive both forms of the Eucharist: the body *and* the blood of Jesus Christ. Since the time of the Apostles, the Christian East has offered the full Eucharist to all baptized Christians: young and old, laypeople and ordained clergy alike. Luther himself countered the Roman Catholic practice in his day by pointing to the Orthodox, exclaiming boldly that the "Greeks . . . are the most Christian people and the best followers of the Gospel on earth."[11] In *The Spirit of Eastern Christendom*, Pelikan (writing at that time as one of the most notable twentieth-century Lutheran scholars) notes that "Martin Luther appealed to the example of the East as proof that one could be catholic and orthodox without being papal."[12]

It is important to highlight, in case it is not apparent, that the Protestant Reformation took place on the Roman Catholic side of history after the split from Eastern Orthodoxy. By the time of the Reformation, however, the Eastern Christian world was under the hostile and oppressive subjugation of the Ottoman Turkish Empire, and thus the freedoms of and communication with and by the Orthodox were drastically limited.[13] Despite the geopolitical and theological distance between East and West in the sixteenth century,

9. Indulgences in the Roman Catholic Church are seen as a means of purification from sin that can reduce one's time in purgatory. Indulgences come in many forms and are still practiced in the Roman Catholic Church today, although they are no longer earned by monetary payment. For example, Pope Francis declared December 8, 2015, to November 20, 2016, to be a Jubilee Year of Mercy and offered indulgences to those who made pilgrimages to sacred basilicas and those who walked through designated doors of mercy in churches around the world. See Robert L. Fastiggi, *The Sacrament of Reconciliation: An Anthropological and Scriptural Understanding* (Chicago: Hillenbrand, 2017), 126–30.

10. Purgatory, which is an essential Roman Catholic belief, is the intermediate state after death where Christians work out "venial sins" that are not forgiven by sacramental confession before death. See Thomas P. Rausch, *Eschatology, Liturgy and Christology: Toward Recovering an Eschatological Imagination* (Collegeville, MN: Liturgical Press, 2012), 110.

11. Martin Luther, "An Article in Defense of All the Articles of Dr. Martin Luther Wrongly Condemned in the Roman Bull," Article 16, *Luther's Works*, vol. 32, *Career of the Reformer II*, ed. Helmut T. Lehmann and George W. Forell (Philadelphia: Fortress, 1958), 59.

12. Robert Louis Wilken, "Jaroslav Pelikan and the Road to Orthodoxy," *Concordia Theological Quarterly* 74 (2010): 97.

13. See Steven Runciman, *The Great Church in Captivity: A Study of the Patriarchate of Constantinople from the Eve of the Turkish Conquest to the Greek War of Independence* (London: Cambridge University Press, 1968).

there was nevertheless an interest among the second generation of Protestant Reformers to gain the approval of the Orthodox. In the late sixteenth century, a group of Lutheran scholars from the University of Tübingen in Germany approached the Greek Orthodox Patriarch of Constantinople, Jeremias II. They expressed great respect for the Patriarch and the Orthodox Christian Faith in their letters and asked for his support for their new Augsburg Confession. The Lutherans had actually translated this foundational Protestant document into Byzantine-style Greek with the expressed hope of garnering a favorable response from the Patriarch. Patriarch Jeremias welcomed the discussion and complimented the Lutheran scholars' enthusiasm for pursuing correct theology and practice.

Nevertheless, after a few exchanges of letters that lasted about five years (1575–1581), the Patriarch replied that he could not agree with many of the theological ideas promoted by the confession of the new Lutheran faith because these ideas departed from the teachings of the Apostles, the witness of the early **Church Fathers**, and the Ecumenical Councils of the unified Church. Neither could he agree, however, with many of the new Roman Catholic teachings, especially papal supremacy.[14] The Lutherans, clearly disappointed in the realization that their new confession would not receive acceptance from the Orthodox, thanked the Patriarch and politely ended the exchange.

For the most part, this same "partial agreement" and "partial disagreement" characterizes how Orthodox theology compares to the Roman Catholic and Reformation traditions. There are many essential and ecumenically hopeful similarities, such as the belief in the divinity of Jesus Christ (in Roman Catholicism and most Protestant denominations), in our need for a Savior as a result of humanity's Fall, and in the historical reality of Christ's Crucifixion, **Resurrection**, Ascension, and promised Second Coming. The basic dogmas of the undivided Church of the first millennium are affirmed by most Christian traditions today, but it was the ancient Church that fought the theological battles necessary to prevent the spread of error in teachings about the Christian Faith, "to contend earnestly for the faith which was once for all delivered to the saints" (Jude 1:3). Consequently, contemporary Christians share the opportunity to affirm their debt to the members of the early Church who defended core Christian beliefs at early and fragile stages.

14. For the details of this most fascinating exchange, see George Mastrantonis, *Augsburg and Constantinople: The Correspondence between the Tübingen Theologians and Patriarch Jeremiah II of Constantinople on the Augsburg Confession* (Brookline, MA: Holy Cross Press, 1982).

East Is East and West Is West

Oh, East is East, and West is West, and never the twain shall meet, / Till Earth and Sky stand presently at God's great Judgment seat. (Rudyard Kipling, "The Ballad of East and West")

Where do East and West actually meet? The Nobel prize–winning story-teller and poet Rudyard Kipling suggests that the East and the West are so completely different from one another that they will never meet until eternity.[15] The psalmist, too, ponders the great distance between East and West, yet as an analogy of the magnitude of God's great mercy: "As far as the east is from the west, so far has He removed our transgressions from us" (Ps. 103:12). Both Kipling and the psalmist express facets of the genuine dichotomies between East and West: geographical, ethnic, political, social, and, of course, religious. There is no question that the Eastern Orthodox Christian world has experienced a very different history than the Western Christian world on these five counts. Yet it is equally true that there is only one God, in whom there is neither Greek nor Jew (Col. 3:11). On the crucial issues of Christianity, one of the foremost Orthodox scholars today, Metropolitan Kallistos Ware, affirms that the "Orthodox agree in their doctrine of God with the overwhelming majority of all who call themselves Christians."[16]

Nevertheless, it can be pedagogically helpful to understand what something is not, in order to have a better sense of what it is. This is especially the case with the Christian East. As Payton observes, "The emphasis for Eastern Christianity is not on explanation but on mystery—on adoration of truth rather than its clarification."[17] As one might expect, "mystery" and "adoration" are far more difficult to express in a book than "explanation" or "clarification." Since Orthodox theology is less about propositional logic and more about offering God "proper glory," theology is to be experienced and not merely studied.

Orthodox theology is not monolithic, however. There is no one "Orthodox view" on many issues, especially with regard to pastoral concerns. Some theological ideas are also just theologoumena—pious ideas or opinions that may or may not be true, and thus should not be taught. For example, as already mentioned, Roman Catholicism has a well-defined "after death" dogma of

15. Rudyard Kipling, "The Ballad of East and West," first published in *Pioneer*, December 2, 1889. The poem tells how an Afghan horse thief and an English colonel come to respect one another's courage. In the end, ethnic and geographical differences will not matter on judgment day.

16. Timothy Ware (Metropolitan Kallistos of Diokleia), *The Orthodox Church: An Introduction to Eastern Christianity*, 3rd ed. (London: Penguin, 2015), 204.

17. Payton, *Light from the Christian East*, 67.

purgatory. But purgatory is not an Orthodox concept, and there is no parallel, detailed after-death dogma in the Orthodox Church beyond the little that Scripture describes.

There are also semantic complications between East and West. In fact, the terms "East" and "West" are problematic in themselves. These two terms once had a particular historical meaning within the Church to denote the Greek-speaking East and the Latin-speaking West, but they are no longer accurate in that usage. The Orthodox Church in Russia is not located in the East, nor are Orthodox Christians in western Europe and the Americas, but they are all nevertheless called "Eastern Orthodox." Most theological writers use these terms as technical shorthand, as I will continue to do as well: "Eastern" and "the East" refer to the Orthodox Church and family of Orthodox churches, and "Western" and "the West" refer to Roman Catholicism and the Protestant denominations that arose from the protest against medieval Roman Catholicism.

The Way It Has Always Been?

There are well-established teachings in Christian circles today that many faithful believers take for granted under the precepts that (1) this has always been the Christian teaching everywhere, and (2) this is the only way to think about the concept. These two affirming principles, however, cannot be stated unequivocally for all Christian teachings today, and not even for many common teachings. One of the specific goals of this book, therefore, is to shake things up a bit and offer a glimpse into other ways of thinking about basic Christian concepts from an Eastern Christian vantage point. Many of these other ways of thinking can certainly be assimilated by those who are not members of the Orthodox Church.

For example, when asked, "What did Jesus do to save you?" many Christians will immediately answer something like, "He died on the Cross to pay the price for my sins." Yet the idea that God the Father required repayment from Jesus to satisfy humanity's debt to God has not always been a Christian teaching. It is also not the only way to think about salvation in Jesus Christ. This atonement model developed in the West on a trajectory from the teachings of Anselm, an eleventh-century Roman Catholic bishop. The so-called satisfaction model of Anselm has not held sway in the Orthodox Church for several reasons, including that Orthodox theology is not transactional in nature (e.g., there are not even "vows" or promises in the Orthodox **Sacrament** of Holy Matrimony). The main reason, however, is that a sharp and narrow focus on the Cross obscures all that the Son of God has accomplished for

His fallen creation. In an Orthodox worldview, the full scope of what Jesus Christ has done must also include His Incarnation, His Resurrection, and even Pentecost.

A Different Worldview and a Different History

The Roman Catholic Scholastic thinker Thomas Aquinas (1225–1274) wrote in his massive work, the *Summa Theologiae*, that theology is the "highest *scientia*" since a high degree of rationality is required to understand the most important and complex philosophical concepts about God.[18] The universities that developed during the Scholastic period in the Christian West were intended to teach students how to deal in this "science" of theology through rigorous conceptual analysis. Theology was considered to be the preeminent Scholastic endeavor, a good thing in many ways. Yet, as a result of the high regard for logic and rationality in medieval Roman Catholicism, those who studied and taught (the "doctors") came to be more highly regarded than the monks and nuns (the "religious") whose main vocation was to pray.

Theology began to be expounded by scholars outside of the context of prayer, pastoral ministry, and liturgical worship. Pelikan traces this specific change in the West through the changing job description of the theologian. He notes that, between AD 100 and 600, most theologians were bishops; from 600 to 1500 in the West they were monks. But after 1500, Western theologians are university professors: "Gregory I, who died in 604, was a bishop who had been a monk; Martin Luther, who died in 1546, was a monk who became a university professor. Each of these lifestyles has left its mark on the job description of a theologian."[19] After the sixteenth century in the West, the task of theology increasingly became separated from its earlier moorings to the worship of the community and the spiritual disciplines.

From an Eastern Orthodox point of view, knowledge of God comes only from an encounter with the God who has revealed Himself: "What may be known of God is manifest in them, for God has shown it to them" (Rom. 1:19). Thus, theology can never be separated from prayer, worship, and contemplation of the Holy Trinity. Metropolitan Ware affirms that all true Orthodox theology is mystical: "Just as mysticism divorced from theology becomes

18. Brian Davies, *Thomas Aquinas's* Summa Theologiae: *A Guide and Commentary* (New York: Oxford University Press, 2014), 19–20.

19. Jaroslav Pelikan, *The Christian Tradition: A History of the Development of Doctrine*, vol. 1, *The Emergence of the Catholic Tradition (100–600)* (Chicago: University of Chicago Press, 1971), 5.

subjective and heretical, so theology, when it is not mystical, degenerates into an arid scholasticism, 'academic' in the bad sense of the word."[20] That is to say, Orthodox mystical theology guards against either unacceptable extreme: subjective and heretical, or arid and academic.

The separation of religious sensibilities and disciplines became even more exaggerated by the seventeenth and eighteenth centuries in western Europe, in a period historians refer to as the Enlightenment or the Age of Reason. This time, the chasm arose between (1) that which could be proved by scientific method and observation and (2) the mystical claims of Scripture. Thinkers such as H. S. Reimarus, an eighteenth-century deist, insisted that no human testimony could prove something that present-day experience could not support. For example, if water is not being changed into wine in the present day, one should not expect that it occurred in the past at the wedding at Cana (John 2:1–12). In the Age of Reason, the truly rational person should be able to recognize not only that divine revelation is no longer needed but also that it was probably a human fabrication in the first place. The consequences of Enlightenment humanism were the seeds from which full-grown Protestant liberalism would sprout in the twentieth century.

During the nineteenth and twentieth centuries in the Protestant West, the Jesus of history became more like a data point to be studied as an example of ethical living than the Incarnate Son of God who taught, performed signs and wonders, was crucified, rose from the dead, ascended to heaven, and sent the Holy Spirit to the Church. Many thought of Jesus as a regular man who lived correctly and, in doing so, gained higher insights and knowledge that one might even think of as "divine." The famous twentieth-century missionary doctor Albert Schweitzer, for example, did not believe that the Resurrection of Christ happened. Yet Schweitzer considered himself a Christian, believing that Jesus was an important role model for humanity since Jesus exhibited a life of self-sacrifice for those in need.[21]

The liberal Protestant skepticism about miracles and the loss of unwavering belief in an eternal, omniscient, omnipresent, and loving God-become-man was the environment from which Protestant fundamentalism emerged in vocal and staunch opposition. When popular liberal Protestants like Rudolf Bult-

20. Ware, *Orthodox Church*, 200.
21. "Schweitzer stands at some distance from versions of Christianity that are based on the New Testament witness, and so from New Testament theology that describes that witness historically in order to guide Christian teaching and identity." Robert Morgan, "Albert Schweitzer's Challenge and the Response from New Testament Theology," in *Albert Schweitzer in Thought and Action: A Life in Parts*, ed. James Carleton Paget and Michael J. Thate (New York: Syracuse University Press, 2016), 73.

mann began calling the entire thought-world of the Bible "mythological,"[22] Protestant fundamentalists went public in their challenge with a formal statement acknowledging the Bible to be "fully inerrant" on all matters, including science and history.[23] From this Protestant family arose the "Young Earth" or literal interpretation of creation, whose proponents believe that each "day" of creation was a literal twenty-four-hour day that took place about six thousand years ago. A supreme trust in the Bible as "God's inerrant Word" and in the power of a sovereign Creator continues to uphold Young Earth creationist views, even though the preponderance of scientific evidence shows that the earth is at least four billion years old and probably originated with one or more cosmic explosions known as the Big Bang.[24]

As will be discussed in chapter 3, the Orthodox hermeneutic for interpreting Holy Scripture is different from that of most Western Christian traditions; it is neither strictly literal nor strictly allegorical (although there is room for both kinds of readings). As a result, there is no Orthodox dogma asserting how God must have created, except that it was God who created (Gen. 1:1). This means that there is room in Orthodox theologoumena for many possible creation scenarios, without stating one definitively and without discounting any view on the grounds that the Bible does not describe it specifically.

The main point of this brief summary of major movements in Western religious culture since the twelfth century is that none of these challenges were part of the history of Eastern Orthodox Christianity. Scholasticism was exclusively Latin and did not involve the Eastern Orthodox Sees, from which Rome had already separated by the mid-eleventh century. Similarly, the sixteenth-century Protestant Reformation—the break from, or "reform" of, Roman Catholicism—also did not involve the Orthodox Church in any way whatsoever. Nor did the unbiblical worldview of the Enlightenment and the pendulum swings of liberal Protestantism and Protestant fundamentalism affect or alter the Apostolic Faith and practice in the Orthodox Church.

The Primacy of Worship

One of the prevailing themes woven throughout most topics in this book is that worship is primary in the Orthodox Church and that theological reflection,

22. Rudolf Bultmann, *New Testament Mythology and Other Basic Writings* (Philadelphia: Fortress, 1989).

23. "Chicago Statement of Biblical Inerrancy," in *Evangelical Dictionary of Theology*, ed. Walter A. Elwell (Grand Rapids: Baker Books, 2001), 226–27.

24. Hugh Ross, *Why the Universe Is the Way It Is* (Grand Rapids: Baker Books, 2010), 52.

while important, is nonetheless secondary. Reading this or that book on theology or being in a class that discusses theology is not "doing theology" in an Orthodox context, no matter how insightful the ensuing discussions. Metropolitan John Zizioulas, one of the most influential Orthodox bishops and scholars of the present day, articulates the centrality of worship in the Orthodox Church in this way: "Academic theology may concern itself with doctrine, but it is the communion of the Church which makes theology into truth."[25] This means that in order to go beyond ideas about God, truth is revealed most fully by the Holy Spirit in and through worship, and especially in the Church's celebration of the Holy Eucharist. The consensus of belief about the nature of the triune God has always arisen in and through the direct and personal experience of God—through prayer and worship—and not through academic study.

Doctrinal affirmations of the Ecumenical Councils of the Orthodox Church were expounded not by professional theologians or by academics but by those who were "overseers" (Greek: *episkopoi*) of the Eucharist, the bishops whose sacred liturgical role was to call upon the Holy Spirit to descend on the people and the gifts being offered, in order to make them both holy. One of the many blessings of studying Orthodox theology is that we are reminded again and again that one's direct relationship with God through prayer and worship is what informs "head knowledge" about God.

Throughout its more than two thousand years of history, Orthodox Christianity has tried not to separate spirituality from theology or rational thought from faith. True theology is really true worship: both theology and worship arise only through actual encounters with God. An early New Testament encounter with God is Pentecost, described by St. Luke the Evangelist in chapter 2 of the Acts of the Apostles—a watershed and cosmic event that changed the course of history. The Apostles and others were gathered in an upper room in Jerusalem. As Jesus Christ had promised them (John 14:16) and as the Prophet Joel had prophesied (Joel 2:28–29), God dramatically poured out His Spirit with the rush of a great wind and tongues of fire. Those who were in that room, and the multitude that had gathered around the home, were from a variety of nations, and they all heard the Gospel message wondrously being preached in their own languages.

Those in attendance were awestruck by the enormity of God's mercy and power—a power that had now been fully released into the world. The very next thing that happened is that St. Peter, who had been a fisherman by trade,

25. John D. Zizioulas, *Being as Communion: Studies in Personhood and the Church* (Crestwood, NY: St. Vladimir's Seminary Press, 1985), 118n120.

immediately stood up and miraculously preached an articulate, logical, and inspirational sermon summarizing salvation history with erudition far above the typical level of education of a simple fisherman. Filled with divine inspiration, Peter proclaimed boldly that Jesus Christ fulfilled all the prophecies about the Messiah contained in the Jewish Scriptures.

Then as now in the Orthodox Church, the "wise" are not necessarily those who have the most academic credentials, but those who have received—and who follow—the Holy Spirit. This seminal day of Pentecost is also considered by the Orthodox to be the formal inauguration of the Church—the day on which the Church established by Jesus Christ was given new warmth and power by the indwelling of the Holy Spirit to make it grow and spread like wildfire throughout the inhabited earth.

The event of Pentecost in Acts 2 also illustrates one of the most important principles of Orthodox theology: worship of the uncreated Creator is the Church's primary task. To this point, imagine that you are one of the Apostles of Christ, or even one of the faithful in that upper room on the day of Pentecost. You have just been filled with the gifts of the Holy Spirit beyond what you can describe or even fully understand. Now imagine a reporter who has witnessed the scene excitedly rushing up to you afterward and exclaiming, "You have just received the gifts of the Holy Spirit, and miraculously preached the Gospel of Christ heard by all the people there in their own language! What are you going to do next?" Would you say, "I am going to go sit down with pen and parchment and write a theological reflection on the concepts I have just experienced"? This is not very likely. What is more likely, after having been filled with the Holy Spirit, is an answer like

The Great Feast of Pentecost

Pentecost is one of the Twelve Great Feasts of the Lord in the Orthodox Church and is commemorated annually through the Church's liturgical worship on the fiftieth day after Christ's Resurrection on **Pascha** (Easter). The Orthodox hymn for the Great Feast of Pentecost tells of the simple fishermen who were thereafter revealed as "all-wise" because they were filled with the Holy Spirit:

> Blessed are you, O Christ our God, who have revealed the fishermen as most wise by sending down upon them the Holy Spirit; through them you drew the world into your net. O Lover of man, glory to you![a]

a. *The Incarnate God: The Feasts of Jesus Christ and the Virgin Mary*, ed. Catherine Aslanoff, trans. Paul Meyendorff, 2 vols. (Crestwood, NY: St. Vladimir's Seminary Press, 2002), 2:209.

this: "I am going to thank God for His generosity and mercy, and offer Him praise and worship always!"

The great seventh-century mystic St. Isaac the Syrian writes that when the Holy Spirit dwells in us we will never cease to pray, because the Spirit will constantly pray in us.[26] Indeed, the first activity of the Apostles and the thousands who were baptized on that day was not to begin developing a doctrine, or even to reflect in writing on their shared yet personal experience of the Spirit. As the New Testament shows, "they continued steadfastly in the apostles' doctrine and fellowship [*koinōnia*, or communion], in the breaking of bread, and in prayers" and they continued praising God "daily with one accord in the temple" (Acts 2:42–47). For Orthodox Christianity, worship is primary, because the Holy Spirit abides in the Church through its corporate prayer and worship. But also (and more importantly), the Orthodox understand that the rational and intellectual gifts needed to pursue theological reflection are themselves gifts of the Holy Spirit, as in the Orthodox hymn of Pentecost: the fishermen are now all-wise because Christ sent down His Holy Spirit upon them.

Come and See!

I will gather all nations and tongues; and they shall come and see My glory. (Isa. 66:18)

Come and see the works of God; He is awesome in His doing toward the sons of men. (Ps. 66:5)

After Philip meets Jesus, he tells Nathanael that he has met the Messiah of whom Moses and the Prophets foretold. Nathanael is suspicious, though, that anything good could come out of Nazareth. "Come and see," says Philip (John 1:46). Sometimes "come and see" (Ps. 66:5; John 1:39, 46) is the best way to understand. A fascinating historical example of the value of "come and see" as well as of the primacy of worship in the Orthodox Church comes from the story of how Russia became Christianized. Around AD 987, the pagan prince of Kiev, Vladimir, wanted to provide his subjects with a better religion as an alternative to paganism. The story goes that Vladimir charged his envoys to visit and experience the four Abrahamic religions—Judaism, Islam, Roman Catholicism, and Greek Orthodoxy—and return with a full report of what they saw and experienced.[27]

26. *Mystic Treatises by Isaac of Nineveh*, trans. A. J. Wensink (Amsterdam: Koninklijke Akademie van Wetenschappen, 1923), 174.
27. Ware, *Orthodox Church*, 257.

Their first stop was with the Bulgarian Muslims in the Volga region. The envoys reported that the Muslims had no gladness in their religion, "only sorrow and a great stink." (Apparently Vladimir also did not care for the Muslim ban on alcohol and pork!) Traveling on to Germany and Rome, the envoys found the Latin Masses and ceremonies more satisfactory, but not beautiful. But the emissaries of Vladimir had a completely different experience when they attended the Byzantine (Greek Orthodox) Divine Liturgy at the Church of Holy Wisdom (the Hagia Sophia) in Constantinople, as evidenced by their report:

> We knew not whether we were in heaven or on earth, for on earth there is no such splendor or beauty, and we are at a loss to describe it. We only know that God dwells there among humans, and their worship is fairer than the ceremonies of other nations. . . . And we cannot forget that beauty. Every man who has partaken of sweetness will not afterwards accept bitterness, and so we can no longer remain apart from it.[28]

As a result of the envoys' report, Vladimir declared in AD 988 that the Orthodox Christian Faith would become the religion of Russia. Byzantine

St. Vladimir, Equal to the Apostles

A *troparion* is a special hymn sung in commemoration of a **saint** or event. The troparion is chanted annually on the feast day of the saint or event and at every liturgy celebrated in churches named for the saint or event.

The Troparion of St. Vladimir offers poetic highlights of Vladimir's life—the search for the priceless pearl of truth for his people and his coming to Christianity later in life through **repentance** and **Baptism**:

> Holy Prince Vladimir, you were like a merchant in search of fine pearls. By sending servants to Constantinople for the Orthodox Faith, you found Christ, the priceless pearl. He appointed you to be another Paul, washing away in baptism your physical and spiritual blindness. We celebrate your memory, asking you to pray for all Orthodox Christians and for us, your spiritual children.[a]

a. English translation by the Orthodox Church in America, https://www.oca.org/saints/troparia /2020/07/15/102031-equal-of-the-apostles-great-prince-vladimir-in-baptism-basil-enl. Used with permission.

28. From the *Russian Primary Chronicle* (ca. 1113), as presented in Ware, *Orthodox Church*, 257–60.

Orthodoxy would soon transform the entire Russian culture, not merely that of Kiev and not merely its religious worldview. Greek learning and culture would also be fully adopted throughout Russia. The significance of this example lies in the way in which Orthodox Christianity was chosen above the other religious options. Prince Vladimir never asked his envoys to study or to report on the beliefs or moral teachings of the various religions, but only to experience the religions in worship. Because of the beauty of Orthodox worship and the envoys' experience of God's presence among humans, Russia became Christian. Today St. Vladimir, prince of Kiev, is called "equal to the Apostles" because of his Christianization of the Russian lands, and he is remembered liturgically in the Orthodox Church every year on July 15.[29]

This story of Vladimir and the Christianization of Russia indeed exemplifies the invitation to "come and see," since the Orthodox Christian Faith is found not in theology books but in worship. This story also highlights a Patristic rule, *legem credendi lex statuat supplicandi* (paraphrased as *lex orandi, lex credendi*), which states that the law of worship establishes the law of belief.[30] Belief is constituted by worship, which is an encounter with God. Roman Catholic liturgical scholar Fr. Aidan Kavanagh shows why the reverse is not the case: "It was a Presence, not faith, which drew Moses to the burning bush, and what happened there was a revelation, not a seminar. It was a Presence, not faith, which drew the disciples to Jesus, and what happened then was not an educational program but his revelation to them of himself as the long-promised Anointed One."[31] Belief arises from encounter.

"Doing Theology" in Orthodox Christianity

How does the Orthodox Church do theology? "Theology" (Greek: *theologia*) is composed of two words: *Theos* (God) and *Logos* (Word). The earliest understanding of *theologia* was the contemplation of God in Godself, without images or words. Often quoted in this regard are the words of an influential fourth-century monk, Evagrius of Ponticus, who states, "If you are a theologian you truly pray. If you truly pray, you are a theologian."[32]

---

29. See *The Legacy of St. Vladimir: Byzantium, Russia, America*, ed. John Breck, John Meyendorff, and Eleana Silk (Crestwood, NY: St. Vladimir's Seminary Press, 1990).

30. Latin *statuat* = "makes stand." In other words, it is only through worship that beliefs stand.

31. Aidan Kavanagh, *On Liturgical Theology* (Collegeville, MN: Liturgical Press, 1984), 91–92.

32. Evagrius of Ponticus, "Chapters on Prayer," in *Evagrius of Ponticus: The Praktikos, Chapters on Prayer*, trans. J. E. Bamberger (Spencer, MA: Cistercian Publications, 1970), 65.

Prayer and worship are the most important activities of a Christian, and true theology includes praise and contemplation. A popular twentieth-century spiritual father, Silouan of Mount Athos (1866–1938), who was recognized by the Ecumenical Patriarchate as a saint in 1988, summarizes well the role of theology in Orthodoxy: "It is one thing to speak of God; it is quite another thing to know God."[33] The Orthodox belief is that no one can begin to have an understanding of God's nature or God's will without an encounter.

The Orthodox Church has formally given the appellation of "Theologian" to only three people in two-thousand-plus years. It is not the case that no one else can discuss theology in the Orthodox Church, but these three were so called because of their incomparably beautiful God-inspired theological orations, derived through the **ascetic** disciplines of prayer, fasting, repentance, contemplation, and worship. The three who are honored with the title "Theologian" are John the Evangelist and Theologian (first century), Gregory (of Nazianzus) the Theologian (fourth century), and Symeon the New Theologian (eleventh century). (Yes, in the Eastern Orthodox worldview, the eleventh century is considered "new"!) Each Theologian used words, but the words pointed beyond their own limits. A theological theme present in the works of all three Theologians is the theme of light: "God is light—and so reaches out towards us and makes the incomprehensible God knowable, but through participation and experience rather than academic enquiry."[34]

The Troparion of St. Gregory the Theologian, Archbishop of Constantinople (Commemorated on January 25)

The sweet-sounding shepherd's pipe of your theology overpowered the trumpeting of the orators; for having searched the depths of the Spirit eloquence was also bestowed upon you. Pray to Christ God, Father Gregory, that our souls may be saved.[a]

a. English translation by the Orthodox Church in America, https://www.oca.org/saints/troparia /2020/01/25/100298-saint-gregory-the-theologian-archbishop-of-constantinople. Used with permission.

---

33. Quoted in His All Holiness Ecumenical Patriarch Bartholomew, *Encountering the Mystery: Understanding Orthodox Christianity Today* (New York: Doubleday, 2008), 41–42.

34. John Binns, *An Introduction to the Christian Orthodox Churches* (Cambridge: Cambridge University Press, 2002), 72.

Apophatic Theology

Theology may be understood by the Orthodox as the experience of God, but of course "theology" also refers to the words used to describe ideas about God. Yet words from a finite being will always fall short of expressing the mystery of the infinite God. Though we can communicate in words (this book is filled with words about theology), it is wise to recognize in humility that our words will never begin to approach the reality of God's unknowable essence: "The mystical presence of God . . . transcends the possibility of being defined in words."[35] In order to resolve this seeming **paradox** of needing to use words, when words will always fail to hit the mark, the Orthodox make use of what is referred to as **apophatic theology**. The apophatic theology of Orthodoxy is based on a position of humility that human reasoning will never approach the fullness of God. As the Lord God revealed to the Prophet Isaiah, "For as the heavens are higher than the earth, so are My ways higher than your ways, and My thoughts than your thoughts" (Isa. 55:9). Similarly, St. Paul told his spiritual son Timothy that God alone dwells "in unapproachable light" (1 Tim. 6:16).

One type of apophatic approach is to speak about what God is *not* by "the way of negation."[36] For example, we humans are mortal, finite, and created, but God is *im*mortal, *in*finite, and *un*created. One of my favorite apophatic statements is from the Byzantine scholar St. John of Damascus: "God, then, is infinite and incomprehensible, and all that is comprehensible about Him is His infinity and incomprehensibility."[37]

Mainly, however, the Orthodox use apophatic theology not as a counterbalance to positive statements about God, but rather to avoid forming concepts about God altogether. The fourth-century Church Father Gregory of Nyssa taught that it is not only wise but safer and more reverent to believe that the majesty of God is greater than we can understand. The disciple who has an experience of God will not go through the door of speculation. But if one does attempt knowledge of God beyond one's finite abilities, Gregory

---

35. Dumitru Stăniloae, *The Experience of God*, vol. 1, *Revelation and Knowledge of the Triune God*, trans. Robert Barringer and Ioan Ioniţă, Orthodox Dogmatic Theology (1994; repr., Brookline, MA: Holy Cross Orthodox Press, 1998), 95–96.

36. The great Roman Catholic Scholastic thinker Thomas Aquinas referred to the way of negation (Latin: *via negativa*) as a corrective to affirmations about God. See Gregory P. Rocca, *Speaking the Incomprehensible God: Thomas Aquinas on the Interplay of Positive and Negative Theology* (Washington, DC: Catholic University of America Press, 2004), 49–68.

37. John of Damascus, *An Exact Exposition of the Orthodox Faith* 1.4, in *A Select Library of Nicene and Post-Nicene Fathers of the Christian Church*, 2nd series, ed. Philip Schaff and Henry Wace, 14 vols. (1890–1900; repr., Grand Rapids: Eerdmans, 1952), 9:3. See https://www.newadvent.org/fathers/33041.htm.

believed that error rather than truth is the likelier outcome: "The desire of investigating what is obscure and tracing out hidden things by the operation of human reasoning gives an entrance to false no less than to true notions, inasmuch as he who aspires to know the unknown will not always arrive at truth, but may also conceive of falsehood itself as truth."[38] In other words, it is best not to speculate at all about God's being, since limited human reasoning may perceive falsehood as truth.

Consider the profound self-defining statement the Lord made to Moses from within the burning bush: "I AM THAT I AM" (Exod. 3:14 KJV). Even though this was a direct statement from the Lord God Himself, no concepts can be formed about God except that God has being and is present. The Orthodox mind is comfortable in the apophatic tension of God being far beyond us in "unapproachable light" and yet also fully with us.[39] The same apophatic reserve is present in the writings of two of the most highly regarded Orthodox authors of the twentieth century, the Romanian priest Dumitru Stăniloae (1903–1993) and Russian lay scholar Vladimir Lossky (1903–1958). Both agree that knowledge of God can never be abstract, as if God is a concept rather than a personal being. The apophatic approach instead seeks to raise the mind "to those realities which pass all understanding."[40]

Apophatic theology does not discount the importance of positive or **cataphatic** statements. Positive statements (e.g., God is love, God is good) are the starting points that enable us to contemplate the divine realities far beyond human experience. Finite human language may not fully reach the infinite God, but God reaches out to His creation. Apophatic theology is about God's presence, not God's distance. God is with us, even "where human understanding cannot reach."[41] The God who is perceived cannot be defined, even though the uncreated glory of God can be experienced in a way that transcends all possibility of definition.[42]

38. Gregory of Nyssa, "Answer to Eunomius' Second Book," in *A Select Library of Nicene and Post-Nicene Fathers of the Christian Church*, 2nd series, ed. Philip Schaff and Henry Wace, 14 vols. (1890–1900; repr., Grand Rapids: Eerdmans, 1952), 5:260. See https://www.newadvent.org/fathers/2902.htm.

39. Maximus the Confessor, *Centuries on Theology and the Incarnate Dispensation of the Son of God* 2.8, cited in Andrew Louth, *Maximus the Confessor* (New York: Routledge, 1996), 43.

40. Vladimir Lossky, *The Mystical Theology of the Eastern Church*, trans. The Fellowship of St. Alban and St. Sergius (Crestwood, NY: St. Vladimir's Seminary Press, 1976), 43.

41. Gregory of Nyssa, *The Life of Moses* 1.46–47, quoted in Payton, *Light from the Christian East*, 77.

42. Stăniloae, *Experience of God*, 99.

An Open Hermeneutic

From the time of Scholasticism in the eleventh century, the Christian West considered theology to be the "highest *scientia*," and the medieval Roman Catholic Church had become the arbiter of all academic disciplines, theological and otherwise. The Bible was being interpreted as something like a scientific text, and scientific discoveries or opinions could not contradict the Roman Catholic teaching. For example, Roman Catholicism taught that the earth was a static body at the center of the universe and that the sun revolved around the earth. When in the seventeenth century Galileo insisted that he had scientific and mathematical evidence to prove Copernicus's theory that the earth revolves around the sun, not the other way around, the Roman Inquisition declared him to be a heretic and imprisoned him until his death. "Geocentric" views persisted even into the twentieth century: the Missouri Synod Lutheran tradition officially held such a view until 1920.[43] In both of these cases, the problem was ultimately not an "ungodly" science but a closed theology derived from a particular scriptural hermeneutic.

Despite our many twenty-first-century technological advances, there is still discord in the present day between empirical scientific evidence and the beliefs of some Christians. I am thinking again of the Young Earth creationists mentioned earlier, who hold to a strictly literal interpretation of the Bible and believe that the Bible supports an earth age of between six thousand and ten thousand years old. This view is in stark contrast to the belief of scientists in several disciplines today who are fairly consistent with one another in suggesting that the earth is 4.5 billion years old, give or take a few million years. For example, physical cosmologists and astrophysicists believe they have uncovered evidence in space about the earth's age that aligns with the claims of geologists to have discovered rocks that have been on earth for four billion years. Geologists have also unearthed evidence that catastrophic volcanic eruptions took place on earth at least three billion years ago.

Once again, "East is East and West is West." With intentional apophatic reserve, Eastern Orthodoxy has never officially stated more than finite humans can possibly know about how God created. We can indeed know and proclaim with certainty *that* God created, but we are not able to know exactly *how* God created. The early Church Fathers and contemporary Eastern Orthodox scholars have tried to leave room for God to be God without the need

---

43. Ron Miller, *Recentering the Universe: The Radical Theories of Copernicus, Kepler, Galileo, and Newton* (Minneapolis: Twenty-First Century Books, 2014), 689. The Roman Catholic Church burned Giordano Bruno at the stake for supporting Copernicus's heliocentric view, but Galileo was more popular with the people and thus was merely imprisoned for life.

to explore or explain details. In this way, the latest scientific discoveries or trends need be neither shunned nor affirmed. Vladimir Lossky writes that "the Church always freely makes use of philosophy and the sciences for apologetic (explanatory) purposes, but she never has any cause to defend these *relative* and *changing* truths as she defends the *unchangeable* truth of her doctrines."[44] Science discoveries and theories change, but God's truth does not.

The unchanging truth of creation is that "in the beginning God created the heavens and the earth" (Gen. 1:1). In order to distinguish this God from the Gnostic deities who were thought to have created the universe from preexisting materials, the Fathers of the First Ecumenical Council affirmed that God created everything "visible and invisible." The Orthodox hold it as incontrovertible dogma that God spoke everything that exists into being out of nothing: "For He spoke, and it was done; He commanded, and it stood fast" (Ps. 33:9). But there is no official Orthodox narrative about creation beyond the fact *that* God created everything at the beginning. This allows room for the Orthodox to entertain many possible creation scenarios without stating one definitively and without discounting any view on the grounds that the Bible does not specifically describe it. An open hermeneutic has also prevented the Orthodox Church from falling into the same error as geocentrists of the past who used the Bible as a scientific textbook, while still affirming the absolute truth of the Bible.

Astrophysicist Christopher Knight affirms that Orthodoxy has had no problem putting God at the origin of what scientists perceive as natural processes: "God may be seen as having worked as creator in and through the naturalistic processes that are perceived by scientists as providing a valid explanation of the cosmos's development from the Big Bang to the present time."[45] Science should never drive Christian theology, however, and scientific knowledge can never lead to the meaning, purpose, or end (telos) of cosmology. Science needs Christian theology to supply answers to the "black box" questions of science, such as this one: If the Big Bang theory of the universe has scientific merit, what (or who) caused the Big Bang? The apophatic nature of Orthodox theology lends itself to this type of dialectic with science since, as Lossky writes, Christian theology "is able to accommodate itself very easily to any scientific theory of the universe."[46] What he means is that no advance

44. Lossky, *Mystical Theology*, 104.

45. Christopher Knight, "Divine Action and the Laws of Nature: An Orthodox Perspective on Miracles," in *Science and the Eastern Orthodox Church*, ed. Gayle Woloschak and Daniel Buxhoeveden (Abingdon, UK: Routledge, 2016), 42. Rev. Dr. Knight is the executive secretary for the International Society for Science and Religion in Cambridge, England.

46. Lossky, *Mystical Theology*, 106.

of science will change theology; but theology can ultimately provide meaning and insights into the purpose of whatever science may discover to be true.

Alexei Nesteruk, in his book *Light from the East: Theology, Science, and the Eastern Orthodox Tradition*, concludes that scientific research and activity can even be thought of in the context of religious experience: "Science thus cannot be detached from theology; it is in the complex with theology that it can be properly understood and treated."[47] The Orthodox interpretive hermeneutic makes room for God to be God, without limiting Him to whatever might be the current level of human understanding of the cosmos. There is also no battle between the Orthodox Church, the Bible, and science. The Orthodox reading of Genesis uncovers literal truth, but Genesis is not understood as a scientific textbook. Fr. Lawrence Farley states in an Orthodox context what many Western biblical scholars are also saying about the creation narratives: that the stories of Genesis should not be read apart from their original cultural context, which affirms that Israel's God is the intentional cause of all that exists. "When we read them as they were meant to be read, we see that the creation story was a gauntlet thrown down before the prevailing culture of its time. The creation stories affirmed that the Jewish God, the tribal deity of a small and internationally unimportant people, alone made the whole cosmos."[48] The Orthodox scriptural hermeneutic will be discussed further in chapter 3 and generally throughout the remainder of the book.

▪ DISCUSSION QUESTIONS ▪

1. Share something that you never knew about Eastern Orthodox Christianity before reading this chapter, or something in the chapter that surprised you.

2. How might the apophatic approach to theology in Eastern Orthodoxy be both a benefit and a challenge?

3. This chapter briefly summarizes the biblical account of the descent of the Holy Spirit on Pentecost. How does the Orthodox hymn of Pentecost reflect the meaning of the biblical event? What would have been your response had you actually been there?

4. In your opinion, what is the proper relationship between theology and science?

47. Alexei V. Nesteruk, *Light from the East: Theology, Science, and the Eastern Orthodox Tradition* (Minneapolis: Fortress, 2013), 7.
48. Lawrence Farley, *In the Beginning: The True Message of the Genesis Origin Stories* (Chesterton, IN: Ancient Faith Publishing, 2018), 13.

The Church

We, being many, are one body in Christ, and individually members of one another.

—Romans 12:5

Joined Together in the Church

Some Christian concepts evoke different understandings from believers in different traditions. Although it may seem counterintuitive to even suggest it, "Church" is one of those concepts. It is a prevailing idea in many Protestant circles, for example, that when people give their lives over to Jesus Christ, they are considered to be Christians from that point forward. Some consider that salvation has been accomplished at that very moment. In that case, belonging to a church congregation may not be essential, or at least it may be far less important than one's individual faith in Christ.

An individualistic Christianity is a contradiction in terms to the Orthodox. Although the Christian God is a personal God and desires to have a personal relationship with each believer, Orthodox Christians believe they are being saved together in the Church, not in isolation. In fact, it is impossible even to think about being an Orthodox Christian without being a member of the Church. James Payton has quite a bit to say about the example that Orthodoxy sets by its communal emphasis: "Christ died for his church. He gives his salvation to his people, not just to discrete persons—and he gives it to them in concert with and interaction with the others of the church."[1] It is only in the Church that Christians become members of the Body of Christ. The New Testament clearly reflects the interconnectedness of Christians in Christ through the Holy Spirit, as the Body of Christ with many members. For example, "for by one Spirit we were all baptized into one body" (1 Cor. 12:13) and "we, being many, are one body in Christ, and individually members of one another" (Rom. 12:5).

The Body of Christ is not a theoretical idea in Eastern Orthodoxy. While on the surface the analogy of "body" describes the obvious aspects of a shared unity of purpose in Christ, the Orthodox see a genuine physical and spiritual communion of the faithful with one another as comembers of the Body of Christ, especially through the Eucharist.[2] Payton is also especially insightful in expressing that in the Orthodox understanding of the Church, "we collectively do something that we could not possibly do otherwise, and in doing it, we are something that we could not otherwise be."[3]

What Is the Church? Where Is the Church?

What is the Church? Where is the Church? Is the Church "one," or are there many churches? How was the Church founded? Is the Church a historical reality or only a spiritual reality? How can the Church be holy if it is composed of sinful people? How does one become part of the Church? As with other theological concepts, these questions are often answered differently outside and inside the Orthodox Church. The Orthodox understanding of the Church is interconnected with a theological worldview that cannot be fully apprehended in one chapter, much less one book. Nevertheless, I will sketch out some of the distinctive contours of the theology of the Church in Eastern Orthodoxy.

The Church in the New Testament

The study of the doctrine of the Church is called "ecclesiology," derived from the New Testament Greek word *ekklēsia* (usually translated either as "assembly" or "church") and formed from two Greek words: *ek* (out from)

---

1. James Payton, *Light from the Christian East: An Introduction to the Orthodox Tradition* (Downers Grove, IL: IVP Academic, 2007), 173.
2. The created purpose of humankind is discussed in greater detail in chap. 6 in the section "Created for Communion." The importance of the Eucharist in Eastern Orthodoxy is discussed in greater detail in chap. 8 in the section "The Holy Mysteries."
3. Payton, *Light from the Christian East*, 173.

and *kaleō* (to call). Thus, *ekklēsia* literally refers to being "called out" from the world. According to St. Peter, the *ekklēsia* is a structure of "living stones" that are built into "a spiritual house, a holy priesthood" (1 Pet. 2:5). St. Paul seems to suggest that the Church is actually formed *by* the gathering of the people: "when you come together as a church" (1 Cor. 11:18). This dynamic understanding of the Church being "formed" is especially important in Orthodoxy. The Church is not a physical place, but it is constituted by people who are being called out from the world to be formed together into the Body of Christ by the Holy Spirit, in worship of the Father.

In his letters, St. Paul often speaks about the *ekklēsia* in the singular as the one Body of Christ.[4] Yet Paul also uses the term *ekklēsia* in the plural to refer to the various local congregations in Greece and Asia Minor. For example, Paul tells the believers in Rome that the "churches of Christ" send their greetings to them through him (Rom. 16:16). He also greets believers in the "churches" at Ephesus, Thessalonica, Rome, Galatia, and Colossae in a similar fashion. Clearly, the Church can be one and many at the same time!

The key to any inconsistency is the distinction made by location. There is only one Church because there is only one Christ. When St. Luke and St. Paul use the specific term "the Church of God" (Greek: *Ekklēsia tou Theou*),[5] they mean only the one Church—the one Body of Christ—wherever it is to be found. Paul wrote two letters to the Church at Corinth, to which I happen to have a personal connection. All four of my grandparents were Orthodox Christians born in villages in southern Greece, and two were actually from the Corinth region. When Paul wrote to my ancestors there two thousand years ago, addressing his letter "to the church of God which is at Corinth" (1 Cor. 1:2; 2 Cor. 1:1), he meant that the one Body of Christ was present in the local eucharistic Body of Christ located in Corinth.

The one Apostolic *Ekklēsia tou Theou* is constituted wherever and whenever the eucharistic community—the Body of Christ—assembles. The contrast is sometimes expressed in English writings with a capital *C* when referring to the one universal or cosmic Church, which is fully present in the lowercase *c* local Orthodox churches. The two are not separate realities. The local church is not a subset of the one Church; neither is it a segment of a divided larger reality. From the time churches began to be planted by the Apostles until now, there has been an identity between the local church and the one universal Body of Christ.

4. See Rom. 12:4–5; 1 Cor. 10:17; 12:12–13, 20; Eph. 2:16; 3:6; 4:4, 25; Col. 3:15.
5. See Acts 20:28; 1 Cor. 1:2; 10:32; 11:16, 22; 15:9; 2 Cor. 1:1; Gal. 1:13; 1 Thess. 2:14; 2 Thess. 1:4; 1 Tim. 3:5.

In an admittedly paradoxical way of thinking, the local Orthodox church *is* the universal Orthodox Church. When St. Peter first planted the Church in Antioch, for example, it was not a fractional piece of the Church originally planted in Jerusalem, like a slice of pie. Nor was it understood as a "branch" of the "tree" of the one Church.[6] Rather, there was identity of that local eucharistic congregation with the one Church of God. It is in the local eucharistic congregation where all ministry occurs. The individual struggles of life are worked out together with one's church family in the local congregation, in which the one Church of God is manifested.

In confessing itself to be the "One, Holy, Catholic, and Apostolic Church" of God, the Orthodox Church claims an absolute identity with the one Christian Church in history. The historical Church has mystical and spiritual aspects, but it is also physical and visible. The Orthodox do not imagine—as did John Calvin, the father of the Protestant Reformed tradition—that the true Church is an invisible reality on earth, waiting to be constituted in heaven in the future.[7] Just as Jesus was a historical person with a genuine bodily form— and even His resurrected body was physical, tangible, and visible—the Church of God that is His body on earth must also be physical, tangible, and visible.

What does all this mean for Christians who do not happen to be members of the Orthodox Church? In saying that the Orthodox Church is the visible and historical New Testament Church two thousand years later, the Orthodox are not also suggesting that other Christians are not following Christ with fervor. Clearly, Western Christians are preaching and following the Gospel of Christ and serving the world in His name. My own Christian formation speaks to the nurturing influence of non-Orthodox Christian teachers at a Lutheran elementary school and a Baptist vacation Bible school, and much later to the witness of devout Christian scholars at Fuller Theological Seminary. Because of the visible, outward form of the historically continuous Apostolic Church, Metropolitan Kallistos Ware writes that "we know where the Church is but we cannot be sure where it is not."[8] That is to say, the Orthodox do not equate the

---

6. This is not at all the same idea as the "branch theory" propagated by William Palmer, an Anglican in the nineteenth century, which suggested that Roman Catholicism, Eastern Orthodoxy, and the Church of England were mere branches of the one Church. Even on its surface, the idea that bodies not in communion with one another, and that teach different doctrines of faith, could somehow form one Church is inconceivable.

7. For example, Calvin writes, "We must leave to God alone the knowledge of his church, whose foundation is his secret election," and "God miraculously keeps his Church as in hiding places." John Calvin, *Institutes of the Christian Religion* IV.1.2, ed. John T. McNeill, trans. Ford Lewis Battles (Louisville: Westminster John Knox, 1960), 2:1013–14.

8. Timothy Ware, *The Orthodox Church: An Introduction to Eastern Christianity*, 3rd ed. (London: Penguin, 2015), 301.

ecclesial boundaries of the Orthodox Church with salvation, since one should never speak for God. "It may be that in His mercy He will grant salvation to many people who in this present life have never been visibly members of any church community."[9] To phrase this view another way, being joined to the Body of Christ is considered by the Orthodox to be essential for salvation, but it may well be the case that God accepts those outside the Orthodox Church into communion in His heavenly Kingdom. Alexei Khomiakov (1804–1860), a Russian Orthodox scholar noted especially for his writings on Orthodox ecclesiology, indicates that because the earthly and visible Church has limits, it can only judge within its limits:

> She acts and knows only within her own limits; and (according to the words of Paul the Apostle to the Corinthians, 1 Cor. 5:12) does not judge the rest of mankind, and only looks upon those as excluded, that is to say, not belonging to her, who have excluded themselves. The rest of mankind, whether alien from the Church, or united to her by ties which God has not willed to reveal to her, she leaves to the judgement of the Great Day.[10]

There is a prevailing attitude of humility, evident both in Orthodox theology and among Orthodox people, that salvation can only be declared by the one who saves. It is due to a high regard for God's "longsuffering toward us, not willing that any should perish" (2 Pet. 3:9) and God's desire that all should "be saved" and "come to the knowledge of the truth" (1 Tim. 2:4) that the Orthodox simply refrain from the judgment that salvation is impossible for anyone.

Theandric Mystery

There are some people whose impression is that "the Church" is something like a religious megacorporation—a human institution with established rules of operation. This organization might even conduct market research to attract its congregants. But the Orthodox Church is nothing like this. First of all, it is not very "organized" in the corporate sense. Mainly, the Orthodox Church is not a human institution at all—not even a human institution that directs its efforts toward God. Eastern Orthodoxy considers the Church to be a theandric mystery. "Theandric" is composed of the Greek words for God (*Theos*) and man (*andros*), and therefore simply refers to something that is

9. Kallistos Ware, *How Are We Saved? The Understanding of Salvation in the Orthodox Church* (Minneapolis: Light and Life Publishing, 1996), 68.
10. Alexei Khomiakov, *Russia and the English Church*, 194, quoted in Georges Florovsky, "The Limits of the Church," *Church Quarterly Review* 117, no. 233 (1933): 131.

both divine and human. Since Jesus Christ Himself is simultaneously divine and human, the Church that is His Body on earth is also divine and human.

Vladimir Lossky calls the Church an "incarnational organism." Just like the incarnate Christ, the Church has "two natures, two wills and two operations which are at once inseparable and yet distinct."[11] It is not a human institution, and it is certainly not a business, yet it has a human form, and it must function as a nonprofit corporation in a practical, legal sense. Fr. Thomas Hopko, who was Professor of Dogmatics and Dean of St. Vladimir's Orthodox Seminary, provides a helpful definition of the Church as "a divine reality with a human form made divine by **grace**."[12]

The Orthodox Church Today

At the time of this writing, there are approximately 2.5 billion Christians in the world. It is probably no surprise that the largest single grouping of Christians in the world is found in the Roman Catholic Church. One might nevertheless be surprised to learn that the second largest grouping of Christians in the world is the Orthodox Church, with nearly 300 million.[13] The Orthodox Church is actually a family of churches throughout the world that are in full communion with one another. They are identified by their location and recognize one another, through their bishops, as holding to the same Apostolic Tradition.

Besides the original four ancient Orthodox Sees—Constantinople (now called Istanbul), Alexandria, Antioch, and Jerusalem—today there are also self-headed or **autocephalous** Orthodox churches. Each self-headed Orthodox church is led by a bishop who might be referred to as "archbishop," "metropolitan," or "patriarch" (titles that refer to a bishop with oversight of an even larger area, usually a country or a continent). These self-headed churches include Russia, Serbia, Romania, Bulgaria, Georgia, Cyprus, Greece, Poland, Albania, Ukraine, and the Czech lands and Slovakia.[14] Being in full communion with one another means that any member of one self-headed Orthodox

11. Vladimir Lossky, *The Mystical Theology of the Eastern Church*, trans. The Fellowship of St. Alban and St. Sergius (Crestwood, NY: St. Vladimir's Seminary Press, 1976), 187.
12. Thomas Hopko, *All the Fullness of God* (Crestwood, NY: St. Vladimir's Seminary Press, 1982), 93.
13. "Status of Global Christianity," Gordon-Conwell Theological Seminary, accessed July 1, 2020, https://www.gordonconwell.edu/center-for-global-christianity/resources/status-of-global-christianity/.
14. See the list at "Patriarchates and Autocephalous Churches," Greek Orthodox Archdiocese of America, http://www.goarch.org/patriarchates.

church may participate in the worship of any other Orthodox church, including receiving the Eucharist. Even today, each local eucharistic congregation in the recognized family of Orthodox churches in the world is considered to have essential identity with the one Body of Christ. The one Church of God (*Ekklēsia tou Theou*) is fully present in the many Orthodox churches.

Still, a local eucharistic congregation must possess certain criteria in order to be "in communion" with other local Orthodox churches. One of the criteria is that each local Orthodox Church family must have kept both a historical and a liturgical continuity with the Church of the Apostles by Apostolic succession, and must profess and live the same Orthodox Faith. Apostolic succession means that each local Orthodox community has been led by a bishop who can trace his eucharistic leadership back to the Apostles. The Orthodox bishop must also lead his congregation in maintaining the Apostolic worship, beliefs, and practices "in communion" with other Orthodox bishops worldwide. These interrelated ideas of unity, conciliarity, and Apostolic succession will be discussed in greater detail in chapter 3.

To summarize the Orthodox view of the Church:

1. There is one Church, since the Church is the Body of Christ and Jesus Christ is one.
2. The one Church is present in each local church that has maintained a historical connection with the Apostolic Church in faith and practice.
3. Jesus Christ is inseparably human and divine, so the Church as the Body of Christ has the same two natures, inseparable and yet distinct.
4. Since the Body is made up of many members, Orthodox Christians believe that they are being saved together in the Church.
5. Although the Church has mystical aspects that are not always visible, the Church has been a historically continuous and visible reality since its institution by Jesus Christ.

What Is "This Rock"?

Jesus Christ Himself instituted His Church. St. Matthew's Gospel recounts how Jesus told the Apostle Peter, "You are Peter, and on this rock I will build My church" (Matt. 16:18). What is this rock? Throughout history, commentators have interpreted this passage in two distinct ways: (1) the rock is Peter; or (2) the rock is Peter's faith in Christ. Christian commentators in both the East and the West, past and present, usually emphasize one option over the other. Roman Catholicism eventually narrowed its focus on the first interpretation:

the rock is the person of Peter. For example, the *United States Catholic Catechism for Adults* states that "Jesus then proceeded to make Peter the rock on which he would build the Church."[15] The logic is that because Peter's name (*Petros*) means "rock" in Greek, Jesus must have been referring specifically to the person of Peter. The next step in the Roman Catholic logic is to make a direct identification between the Apostle Peter—who was initially the first bishop of Antioch, but later the first bishop of Rome—and every bishop of Rome thereafter.[16] And finally, Roman Catholics believe that each succeeding pope has been given universal authority over the whole Church because they believe that the "keys of the kingdom" (Matt. 16:19) were given by Christ only to Peter.

In rather stark contrast to the Roman Catholic view, the Eastern Orthodox Church affirms that the rock in Matthew 16:18 is not Peter but rather Peter's faith in Jesus as Israel's expected Messiah—the Christ. This interpretation first takes into consideration the entire context of Peter's encounter with Jesus, noting that Christ's comment was an immediate response to Peter's confession of faith: "You are the Christ, the Son of the living God" (Matt. 16:16). Also, Jesus Christ is the "chief cornerstone" of the Church, which has been "built on the foundation of the apostles and prophets" (Eph. 2:20). Fr. Theodore Stylianopoulos, Professor Emeritus of New Testament at Holy Cross Orthodox Seminary, states the consensus Orthodox view: "Peter is the first confessor, the foundation upon which others are added and thus the Church is built on the confession of all believers."[17]

Also, since the Orthodox Christian understanding of the Church is that it is a theandric (human and divine) mystery, the Church could not have been founded solely upon a human element. Orthodox commentators are unanimous in stating emphatically that the Church was established by Christ Himself (the divine element) upon the confession of faith by Peter, who was the leader of the Apostolic council (the human element)—but not exclusively upon the individual person of Peter. The foundation of the Church is the faith of all the Apostles, with Christ as the cornerstone: "No other foundation can anyone lay than that which is laid, which is Jesus Christ" (1 Cor. 3:11).

15. *United States Catholic Catechism for Adults* (Washington, DC: United States Conference of Catholic Bishops, 2007), 111.

16. For details, refer to the authorized Catholic Catechism by Peter Kreeft, *Catholic Christianity: A Complete Catechism of Catholic Beliefs Based on the Catechism of the Catholic Church* (San Francisco: Ignatius, 2011).

17. Theodore Stylianopoulos, "Concerning the Biblical Foundations of Primacy," in *The Petrine Ministry: Catholics and Orthodox in Dialogue*, ed. Walter Kasper (New York: Newman, 2006), 46.

One of the most respected preachers and biblical commentators of the Patristic era was St. John Chrysostom (347–407), the "golden-mouthed" preacher and Archbishop of Constantinople. Chrysostom observes that, in Matthew 16:18, Jesus Christ was acknowledging Peter's preceding statement of faith in Matthew 16:16: "He did not say 'upon Peter' for it is not upon the man, but upon his own faith that the Church is built. And what is this faith? 'You are the Christ, the Son of the living God.'"[18] Australian theology professor Philip Kariatlis agrees with Chrysostom's view and summarizes the general Patristic witness in this way: "Whilst not denying the identification of the 'rock' with Peter, one must immediately qualify, in line with the early Patristic witness, that it is the *confessing* Peter that is being referred to in this case—specifically Peter's christological profession of faith and not with the person of Peter *per se*."[19]

There is again a contrast between how the Eastern Orthodox and Roman Catholics understand the very next verse. In Matthew 16:19, Jesus tells Peter, "I will give you the keys of the kingdom of heaven" so that "whatever you bind on earth will be bound in heaven, and whatever you loose on earth will be loosed in heaven." This same language is found again later in the same Gospel, where Jesus is clearly speaking to all His disciples (Matt. 18:18). It is obvious from the latter passage that the authority to bind and loose was given by Christ to all the Apostles, as well as to Peter. Yet this specific passage has undergirded the Roman Catholic notion that only Peter is the foundation of the Christian Church and that every successor bishop of Rome enjoys supreme authority over all bishops in the Christian world. This has never been the Orthodox belief.

One, Holy, Catholic, and Apostolic

Imagine being given the task of describing something that is not only historical and global but also prehistoric and cosmic (since Christ is eternal God and the Church is His Body), and in as few words as possible. The Fathers of the First Ecumenical Council held in Nicaea in AD 325[20] took on such a task when they began to compile a brief statement of the Orthodox Christian

18. John Chrysostom, *Pentecosten*, quoted in Laurent Cleenewerck, *His Broken Body: Understanding and Healing the Schism between the Roman Catholic and Eastern Orthodox Churches* (Washington DC: Euclid University Consortium Press, 2007), 263.

19. Philip Kariatlis, *Church as Communion: The Gift and Goal of Koinonia* (Adelaide, Australia: ATF Press, 2011), 57n89.

20. See chap. 5 for a discussion of the importance of the Ecumenical Councils in the Orthodox Church.

Faith. The resulting Creed is most often referred to as the "Nicene Creed" or simply "the Creed," and has been proclaimed in the Orthodox Church at every Divine Liturgy continually since the fourth century.[21] Of note for this present discussion is how the Fathers of the First Ecumenical Council brilliantly (and succinctly!) described the Church of God with four scriptural terms: "One, Holy, Catholic, and Apostolic." One helpful way to think about these four identifying features of the Church is to consider them as both "gift" and "task."

One

The Orthodox Church is "one" because God is one: "There is one body and one Spirit, just as you were called in one hope of your calling; one Lord, one faith, one baptism; one God and Father of all, who is above all, and through all, and in you all" (Eph. 4:4–6). The Church has also been charged with the task to endeavor to "keep the unity of the Spirit in the bond of peace" (Eph. 4:3), living out the mystery of unity in diversity. Christ is one, even though His Body, the Church, is constituted by the many.

Holy

The Greek word for "holy" in the New Testament is *agios*. In Greek, an *a* in front of a word negates the word. The root *gios* means "earth" or "world" (think "geography" or "geology"), so *agios* literally means "not of the world." If something is holy, it has been set apart from the world or blessed for a special purpose. In the New Testament, believers are set apart as a holy nation in Christ: "But you are a chosen generation, a royal priesthood, a holy nation, His own special people" (1 Pet. 2:9).

Orthodox Christianity considers the Church of Christ to be holy and perfect (one might even use the term "infallible") because it is Christ's perfect Body. Despite the fact that its individual members are not all righteous, the belief is that the Holy Spirit constitutes the perfect Body of Christ from imperfect and sinful human beings at each celebration of the Eucharist in the Divine Liturgy. In response to the gift of holiness, the Church must also follow Christ in holiness: "Be holy, for I am holy" (1 Pet. 1:16). Christians are admonished to pursue holiness, "without which no one will see the Lord" (Heb. 12:14).

21. Much of the Creed of Nicaea was already present in the first-century Church, such as in the creedal statements of 1 Cor. 15:3–5. Justin Martyr wrote in his *First Apology* (section 61), around AD 150, that Baptism was accompanied by a similar confession of faith.

Catholic

The Greek word in the Creed translated as "catholic" is *katholou*, and it means "according to the whole." St. Ignatius of Antioch was the first to use it to describe the Church in his *Letter to the Smyrnaeans* in AD 110.[22] Ignatius's meaning in the context of this letter is that the catholic Church has the whole Christ and everything needed for salvation. "Catholic" also eventually came to mean "universal," but this was not Ignatius's understanding when he first used the phrase, nor was it the meaning intended by the Church Fathers who formulated the language of the Creed. The Church has received the gift of catholicity, which is the fullness of Jesus Christ, the "head over all things to the church, which is His body, the fullness of Him who fills all in all" (Eph. 1:22–23), as well as the task of maintaining the fullness of Christ.

Apostolic

An apostle (Greek: *apostolos*) is literally "one who is sent." Christ's command to the Apostles to "go . . . and make disciples of all the nations" in the Great Commission (Matt. 28:19) expresses the Apostolic imperative to be sent into the world to proclaim the Good News. There are several other layers of meaning in the Orthodox understanding of apostolicity. The mystery of Christ was first revealed to the Apostles (Eph. 3:5), and the Church was founded on their teachings. Therefore, an important aspect of the task of maintaining apostolicity in the Orthodox Church is to teach and live the same faith as the Apostles: "Therefore, brethren, stand fast and hold the traditions which you were taught, whether by word or our epistle" (2 Thess. 2:15).

According to twentieth-century British church history scholar J. N. D. Kelly, the Nicene Fathers wanted to "affirm the apostolicity of the Church in the sense that it was continuous with the apostles, not only in the faith to which it witnessed but also in its structure, organization and practice."[23] Consequently, another layer of apostolicity requires maintaining the Apostolic structure, organization, and practice of the Faith. Finally, "Apostolic" indicates a historically continuous connection to the Church of the Apostles, which in the Orthodox Church has been guarded through the succession of the eucharistic leaders (bishops) and their communities.[24] All of these together constitute apostolicity for the Orthodox Church: (1) maintaining the teaching

---

22. Ignatius of Antioch, *Letter to the Smyrnaeans* 8. Excerpts from this letter are included in the appendix.
23. Quoted in Thomas P. Rausch, *Towards a Truly Catholic Church: An Ecclesiology for the Third Millennium* (Collegeville, MN: Liturgical Press, 2005), 145.
24. See the discussion of Apostolic succession in chap. 4.

of the Apostles; (2) maintaining the structure, organization, and practice of the Apostolic Church; (3) maintaining an unbroken, visible, and historical connection to the Eucharist of the Apostolic Church; and (4) sharing the Good News of Jesus Christ with all nations.

■ DISCUSSION QUESTIONS ■

1. Eastern Orthodoxy considers the Church to be holy and perfect. How do the Orthodox believe this is possible, since the Church's human members are not all righteous?

2. "Apostolicity" is one of the marks of the Church, expressed in the Nicene Creed. How does Eastern Orthodoxy define and live out its apostolicity?

3. How does the Orthodox Church consider the Church of God to be one and many at the same time?

4. What did the Church Fathers mean when they called the Church "catholic"?

3

Communion and Revelation

What Holds the Orthodox Church Together?

What holds the Orthodox Church together? The question seems simple enough, but it will take a few interrelated steps to arrive at a cohesive paradigm. I have already outlined the idea that the Orthodox Church is a family of local self-governing churches that elect their own bishops and administer their own organizations. Unlike, for example, the pope in Roman Catholicism, there is no one central authority in the Orthodox Church. Earthly administration of the Orthodox Church is entirely decentralized. In light of human nature and history, it seems unlikely that anything without a central earthly power could have been maintained intact for more than two thousand years. But it has. The local self-governed Orthodox churches have all maintained the same Apostolic Faith, use the same Bible, govern under the same **canons**, acknowledge the authority of the same seven Ecumenical Councils, and worship using basically the same liturgy, though in different languages. So a better question here might be, "*How in the world* has the Orthodox Church maintained unity for over two thousand years?"

The key to Orthodox unity is that the essential nature of the Church is pneumatological. What holds the Orthodox Church together is the Holy Spirit guiding all the local churches to the same Faith and the same worship—the same "proper glory" or "orthodoxy." There is an obvious circular reasoning in this logic: it is the same Faith and worship because it is the same Faith and worship. It will be helpful to walk through a few additional steps to gain a clearer vision of how the Orthodox Church has maintained unity—or communion—for more than two thousand years.

Communion and Conciliarity

> The grace of the Lord Jesus Christ, and the love of God, and the communion of the Holy Spirit be with you all. Amen. (2 Cor. 13:14)

Metropolitan John Zizioulas writes that "it is the communion of the Church which makes theology into truth."[1] Communion (Greek: *koinōnia*) is fundamental to every aspect of Orthodox thought and life and is mentioned more than twenty times in the New Testament. *Koinōnia* in the New Testament conveys the highest intimacy of mutual sharing and union; for example, "Do not be unequally yoked together with unbelievers. For . . . what communion [*koinōnia*] has light with darkness?" (2 Cor. 6:14). Unfortunately, in some English versions, the powerful message conveyed by the word *koinōnia* is weakened. For instance, the New International Version of the Bible translates *koinōnia* only as "fellowship" or "participation," which dilutes its intimate spiritual implications. This also means that its readers have likely missed the frequency and importance of *communion* to the New Testament Church. The desire to reflect the full intentions of the biblical authors expressed by *koinōnia*, as opposed to the various English substitutes, is one of the reasons why the World Council of Churches chose to use the original Greek in the title of an important study: "The Unity of the Church as Koinonia: Gift and Calling."[2]

In Communion

The Orthodox believe that when they gather for worship in the Divine Liturgy, they are not beginning a new worship service but are instead "entering into" the eternal heavenly worship around the throne of Jesus Christ. This is a notable distinction. More will be discussed about the "earthly heaven" of Orthodox worship in chapter 8, but for now just keep the idea in mind. The implication of "entering into" heavenly worship means that when any local Orthodox Church, anywhere on earth today, celebrates the Divine Liturgy, it does so in the belief that it is "in communion" with the Orthodox Church in

---

1. John D. Zizioulas, *Being as Communion: Studies in Personhood and the Church* (Crestwood, NY: St. Vladimir's Seminary Press, 1985), 118n120.
2. World Council of Churches, "The Unity of the Church as Koinonia: Gift and Calling," in *The Ecumenical Movement: An Anthology of Key Texts and Voices*, ed. M. Kinnamon and B. E. Cope (Grand Rapids: Eerdmans, 1996), 124ff.

every other location (across space) and also with the same Orthodox Church in history (across time).

As the former Oxford University professor Nicholas Zernov (1898–1980) writes, "The Holy Spirit keeps watch and reveals the same truth to every age and race."[3] Therefore, when an Orthodox congregation in Seoul, South Korea, worships the triune God in the Orthodox Divine Liturgy, they are worshiping the same God in the same way as the Orthodox Church in Corinth, Greece, or as the Orthodox congregation in Modesto, California, or even as a congregation celebrating the Divine Liturgy outdoors in the arid desert of Turkana, Kenya—and so on. St. Athanasius indicates the same notion of communion across time and space in his tenth *Festal Letter* (AD 338):

> For although place separate us, yet the Lord the Giver of the feast, and Who is Himself our feast, Who is also the Bestower of the Spirit, brings us together in mind, in harmony, and in the bond of peace. For when we mind and think the same things, and offer up the same prayers on behalf of each other, no place can separate us, but the Lord gathers and unites us together. For if He promises, that "when two or three are gathered together in His name, He is in the midst of them [Matt. 18:20]," it is plain that being in the midst of those who in every place are gathered together, He unites them, and receives the prayers of all of them, as if they were near, and listens to all of them, as they cry out the same Amen.[4]

Athanasius is saying that when the same prayers are offered by those who are of the same mind, united in the Lord by the same Holy Spirit, their worship is received together as one Amen. They are all "in communion" with one another in the Lord, as if they were together.

"Communion" is also at the core of Metropolitan Kallistos Ware's answer to the earlier question of how the Orthodox Church is held together: "not by a centralized organization, not by a single hierarch wielding power over the whole body, but by the double bond of unity in the faith and communion in the sacraments."[5] Each bishop who leads an autocephalous (self-headed) Orthodox jurisdiction is independent, but he is also in full agreement with

3. Nicholas Zernov, *Orthodox Encounter: The Christian East and the Ecumenical Movement* (London: James Clarke, 1961), 97.
4. Athanasius, *Festal Letter* 10.2, in *A Select Library of Nicene and Post-Nicene Fathers of the Christian Church*, 2nd series, ed. Philip Schaff and Henry Wace, 14 vols. (1890–1900; repr., Grand Rapids: Eerdmans, 1952), 4:506–53. See https://www.newadvent.org/fathers/2806010.htm.
5. Timothy Ware, *The Orthodox Church: An Introduction to Eastern Christianity*, 3rd ed. (London: Penguin, 2015), 7.

every other bishop, past and present, on all essential dogmas and is also "in communion" in terms of the sacraments. Orthodox ecclesiology is, above all else, a theology of communion in the Holy Spirit.

Conciliarity

God is the author of peace, but we humans are not always peaceful, even in our churches. Disagreements can lead to division, as we saw with the Great Schism of 1054 as well as with the Protestant Reformation of the sixteenth century and countless other schisms and church splits since then. Disagreement is an unfortunate yet familiar aspect of most human relationships. Whether in the home, the workplace, or the church, how disagreements are resolved is key to whether a relationship will be sustainable. Unresolved conflicts can result in exclusion—siblings who no longer speak to one another, a couple who divorces, an employee who quits in a huff, or a congregation that splits into factions. And yet, if there is an unwavering commitment to staying together, there will also be an unwavering commitment to resolving the conflicts that inevitably arise.

A few years ago, in a large evangelical congregation in my hometown, the board of elders expressed to the senior pastor that his sermons were not resonating with the new demographic these elders wished to attract. The board told him to especially avoid discussing sin and the need for repentance. Apparently, this was not merely a suggestion. Rather than change what he believed God had led him to preach, the senior pastor resigned. By the next weekend, he was already preaching in a local movie theater with a new congregation created from that split. This example is a microcosm of how the disagreements, splits, and divisions of the Protestant Reformation in the sixteenth century began a trend that has continued into the present day. Church splits in evangelical Protestantism are not only common but are statistically on the rise: there are an estimated 44,800 denominations in 2020.[6] The Orthodox Church is certainly not immune to disagreements, but its present-day unity is due to the precedent of conflict resolution established by the Apostles in AD 49.

The Jerusalem Council of Acts 15

The Acts of the Apostles provides a clear insight into occasionally strained relationships, even in the idyllic New Testament Church. You might remember

6. At the turn of the twentieth century, there were approximately 2,000 Protestant denominations, but that number had grown to 31,100 by the turn of the twenty-first century. See "Status of Global Christianity," Gordon-Conwell Theological Seminary, accessed July 1, 2020, https://www.gordonconwell.edu/center-for-global-christianity/resources/status-of-global-christianity/.

reading in Acts that there were some Jewish Christians who thought that Gentile converts to Christianity should first become Jewish. Gentile men, for example, would need to be circumcised, and all male and female converts would need to follow the dietary and other restrictions of the Jewish law before receiving Christian Baptism. But St. Paul and St. Barnabas (and St. Peter earlier) disagreed and pointed to the circumcision of the heart by the Holy Spirit that was already evident in Gentile believers (Acts 14–15). The conflict between the two factions easily could have caused division—two new congregations or "denominations" could have formed out of the one, as happened to the congregation in my hometown. But division did not happen. The New Testament Church did not split into two congregations or sects because of the way they resolved the dispute.

The first thing we should notice in this New Testament disagreement is that the leader of the Apostles, St. Peter, did not make a move to settle the issue himself. Peter is always mentioned first in lists of the Apostles, and he is even mentioned first in Christ's smaller "inner circle" of Peter, James, and John. Peter clearly held a position of honor within the Apostolic council, and yet he was not the "boss." Peter's word would have been the end of the discussion if he (or the other Apostles) truly believed that he alone had been given the authority to make unilateral declarations about the Faith. Instead, it was decided that Paul and Barnabas should consult with the Apostles and elders in Jerusalem about the question of the circumcision of Gentile believers (Acts 15:1–2).

The bishop of Jerusalem at the time was the Apostle James, who was also called "James the Just." Even James, the leader of the Church of God in Jerusalem, did not make the decision unilaterally. Instead, James convened a council composed of "apostles and elders" (Acts 15:6) who met "with one accord" (15:25)—a clear indication that they had each made a commitment to be unified in their witness. How the "apostles and elders, with the whole church" (15:22) viewed their role is evident in their response letter, as recounted in verse 28: "For it seemed good to the Holy Spirit, and to us . . ." They discerned the presence of the Holy Spirit and confessed the "communion of the Holy Spirit" (2 Cor. 13:14) as the guiding principle of the Jerusalem Council. Neither Peter, who was the leader of the Apostles, nor James, who was the bishop of Jerusalem, believed he had the sole authority to make such an important dogmatic declaration about how Gentiles should be received into the Christian Faith. When they had gathered "in one accord" in the Holy Spirit, they waited until they were all directed by the Holy Spirit to the will of God.

The model for the Church that resulted from this event in AD 49 was an unshakable commitment to preserving unity at all costs. Whenever there were disagreements about important teachings of the Faith, the Fathers of the Church obligated themselves to the principle of conciliarity with confidence that the Holy Spirit would reveal the path to truth in the communion of the Holy Spirit, since "God is not the author of confusion but of peace" (1 Cor. 14:33). But the Holy Spirit does not always move at the speed of text messages, and it may take a long time to reach agreement on major decisions. This explains why some of the Ecumenical Councils of the undivided Church met over many months to settle certain theological issues.

You might be thinking that this is not a very practical way to make decisions, especially in the fast-moving climate of the twenty-first century, and you would be correct! Things will move very slowly when everyone—or nearly everyone—must agree. I witnessed the principle of conciliarity firsthand a few years ago at the annual clergy-**laity** leadership assembly of a large Orthodox metropolis. The debate was about a business issue and not a theological issue. Imagine a gathering of two hundred or so delegates who were asked to decide whether to accept a purchase offer on a piece of property that had been acquired by donation. Following *Robert's Rules of Order*, the motion to accept the offer was presented and discussed with fervor on all sides. Some thought the offer should be accepted, and others thought the offer was too low. Still others thought the property should not be sold until the downtown was rebuilt and property values increased. Eventually, the issue was put to a vote, and the ayes prevailed, with a strong majority of 70 percent. Some of the aye voters clapped, and many of the nay voters grumbled. The parliamentarian of the meeting was ready to certify the vote that the property should be sold, when the metropolitan (a bishop who presides over a larger area) stood up and explained, "We Orthodox should not make decisions this way." He explained that the Orthodox tradition was to always seek consensus, not just majority. He tasked the assembly with finding a solution upon which everyone could agree, even if it might take more time to do so. The parliamentarian determined that the meeting could be suspended while other options were pursued. Within a few weeks and with a little more information, a remote vote by the original set of delegates concluded the issue unanimously. It took a lot longer to settle the issue by conciliarity, but this also allowed the assembly to remain "in one accord."

Holy Tradition

> We do not change the everlasting boundaries which our fathers have set, but we keep the Tradition just as we received it. (St. John of Damascus, *On the Holy Icons* 2.12)

Is it healthy to "keep the Tradition," as in the above quotation from St. John of Damascus? To some, the word "tradition" suggests a stuffy churchly mentality that always looks to the past and cannot address the present era or, even worse, hangs onto human customs against which Jesus warned (Mark 7:7–8). The sixteenth-century Protestant Reformers considered the "traditions" of Rome to be responsible for what they deemed to be unscriptural practices.[7] Many Protestants today still think negatively about tradition because of this history. As one of my Protestant students recently shared, "Tradition is a dirty word in my denomination!"

In contrast, Holy Tradition for the Orthodox Church is something quite different from the "tradition of men" (Mark 7:8) that Jesus spoke of so disparagingly. In his book *The Way*, Clark Carlton suggests that readers of the most popular English translation of the Bible, the New International Version, might be surprised to learn that Christians have actually been instructed to *keep* the tradition handed down from the Apostles, not just the teaching.[8] This is because Carlton believes the NIV translators intentionally mistranslated three verses so that "tradition" would never be presented in a positive light. Regardless of the NIV translators' motivation, their choices for English readers have altered the meaning intended by the New Testament authors.

"Tradition" in the Greek of the New Testament is *paradosis*. Searching for the words "tradition" or "traditions" in an NIV New Testament published prior to 2011 brings up only ten references.[9] In each case, the word "tradition" is presented negatively, as something opposed to the truth of God. The Greek word *paradosis*, however, actually occurs fourteen times in the New Testament. It does seem that the NIV translators of that edition made a decision that wherever Scripture uses the term in the negative sense (e.g., Mark 7:8–9; Col. 2:8), the translation would be "tradition." Wherever it is used in a positive sense, the word is translated as "teachings." Here is an example from two parallel English translations of 2 Thessalonians 2:15:

> So then, brothers and sisters, stand firm and hold fast to the teachings [*paradosis*] we passed on to you, whether by word of mouth or by letter. (NIV)

7. For example, Martin Luther wrote, "We should boldly resist those teachers of traditions and sharply censure the laws of popes." Martin Luther, "Freedom of a Christian," in *Martin Luther: Selections from His Writings*, ed. John Dillenberger (New York: Anchor, 1962), 83.

8. Clark Carlton, *The Way: What Every Protestant Should Know about the Orthodox Church* (Salisbury, MA: Regina, 1997), 135–39.

9. The updated 2011 edition of the New International Version includes twelve references to "tradition(s)."

Therefore, brethren, stand fast and hold the traditions [*paradosis*] which you were taught, whether by word or our epistle. (NKJV)

Another example is 2 Thessalonians 3:6: "But we command you, brethren, in the name of our Lord Jesus Christ, that you withdraw from every brother who walks disorderly and not according to the tradition [*paradosis*] which he received from us" (NKJV). The NIV translates the same word, *paradosis*, as "teaching," which could indeed lead readers to believe that "teaching," but not "tradition," should be handed down.

The Life of the Spirit in the Church

If we live in the Spirit, let us also walk in the Spirit. (Gal. 5:25)

According to Vladimir Lossky, Orthodox Holy Tradition is simply "the life of the Holy Spirit in the Church."[10] Holy Tradition is the result of the direct and personal activity of the Holy Spirit as the guiding authority of truth within the Orthodox Church. Lossky adds that Holy Tradition is the Holy Spirit "communicating to each member of the Body of Christ the faculty of hearing, of receiving, of knowing the Truth in the Light which belongs to it, and not according to the natural light of human reason."[11] This is why Fr. Georges Florovsky (1893–1979) argues that Tradition is a "charismatic principle, not a historical principle."[12] To perceive truth requires the divine gift of spiritual perception. The Holy Spirit is recognized by the Orthodox as the ultimate guide of all aspects of the Church—not only theology, but even governance and administration.

Lossky further insists that Holy Tradition should not be thought of in terms of content or even as an expression of truth, whether in words, images, or symbols, but rather as the "unique mode of receiving Truth."[13] This distinction may seem rather abstruse, but it is still important. James Payton's clever characterization of Tradition as both "process" and "package" may help to clarify what Lossky means. For Payton, "process" is the act of handing something down, and "package" refers to the content that is handed down. The content can be anything, such as the Gospel message, the Apostolic teachings, or worship practices. Lossky emphasizes that Orthodox Holy Tradition

10. Vladimir Lossky, "Tradition and Traditions," in *In the Image and Likeness of God*, ed. John H. Erickson and Thomas E. Bird (Crestwood, NY: St. Vladimir's Seminary Press, 1974), 152.
11. Lossky, "Tradition and Traditions," 151.
12. Georges Florovsky, *Bible, Church, Tradition: An Eastern Orthodox View*, Collected Works 1 (Belmont, MA: Nordland, 1972), 47.
13. Lossky, "Tradition and Traditions," 152.

is not the package (Payton's term) or content at all, but is the entire context through which the Holy Spirit communicates and is experienced. There are many differing expressions of the truth of God, such as "words written or pronounced, in images or in symbols liturgical or otherwise." Yet Holy Tradition is most properly understood not as the content or expression but as the light by which it is revealed: "Tradition is not the word, but the living breath which makes the words heard at the same time as the silence from which it came; it is not the Truth, but a communication of the Spirit of Truth outside which the Truth cannot be received. The Holy Spirit is the living breath of the Church, that makes Truth known."[14]

It is a challenge in such a brief discussion to convey just how important Holy Tradition is in the Orthodox Church. It is literally everything! "There is no Orthodoxy without Holy Tradition," according to Orthodox scholar Fr. John Meyendorff.[15] Meyendorff, like Lossky, is also referring not to the content of what has been handed down but to the entire context of the Church's life as "communion in Spirit and in truth with the witness of the apostles and fathers."[16] Because of the power of God, and in spite of human weaknesses, "there was and there is an uninterrupted, consistent and continuous Holy Tradition of faith held by the Church throughout the centuries."[17]

Scripture in Tradition

A common debate is that of the relationship between Tradition and Scripture. As Metropolitan Ware points out, "Scripture exists *within* Tradition. To separate and contrast the two is to impoverish the idea of both alike."[18] Holy Tradition might be thought of as the "umbrella" context under which all aspects of faith and life in the Orthodox Church are properly understood. Holy Scripture exists within Holy Tradition, as does a whole panoply of expressions of the Apostolic Christian Faith: the Niceno-Constantinopolitan Creed, the dogmatic decrees of the seven Ecumenical Councils, the liturgical and sacramental life of the Church, the threefold pattern of ministry, canon law, **icons**, and even the lives and witness of the saints. But Metropolitan Ware also clarifies that not all these aspects of Holy Tradition are of equal importance. "A unique pre-eminence belongs to the Bible, to the Creed, to the doctrinal definitions

14. Lossky, "Tradition and Traditions," 151–52.

15. John Meyendorff, introduction to *The Legacy of St. Vladimir: Byzantium, Russia, America*, ed. John Breck, John Meyendorff, and Eleana Silk (Crestwood, NY: St. Vladimir's Seminary Press, 1990), 15.

16. Meyendorff, "Introduction," 15.

17. Meyendorff, "Introduction," 15.

18. Ware, *Orthodox Church*, 191.

of the Ecumenical Councils: these things the Orthodox accept as something absolute and unchanging, something which cannot be cancelled or revised."[19]

For the Orthodox Church, there is only one source or authority, and it is the Tradition of the Holy Spirit. Since Scripture exists within Tradition, Scripture can never contradict Tradition. Similarly, the Gospel that is "written" in form and color in Orthodox holy images, or "icons," can also never contradict the Gospel in the Bible written with words, or the liturgical hymns, or the dogmatic teachings of the seven Ecumenical Councils. There is harmony and agreement in all forms and in every aspect of Orthodox faith and life since they derive from the same Holy Spirit. Orthodox Tradition could not, therefore, ever be used to justify a teaching that contradicts Scripture, since the practice of the Faith and the witness of Holy Scripture both arise from the life of the Holy Spirit in the Church and the Church's life in the Holy Spirit. Payton refers to Scripture and Tradition in the Orthodox Church as being friends: "There is neither contrast nor rivalry between tradition and Scripture; according to Eastern Christianity, Scripture and tradition do not need to be reconciled because they are friends."[20]

What the Holy Tradition of the Orthodox Church is *not* is an attempt to restore the past for the past's own sake. Orthodox Tradition is not static but dynamic. It is a living experience of the Holy Spirit in the present, as well as an appreciation of the Faith handed down from the past. "Loyalty to Tradition means not primarily the acceptance of formulae or customs from past generations but rather the ever-new, personal and direct experience of the Holy Spirit in the present, here and now. It is a 'witness to the unchanging Truth in a changing world.'"[21] Jaroslav Pelikan famously illustrated the difference between Tradition (positive) and traditionalism (negative) in this way: "Tradition is the living faith of the dead; traditionalism is the dead faith of the living."[22]

Tradition and Traditions

Without a doubt, many diverse customs and local or cultural traditions can be found in Orthodox churches around the world. A favorite distinction among Orthodox commentators is between *Tradition* and *traditions*. *Tradition* (with an uppercase *T*) is the "Holy Tradition" to which Lossky referred

19. Ware, *Orthodox Church*, 191.
20. James Payton, *Light from the Christian East: An Introduction to the Orthodox Tradition* (Downers Grove, IL: IVP Academic, 2007), 201.
21. Meyendorff, "Introduction," 15.
22. Jaroslav Pelikan, *The Vindication of Tradition* (New Haven: Yale University Press, 1984), 65.

as "the life of the Spirit in the Church." This is what makes the continuity of truth and life in the Church, and what also gives the Church stability and unchangeability. Accordingly, *traditions* (with a lowercase *t*) would refer to the concrete and historic manifestations of Holy Tradition, which may change over time and from culture to culture and from place to place.

Just as in the Bible one may distinguish between the letter and the spirit, in the Tradition of the Church one may distinguish between the context and its expression. Expressions of lowercase *t* traditions might include things like the height of the icon screen in front of the altar (very high and solid in Russia; very low and open in Irvine, California) or the commemoration of certain local saints and other liturgical customs, such as the recitation of the **Beatitudes** during the liturgy in the Slavic Orthodox churches but not in the Greek Orthodox churches.

The *Eikōn*

The painted art form that the Eastern Orthodox refer to as "icons" will be discussed later, but here we will talk about the significance of the icon (Greek: *eikōn*) as an important theological concept that applies to many aspects of the Orthodox Christian Faith. *Eikōn* is used to describe a "true image" in the Greek New Testament and also in the Greek **Septuagint** version of the Old Testament. Over the centuries, the Church Fathers have referred to many things as "icons," including human beings, who at the very beginning of the Bible are said to have been created in the **image of God**: "Then God said, 'Let Us make man in Our image [*eikōn*], according to Our likeness" (Gen. 1:26). We may never know exactly what it means to have been created in the image of God, but the Genesis passage nevertheless points to the significant reality that human beings were created to reflect something of God's nature and to be in relationship with God.

Unfortunately, biblical translators confuse the picture by using the English word "image" to describe both positive and negative realities. For example, consider the second commandment that Moses received from the Lord on Mount Sinai: "Thou shalt not make unto thee any graven image" (Exod. 20:4 KJV).[23] If one were to read this commandment in certain English translations, one might think that all images are forbidden by God. This is not the case at all![24] The Hebrew word for "graven image" in Exodus 20:4 is *pesel*, which

---

23. "Graven image" is translated as "idol" in the New Revised Standard Version and as "carved image" in the New King James Version.

24. Just a few chapters later in Exodus, the Lord gives Moses very specific instructions on what images should be used to decorate the tabernacle tent, the holy of holies, and the ark of the covenant.

refers to an **idol**. The parallel word in the Greek Old Testament is *eidōlon*, and it is evident from the transliteration that it refers to an "idol" or "false god." Literally, what was forbidden by the God of Moses was the making and worshiping of carved statues of nonexistent gods—idols (Isa. 44:9–20; Pss. 115:2–8; 135:15–18).

In his letter to the Christians at Colossae, St. Paul refers to Jesus as "the image of the invisible God" (Col. 1:15). The Greek word translated there as "image" is also *eikōn*. In declaring Jesus to be the "true image" of God the Father, Paul was not saying that the Father looks like Jesus (which is impossible since the Father is immaterial). Rather, Paul was commenting on the intimate reality and correspondence between Jesus and His Father, expressed by Jesus Himself: "He who has seen Me has seen the Father. . . . I am in the Father, and the Father [is] in Me" (John 14:9–10). The incarnate Son of God, who is material and visible, has revealed the immaterial and invisible Father to the created world simply by being who He is.

"Icon" for the Orthodox does not have the same meaning as "symbol." A symbol is commonly understood to point to something separate from itself, or to stand in for something not present at all. A contemporary example of a symbol might be the golden arches of McDonald's. When you see the golden arches as you drive down the street, you know that the Big Mac you may be craving (or iced mocha, in my case) is nearby. But there is no presence of the reality—the food—within the symbol of the golden arches; there is no direct correspondence between the symbol and its referent. In contrast, the *eikōn* participates in the reality that it makes visible, even though it was already present. Jesus as *eikōn* of the Father (Col. 1:15) participates in the divine reality of the Father as one of the Holy Trinity and makes visible the Father, who was already present—"He who has seen Me has seen the Father" (John 14:9).

Since we will encounter this concept again, it may be helpful to formulate a brief working model of how *eikōn* or "icon" functions in Orthodox theology. There are two interrelated dimensions of the *eikōn*: (1) the *eikōn* reveals a divine reality that is invisible but is nevertheless present; and (2) the *eikōn* participates in the eternal reality that it presents.

Holy Scripture

The Bible is the preeminent written form of revelation within the Holy Tradition of the Orthodox Church. The Bible is read in all Orthodox worship services, and Orthodox Christians are encouraged to read the Bible independently. The fourth-century Church Father St. John Chrysostom writes that "ignorance of the Scriptures is a great precipice and a deep gulf; to know nothing of the Scriptures, is great betrayal of our salvation,"[25] and further, he believes ignorance of the Scriptures is the cause of heresies.

Metropolitan Ware points out that the Bible "is not just a collection of historical documents, but it is the book of the Church, containing God's word." Since it is "the book of the Church," we are expected to read it as "as members of the Church, in communion with all the other members throughout the ages." Rather than relying upon individualistic or isolated interpretations of Scripture, the Orthodox are concerned to remain faithful to the theological tradition by paying attention to how the Bible has been interpreted by the Church Fathers and saints, and especially to how the Bible has been used in liturgical worship.[26] For example, in addition to formal readings of Scripture during liturgical services, it is estimated that more than 212 direct quotations from the Bible (without mention of chapter and verse) are read, prayed, or sung during the Divine Liturgy.[27] In this way, Scripture becomes an event of communion, not only a text to be read.

Jesus Left a Church

"Jesus left a Church, not a book." This phrase surprised one of my good friends, who was raised as a Southern Baptist, when she heard it mentioned at a Bible study at an Orthodox Church. This very devout and lifelong Christian had simply not given much thought to the origins of the New Testament that she held so dear. Yet it is an objective fact that Jesus established the Church upon the Faith of the Apostles decades prior to the writing of any of the books that would end up in the New Testament. While the New Testament Gospels and Epistles were being written, the Church continued to grow and spread, and the Apostolic teaching and practice of the Faith continued to be faithfully handed down to each new and successive faith community.

The four Gospels and the letters of Paul, John, and Peter were all being circulated in Christian communities by the latter half of the first century and were generally acknowledged as true writings because of their apostolic credentials, because of their harmony with one another, and especially because the narrative and context of Christ's life and ministry resonated with what the Apostles taught and handed down. All four Gospels were also well established

25. John Chrysostom, "Discourse III," in *Four Discourses of Chrysostom, Chiefly on the Parable of the Rich Man and Lazarus*, trans. F. Allen (London: Longmans, Green, Reader, and Dyer, 1869), 67–68.
26. Kallistos Ware, *The Orthodox Way* (Crestwood, NY: St. Vladimir's Seminary Press, 1979), 89.
27. Ware, *Orthodox Church*, 195.

as authoritative Scripture by early Christian bishops such as Clement of Rome, Ignatius of Antioch, Polycarp of Smyrna, and Irenaeus of Lyons.

Even today, the importance of the four Gospels cannot be overstated, as they alone contain the encounter of the incarnate Logos of God, Jesus Christ, with His creation. The four Gospels are bound together in one book and hold a place of honor on the altar of every Orthodox Christian sanctuary (also called a **temple**) today. The Orthodox faithful even come forward to kiss the Gospel book after the Gospel reading in **Matins** and when they enter and leave the temple before and after the Divine Liturgy. The Gospel book itself is **venerated** by Orthodox Christians not because of the paper, ink, or even the "letter" contained therein but because it reflects and conveys the truth of Christ's Incarnation, His ministry, Crucifixion, Resurrection, and Second Coming.

A Canon Develops

It was not until the later part of the fourth century, however, that the twenty-seven books that now constitute the New Testament appeared together in a list. St. Athanasius, the bishop of Alexandria, mentions these twenty-seven books in a letter to his parishes in AD 367 because these books had been recognized as containing the true Christian Faith. Specifically referring to the twenty-seven books as the "New Testament," Athanasius calls them "fountains of salvation, that they who thirst may be satisfied with the living words they contain. In these alone is proclaimed the doctrine of godliness. Let no man add to these, neither let him take [anything] from these."[28]

Athanasius also specifically mentions other writings that had already been rejected by the faithful because of several factors, including the fact that they were written much later yet purported to have an apostolic pedigree. Their content also did not align with the Apostolic teachings and often included fanciful fabrications about the early life of Jesus: "An invention of heretics who write them when they choose, bestowing upon them their approbation, and assigning to them a date, that so, using them as ancient writings, they may find occasion to lead astray the simple."[29] According to Athanasius, it was the gift of discernment from the Holy Spirit that enabled the Church to recognize the true Apostolic teachings, as well as to detect books that were being fraudulently presented as containing the true teachings of Jesus Christ and the Apostles.

---

28. Athanasius, *Letter* 39.5–6, in *A Select Library of Nicene and Post-Nicene Fathers*, 2nd series, ed. Philip Schaff and Henry Wace, 14 vols. (1890–1900; repr., Grand Rapids: Eerdmans, 1955), 4:552. See https://www.newadvent.org/fathers/2806039.htm.

29. Athanasius, *Letter* 39.7.

The writings of Holy Scripture in the Old and New Testaments are often referred to as "the canon of Scripture." "Canon" (Greek: *kanōn*) means "rule" or "straight." In the Church, a canon is a divinely inspired guideline, or standard, which in this case refers to the Church's discernment of the writings to be called "canonical Scripture." It is not accurate to suggest that the Church created the canon, because the Church can only acknowledge which writings the Holy Spirit has brought to light as Scripture. The development of the Christian scriptural canon came about informally—from the established use of books among churches and from lists from bishops (such as Athanasius) and local councils, written out of a concern to limit the spread of heretical documents. In that way, the New Testament canon developed as a grassroots movement rather than a top-down declaration from a council or bishop. Fr. Theodore Stylianopoulos uses the term "firm" rather than "rigid" to describe the "closing of the canon" of Scripture, because the exact number of scriptural books was never "dogmatized" and the Church also valued many other writings and liturgical texts in addition to the Scriptures.[30]

Septuagint: The "Older" Old Testament

As the New Testament was originally written in Greek, the Old Testament version used by the early Church in its worship and teaching was the Greek Septuagint, translated from the Hebrew in Alexandria for Greek-speaking Jews between 275 and 100 BC. Whenever Jesus or the New Testament writers quote from the Old Testament, they quote from the Greek Septuagint version.[31] The Orthodox Church still uses the Septuagint version of the Old Testament, both for worship and in Orthodox Bibles, in its original Greek as well as in translations.

The Septuagint Old Testament includes ten more books than the Protestant Bible, which is based on a much later Hebrew manuscript called the Masoretic Text. The Masoretic manuscript was developed between the fifth and the tenth centuries AD but did not include ten of the books found in the much earlier Greek manuscript. Nevertheless, if these ten books are included in Bibles using the Protestant canon today, they are usually labeled "the **Apocrypha**"—a term that incorrectly implies that the ten books are of questionable validity or authority. These ten books, however, were always part of the ancient Church's

---

30. Theodore G. Stylianopoulos, *The New Testament: An Orthodox Perspective*, vol. 1, *Scripture, Tradition, Hermeneutics* (Brookline, MA: Holy Cross Orthodox Press, 2004), 28.

31. See "Septuagint," in *The Baker Illustrated Bible Dictionary*, ed. Tremper Longman III (Grand Rapids: Baker Books, 2013), 1497.

scriptural canon. They simply were not present in the medieval Hebrew text chosen by the Reformers for their Bible.[32]

The Multidimensional Word

The concept of the *eikōn* and its adjective, "iconic," has been applied by Orthodox theologians to the human person, to ministry, to mosaic and paints, to the Church, and even to Scripture. Sister Nonna Harrison, an independent Orthodox scholar and **monastic**, suggests that the biblical hermeneutic of the Greek Fathers would most accurately be termed "iconic."[33] An iconic interpretation of Scripture supports both "literal" and "symbolic" interpretations, but does not insist on either. Harrison's use of the term "iconic" is supported primarily by a high regard for the actual content of Scripture, with the understanding that there can be many layers and dimensions of meaning being communicated.

An iconic scriptural hermeneutic reflects the Orthodox view that divine revelation is intended to be experienced multidimensionally. St. Ephrem the Syrian (306–373), for example, perceived God's symbols everywhere, and especially in Scripture, because the entire universe contains these symbols: "Wherever you turn your eyes, there is God's symbol; whatever you read, there you will find His types."[34] St. John of Damascus writes that when his thoughts torture him and keep him from profiting from his reading, "I go to the church. . . . My eyes are captivated and push my soul to praise God."[35] Inherent in the Orthodox worldview is this sense that the whole of Christian life is intended to be lived within a vision of the grandeur of God's glory, to whatever degree one is able to perceive it. The interpretation of Scripture, it is believed, should be equally multidimensional, as are all reflections of God in creation.

Ukrainian priest Fr. Anthony Ugolnik believes that while the Protestant mind is culturally and literarily disposed to envision the Word of God in terms of a book, the Orthodox mind "interprets that Word in the light of the image that

32. See Timothy Michael Law, *When God Spoke Greek: The Septuagint and the Making of the Christian Bible* (New York: Oxford University Press, 2013), 99–116.

33. Nonna Verna Harrison, "Word as Icon in Greek Patristic Theology," in *Constructive Christian Theology in the Worldwide Church*, ed. William R. Barr (Grand Rapids: Eerdmans, 1997), 58–70.

34. Ephrem the Syrian, *Hymn on Virginity* 20.12, quoted in Sebastian Brock, *The Luminous Eye: The Spiritual World Vision of Saint Ephrem the Syrian* (Kalamazoo, MI: Cistercian Publications, 1992), 42.

35. John of Damascus, *On the Divine Images* 1.1.16, quoted in Paul Evdokimov, *The Art of the Icon: A Theology of Beauty* (Pasadena, CA: Oakwood, 1990), 178.

reflects it."[36] Stated another way, for the Orthodox the Bible is not the Word, but it is one of many reflections (or "true images" or "icons") of the Word (the Logos, Jesus Christ). For the Orthodox, writes Ugolnik, the Bible is indeed understood as a repository of meaning, yet it is regarded as if it were itself an image—"transforming dead matter into the reflected image of Jesus Christ."[37]

The view of Scripture as icon also means that Scripture is not the totality of God's inexhaustible self-revelation, but is a form of revelation. Contemporary Orthodox scholar Fr. Anton Vrame expresses this point quite well in his book *The Educating Icon*. Scripture is "the verbal record of how God chose to reveal himself to us so that, by faith, it becomes a medium of God's revelation. However, God has chosen to reveal Himself in many ways, through actions and images as well as words."[38] When one thinks of a book, one tends to think of the text itself. But in this Orthodox view, Scripture is not merely a text in the sense of having a bounded meaning. Rather, for the Orthodox, Scripture is understood in a sacramental sense, as conveying the presence of Christ in manifold ways. The Scriptures not only convey but also reflect and interpret other images of God's truth: the pictorial icons, the hymns, and especially the liturgical witness of the Orthodox Church. They are all "of a piece," since the source of all is the same Holy Spirit.

Holy Icons

Payton is correct in stating that "an unsuspecting Protestant who walked into an Orthodox church would be visually assaulted by the plethora of religious imagery within it."[39] The presence of mosaic and painted icons of Christ, the saints, and feasts in Orthodox churches is due to the supreme importance of communicating the Gospel in many and various forms. If the New Testament is a verbal icon of the Gospel message, the Orthodox Holy Icons are the Gospel in form and color—the Gospel that we see. St. Basil the Great writes that "what the word transmits through the ear, that painting silently shows through the image, and by these two means, mutually accompanying one another, we receive knowledge of one and the same thing."[40] The Seventh

36. Anthony Ugolnik, *The Illuminating Icon* (Grand Rapids: Eerdmans, 1989), 50–52.
37. Ugolnik, *Illuminating Icon*, 50.
38. Anton C. Vrame, *The Educating Icon: Teaching Wisdom and Holiness in the Orthodox Way* (Brookline, MA: Holy Cross Orthodox Press, 1999), 51. Rev. Dr. Vrame is director of the Department of Religious Education for the Greek Orthodox Archdiocese of America.
39. Payton, *Light from the Christian East*, 178.
40. Basil the Great, Discourse 19, *On the 40 Martyrs*, quoted in Leonid Ouspensky, "The Meaning and Language of Icons," in *The Meaning of Icons*, ed. Vladimir Lossky and Leonid Ouspensky (Crestwood, NY: St. Vladimir's Seminary Press, 1982), 30.

Ecumenical Council, held in Nicaea in 787, declared that the Holy Icons and the Book of the Gospels should each be venerated (honored) in the same way, since together they represent a complete correspondence between the verbal image and the visual image. Both are part of the single purpose to lead us to salvation. Since the icons visually express certain biblical events and feasts, they have also been used as a form of instruction of the Christian Faith, parallel to a study of written words in the Bible.

The key to understanding Orthodox Holy Icons is the Incarnation of Jesus Christ. In the Incarnation, the Son of God took on the human form and became part of created matter—the stuff of which we humans are made. Jesus Himself is the "icon" of the invisible God (Col. 1:15), revealing and manifesting the presence and divine nature of the Father. Fr. Anthony Coniaris expresses well the role of icons in acknowledging the Incarnation: "To deny the icon is to deny this very basis of our salvation."[41] Because God was revealed in Jesus Christ through the "matter" of His humanity, the Church determined that matter can also be a proper vehicle through which divine realities can be communicated.

The main purpose of Orthodox icons is to create reverence in worship and to make spiritual realities visible. "An icon is not simply a religious picture designed to arouse appropriate emotions in the beholder; it is one of the ways whereby God is revealed to us. Through icons the Orthodox Christian receives a vision of the spiritual world."[42] Leonid Ouspensky (1902–1987), an iconographer (icon painter), refers to the icon as "a constant inexhaustible fountain of knowledge communicated to the Church by the Holy Spirit."[43] This means that the icon is like Holy Scripture in that neither presents one static truth, but rather "inexhaustible" dimensions and facets, since the God from whom truth is revealed is inexhaustible and beyond the limits of human comprehension.

The iconographer must be a member of the Church and an active participant in the sacramental life of the Church, including the ascetic life of prayer and fasting. This is so that what is painted does not come from the individual artist's ego, but rather from the revealed truth of the Holy Spirit. For this reason, icons are also not signed. Just as a priest is forbidden to alter liturgical texts, an iconographer is expected to not include extraneous or emotional content in an icon.[44] This is to allow freedom for each beholder to perceive

41. Anthony Coniaris, *Introducing the Orthodox Church: Its Faith and Life* (Minneapolis: Light and Life Publishing, 1982), 181.
42. Ware, *Orthodox Church*, 200.
43. Ouspensky, "Meaning and Language of Icons," 42.
44. Ouspensky, "Meaning and Language of Icons," 43.

the beauty and meaning of the icon according to his or her own capacity, rather than to be led by the emotions of the painter. Even as iconographers follow the Holy Tradition, in particular the boundaries set by the Seventh Ecumenical Council, they are still expressing something of themselves and their unique proficiencies in **synergy** with the Holy Spirit.

Orthodox iconographers deliberately avoid a realistic, natural look, but rather strive to symbolize the transfigured, resurrected body of Christ and the saints. Icons are, therefore, referred to as "windows to heaven," allowing the viewer to see beyond the earthly reality into the transfigured state. An icon, then, has an intentional sense of "otherworldliness" because "what is 'natural' here, may not be 'natural' there."[45]

For a very brief examination of the theology of an exemplar icon, consider the icon of Jesus Christ on the cover of this book. The iconographer is Fr. Tom Tsagalakis, pastor of a Greek Orthodox Church in Washington State. This icon not only reflects Fr. Tsagalakis's unique creative aesthetic, but it also follows the rules established by the Seventh Ecumenical Council. Every icon of Jesus Christ has a cross in the halo, since "Christianity is the Religion of the Cross."[46] There are typically three letters in the halo, often in Greek. Whether shown in Greek or in another language, these are the two words spoken to Moses by the Lord from the burning bush, as recounted in the Greek Septuagint version of the Old Testament (Exod. 3). They are not easily translatable into English, but "The One Who Is" or the "The I Am" comes close. "The Being" is even closer. The icon tells the viewer that "The I Am" who spoke to Moses in the burning bush was the preincarnate Logos of God, the Second Person of the Trinity.

The letters to the left and right of Christ's head (ICXC) are the first and last letters in the Greek words "Jesus Christ" ('Ιησοῦς Χριστός), which hearken back to the Tetragrammaton (four letters) of Israel that in Hebrew refer to Yahweh: YHWH. Notice that the fingers of Christ's blessing hand are formed to make those four letters: ICXC. The Orthodox priest or bishop will also form his hand into the same four initials when he blesses the congregation in the name of Jesus Christ during worship services.

---

45. Dennis Bell, "Holy Icons: Theology in Color," *Sacred Art Journal* 15, no. 1 (Spring 1994): 5–12.

46. Georges Florovsky, "On the Tree of the Cross," *St. Vladimir's Seminary Quarterly* 1, nos. 3–4 (1953): 11.

■ DISCUSSION QUESTIONS ■

1. James Payton speaks of the relationship between Tradition and Scripture in the Orthodox Church in terms of friendship rather than as contrast or rivalry. How would you describe what he means by this?

2. What does it mean to suggest that Tradition is a "charismatic principle" in the Orthodox Church?

3. What are some theological advantages to viewing Scripture as an *eikōn* of revelation? What are some disadvantages?

4. What is the difference between Orthodox Holy Icons and that which God prohibited in the commandments given to Moses?

4

Ministry and Leadership

Christian history has evidenced three unique expressions of ministry and leadership. On one hand, the Roman Catholic expression emphasizes top-down authority from the pope, who has the sole power to declare dogma and through whom the bishops of the magisterium receive their authority to interpret Scripture for everyone. The Second Vatican Council in the 1960s affirmed that the pope enjoys "supreme, full, immediate, and universal power"[1] and that his word is still the last word on all matters of the Catholic faith. On the other hand, the Protestant expression emphasizes the authority of Scripture alone (*sola Scriptura*), which ultimately allows for scriptural interpretation by each individual, resulting in a panoply of theologies and a variety of leadership styles. Both expressions have intrinsic value and purpose within their own contexts. From an Orthodox perspective, however, they seem like opposite extremes of a pendulum swing.

A third option is the Eastern Orthodox approach, which includes some elements of the other two but has avoided the extremes either of top-down control or of individualism. The seeming paradox of Orthodoxy is that although there is a hierarchy of ordained deacons, priests, and bishops as in Roman Catholicism, Orthodox leadership is conciliar, not papal. There is no central authority in the Orthodox Church like the Roman Catholic pope, and no single earthly person in the Orthodox Church who has any power or authority over another, or even the authority to establish dogma. As the Orthodox Patriarchs

---

1. Vatican II, "Christus Dominus," section 1, October 28, 1965, in *Vatican Council II: The Conciliar and Postconciliar Documents*, ed. Austin Flannery (Collegeville, MN: Liturgical Press, 2014).

wrote in a letter to Pope Pius IX in 1848, "Among us, neither Patriarchs nor Councils could ever introduce new teaching, for the guardian of religion is the very body of the Church, that is, the people (*laos*) itself."[2]

The Orthodox Church is similar to Protestant traditions in that there is no formal body to interpret Scripture. Unlike in many Protestant traditions, however, the boundaries of truth that have been defined by the Holy Spirit are not subject to individual opinion. The seven Ecumenical Councils of the ancient Church hold a priority in the Orthodox Church today because they represent instances of the Holy Spirit's guidance toward a conciliar "unity of the Spirit in the bond of peace" (Eph. 4:3). The historical structure of the Orthodox Church is therefore defined as "conciliar" and "synodal" since doctrine and dogmas have developed through the councils or synods of bishops, and no one person or group can make declarations about doctrine or dogma for the entire Church.

The Royal Vocation of All People

In the Orthodox Church, clergy and laity have always been seen as **ontologically** equal as persons. This is in contrast to the early twentieth-century Roman Catholic understanding of clergy and laity forming an "unequal society."[3] Ministry and worship in Eastern Orthodoxy are the shared work of the clergy and laity together, because they each have a unique and irreplaceable role. The word "liturgy" (Greek: *leitourgia*) actually means "the work of the people," and it refers to all worshipers, not just to the clergy. Every baptized and **chrismated** person has received the Holy Spirit and is a member of the "royal priesthood" of which St. Peter spoke in his first letter (1 Pet. 2:5, 9). His All Holiness Patriarch Bartholomew expresses the Orthodox view of equality thus: "Priesthood is in fact the royal vocation of all people." The Kingdom of God is itself a welcoming and inclusive reality, and "the whole world is a sacred cathedral; no person is unordained for the kingdom, and no place is unhallowed in this world."[4]

2. The Orthodox Patriarchs' response to the writing of Pope Pius IX, "On the Supreme Throne of Peter the Apostle," quoted in Timothy Ware, *The Orthodox Church: An Introduction to Eastern Christianity*, 3rd ed. (London: Penguin, 2015), 244.

3. It was Pope Pius X who stated in *Vehementer Nos* (1906) that the Roman Catholic Church was an "unequal society" in which priests and bishops are a different category of person than the laity and that "the one duty of the multitude is to allow themselves to be led, and, like a docile flock, to follow the Pastors."

4. His All Holiness Ecumenical Patriarch Bartholomew, *Encountering the Mystery: Understanding Orthodox Christianity Today* (New York: Doubleday, 2008), 88.

The Orthodox Church also differs from Protestant traditions in how the *sola Scriptura* teaching of the Reformation has led to individualistic interpretations. *Sola Scriptura* generally means that Scripture is the supreme religious authority. While Holy Scripture in the Orthodox Holy Tradition is the preeminent written form of revelation, it is not the only form by which the Gospel has been revealed and communicated to the Church. More to the point, even the interpretation of Scripture is "conciliar" in Eastern Orthodoxy, and not individualistic. Most Orthodox Bible studies are based on the exegesis and consensus of the early Church Fathers because of their historical proximity to the New Testament Church.

In the mid-nineteenth century, Alexei Khomiakov entered into an exchange of letters with Anglican deacon and scholar William Palmer. Khomiakov focused on pointing out the contrast between, on the one hand, the individualism and rationalism of *sola Scriptura* and, on the other hand, the Orthodox alternative of mutual love. He writes of "the gift of unvarying knowledge (which is nothing but faith) that is attributed, not to individuals, but to the totality of the ecclesiastical body, and is considered as a corollary of the moral principle of mutual love."[5]

Protestant scholar Donald Fairbairn observes similarly that in the Orthodox Church "the prophets and apostles, the early church fathers, the bishops, and the laypeople are all understood as being intimately connected with each other."[6] Since they are connected in mutual love in Christ, it has never become necessary to place one group over another as the locus of authority. "All of them are witnesses to the truth that the entire Church possesses, and Eastern Christianity generally does not attempt to distinguish between them."[7] In noting the absence of authority structures in Eastern Orthodoxy, Fairbairn also considers the reason for the apparent and strong need for authority in both main families of the Christian West. Protestants say that "the Bible alone is authoritative" and Roman Catholicism "insists that the pope has authority over the rest of the Church." Fairbairn reasons that regardless of whether the emphasis is on a book or on a person, the focus is on an individual entity holding final authority, which creates the need to define which entity is in most possession of truth.[8]

5. W. J. Birkbeck, ed., *Russia and the English Church during the Last Fifty Years: Containing a Correspondence between Mr. William Palmer and M. Khomiakoff, in the Years 1844–1854*, vol. 1 (London: Revington, Percivalo & Co., 1895), 94–95.

6. Donald Fairbairn, *Eastern Orthodoxy through Western Eyes* (Louisville: Westminster John Knox, 2002), 13.

7. Fairbairn, *Eastern Orthodoxy*, 13.

8. Fairbairn, *Eastern Orthodoxy*, 13.

Khomiakov explains why the concept of authority is external to the Orthodox Church:

> The Church is not an authority, just as God is not an authority and Christ is not an authority, since authority is something external to us. The Church is not authority, I say, but the Truth—and at the same time the inner life of the Christian, since God, Christ, the Church live in him with a life more real than the heart which is beating in his breast and the blood flowing in his veins.[9]

In other words, the Church is the fulfillment of the prophecy of Jeremiah: "I will put My law in their minds, and write it on their hearts; and I will be their God, and they shall be My people" (Jer. 31:33). It is the Eastern Orthodox emphasis on mystical knowledge and intimate communion with God that helps to explain why Orthodoxy is not as concerned with religious authority as the West is. James Payton offers a helpful analogy in the biblical example of the marital relationship between a wife (the Church) and a husband (God). "In such a relationship, the fundamental issue is the relationship itself, not the structures of authority which sustain it. Something is desperately defective in a marital relationship if the fundamental consideration for it is one of authority."[10] The analogy illustrates why the Orthodox believe there would be something desperately defective in an ecclesial relationship built on authority and not love.

Because of Orthodoxy's emphasis on communion with God and with comembers of the Body of Christ, recognition and respect are also given to holy men and women in the Orthodox Church who are not ordained as clergy. A spiritual father or spiritual mother is such because of the "vivid activity of the Holy Spirit in his or her person, independent of the church's system of hierarchy."[11] Since prophetic insight and wisdom have been given to the holy person as a gift from the Holy Spirit, he or she is "ordained, not by the hand of man, but by the hand of God."[12] There is never a formal or official appointment of a spiritual father or spiritual mother. The faithful simply begin to come to that person for advice or counsel, and the word spreads.

9. Alexei Khomiakov, "On the Western Confessions of Faith," quoted in John Meyendorff, *Living Tradition: Orthodox Witness in the Contemporary World* (Crestwood, NY: St. Vladimir's Seminary Press, 1978), 27.

10. James Payton, *Light from the Christian East: An Introduction to the Orthodox Tradition* (Downers Grove, IL: IVP Academic, 2007), 195.

11. Eugene Webb, *In Search of the Triune God: The Christian Paths of East and West* (Columbia: University of Missouri Press, 2014), 182.

12. Kallistos Ware, "The Spiritual Guide in Orthodox Christianity," in *The Inner Kingdom: Collected Works* (Crestwood, NY: St. Vladimir's Seminary Press, 2000), 129.

The true spiritual father, according to Fr. Steven Tsichlis, is the one who shows such deep compassion for others that "it is he to whom a broken humanity naturally, almost instinctively, turns in order to find the path to God which lay open before us all."[13] In a way, "it is the spiritual children who reveal the spiritual guide to himself."[14] Practically and administratively, the prophetic and institutional roles in the Orthodox Church are intertwined with one another.[15] In many cases holy laypeople are recognized by the Orthodox faithful as "higher in honor" than those who have been ordained. This is certainly the case with the Virgin Mary, who was never ordained and whom the Orthodox call "ever-blessed" according to her own prophetic exclamation:

> My soul magnifies the Lord,
> And my spirit has rejoiced in God my Savior.
> For He has regarded the lowly state of His maidservant;
> For behold, henceforth all generations will call me blessed.
> For He who is mighty has done great things for me,
> And holy is His name. (Luke 1:46–49)

First among Equals

Although the Christian East has always opposed the idea of a universal and supreme papal authority, it has had no qualms in acknowledging the preeminence of honor either of St. Peter or of the Roman See. St. Cyril of Jerusalem (313–386) referred to Peter as "the chief and foremost of the apostles."[16] The ancient bishops all regarded the bishop of Rome as "first among equals" or *prōtos* (first), as Peter himself was identified as the *prōtos* of the Apostolic council in the New Testament (Matt. 10:2). Metropolitan Ware refers to the bishop of Rome with fraternal language as "elder brother" but "not the supreme ruler."[17]

There is, nevertheless, quite a wide chasm between the Eastern Christian understanding of the bishop of Rome as "elder brother" or "first among equals" and Rome's self-understanding of the pope's "full, supreme and universal power over the whole Church."[18] In fact, these two views of Church

13. Steven P. Tsichlis, "The Spiritual Father in the Pachomian Tradition," *Diakonia* 18, no. 1 (1983): 18–30.

14. Ware, "Spiritual Guide," 143.

15. Ware, "Spiritual Guide," 129.

16. Cyril of Jerusalem, *Lecture* 17.27, in *The Catechetical Lectures of S. Cyril* (Oxford: J. H. Parker, 1839), 233.

17. Ware, *Orthodox Church*, 309.

18. "Dogmatic Constitution of the Church" (*Lumen Gentium*) 22. Available at http://www .vatican.va/archive/hist_councils/ii_vatican_council/documents/vat-ii_const_19641121_lumen

leadership are incompatible with each other. In the opinion of the Orthodox bishops, the claim by any bishop to have control over other bishops, and sole universal authority and jurisdiction throughout the world, is above all a breach of the Church's communion in Christ through the Holy Spirit.

It was only after Rome was no longer in communion with the Orthodox bishops that the Archbishop of Constantinople was designated by the Orthodox bishops as the *prōtos* or first among equals of the Eastern Christian Sees. Why is a *prōtos* needed at all? Why not have an egalitarian society of equals? A designated "first in honor" is always necessary, according to Metropolitan John Zizioulas, because diversity of its own accord will always lead to division. The seventh-century teacher Maximus the Confessor expresses a universal and cosmic problem when he says that *diaphora* (difference) must be maintained, for it is good, but that *diaresis* (division), a perversion of difference, is bad.[19] When difference becomes division, we encounter the "fallen" state of existence. The role of the bishop is to be the minister of unity in diversity: one who is needful of "others" and yet capable of protecting difference from falling into division.[20] The Orthodox hierarch therefore is not only a source of unity amid the many but also a source of their conciliarity.

In the present-day Orthodox Church, His All Holiness Bartholomew, the 270th Patriarch of Constantinople, serves as the spiritual leader for Orthodoxy in the world. Even "leader" fails to accurately describe the Patriarch's role within the Orthodox Church, however, since the only actual "leader" of the Church is Christ Himself. Patriarch Bartholomew is afforded a primacy of honor by the other Orthodox bishops but not a supremacy of authority. As with each previous Patriarch of Constantinople, Patriarch Bartholomew has no direct jurisdiction or power over any other bishop in the Orthodox Church, and any primacy is exercised within a synodal context. The Patriarch does not "seek to impose decisions upon the other Orthodox churches, to command or coerce, nor . . . attempt to interfere unasked in their internal affairs."[21] Rather, the role of the Ecumenical Patriarch is "one of presidency, initiative, and coordination."[22]

-gentium_en.html. See also the authorized Catholic Catechism by Peter Kreeft, *Catholic Christianity: A Complete Catechism of Catholic Beliefs based on the Catechism of the Catholic Church* (San Francisco: Ignatius, 2011).

19. John D. Zizioulas, "Communion and Otherness," *St. Vladimir's Theological Quarterly* 38, no. 4 (1994): 350–51.

20. Zizioulas, "Communion and Otherness," 357.

21. Kallistos Ware, foreword to Bartholomew, *Encountering the Mystery*, xvii.

22. Ware, "Foreword," xvii.

Three Orders of Clergy

While every Orthodox Christian is ordained at Baptism as a member of the royal priesthood, there are some who have been given a special calling to lead as clergy through ministerial ordination (called **Holy Orders**). The Orthodox Church maintains the threefold order of ministry—**deacon, priest,** and bishop—which was already well established by the end of the first century. We know this not only because of what is written in the later writings of the New Testament, such as in Paul's letters to Timothy and Titus, but also because of other writings by members of the Church in the first century: *The Didache* (or *Teaching of the Twelve*) and *The Shepherd of Hermas,* both anonymous. Even within the first generation of Christians, and by a date as early as AD 50,[23] the roles and offices of bishop and of deacon had been established as deserving of the honor paid to prophets and teachers:

> Therefore, appoint for yourselves bishops and deacons worthy of the Lord, men meek, and not lovers of money, and truthful and proven; for they also render to you the service of prophets and teachers. Despise them not therefore, for they are your honoured ones, together with the prophets and teachers.[24]

The Church at large also has access to the writings of several first- and second-century bishops such as Ignatius of Antioch, who was born just a year or two after the Resurrection of Christ and who would be martyred during the persecution of Christians by Emperor Trajan.

The New Testament often mentions these three types of formal ministry: deacon (*diakonos*), elder (*presvyteros*),[25] and bishop (*episkopos*) (Acts 14:23; Phil. 1:1). *Diakonos* in Greek literally means "one who serves." Although every Christian should be a servant of Christ, the seven deacons mentioned in Acts were set apart as servants in a special ministerial role. The Apostles saw that the ministry of serving tables at the daily distribution should not take them away from their ministry of preaching, so the community chose seven good men, full of the Spirit and of wisdom, to be responsible for serving. These seven men, all of whom had Greek names, were brought to the

---

23. Recent scholarship suggests that it may have been written as early as AD 50 but not later than 70. For a review of the dating of *The Didache,* see Thomas O'Loughlin, *The Didache: A Window on the Earliest Christians* (Grand Rapids: Baker Academic, 2010), 25.

24. *The Didache* 15. See the full text in the appendix.

25. An alternate English spelling would be "presbyteros." However, there is no *b* in the Greek alphabet. The second letter of the Greek alphabet (β) is pronounced like the English *v,* so I have chosen to use the spelling that more closely reflects the pronunciation.

apostles, who laid hands on them, ordaining them for this special ministry of serving (Acts 6:5–6).

Presvyteros literally means "elder" or "old guy." Today the **presbyter** is called a "priest" in English. In the New Testament, the terms *presvyteros* and *episkopos* are often used interchangeably, since the essential tasks for both were preaching the Gospel, eucharistic leadership, and pastoral care (Acts 20:17–28; Titus 1:5–7). These tasks remain a primary part of the roles of Orthodox presbyters and bishops today. The *episkopos* is literally "one who oversees." Even today, the main ecclesial task of the Orthodox bishop is to consecrate (or oversee) the Eucharist during the Divine Liturgy. The ancient Church also knew of two so-called minor orders, subdeacon and reader, which still exist in the Orthodox Church today.

In the early Church, the celebrant at the Eucharist was normally the bishop, who led only one Christian community and who served at the altar together with presbyters and deacons. As the primitive Church began to grow and spread, it became necessary for each bishop to be responsible for multiple congregations, with priests designated as the leaders of local communities, responsible for presiding at the altar, preaching, teaching, and providing pastoral care.[26] The shift away from a bishop-centered Eucharist to a presbyter-centered Eucharist happened rather early, as evidenced by this comment in the first-century letter of St. Ignatius to the Smyrnaeans: "Let that be deemed a proper Eucharist, which is [administered] either by the bishop, or by one to whom he has entrusted it."[27]

Prayer at the Consecration of an Orthodox Bishop

Grant, O Christ, that this man, who has been appointed a steward of the Episcopal grace, may become an imitator of thee, the True Shepherd, by laying down his life for thy sheep. Make him a guide to the blind, a light to those in darkness, a teacher to the unreasonable, an instructor to the foolish, a flaming torch in the world; so that having brought to perfection the souls entrusted to him in this present life, he may stand without confusion before thy judgment seat, and receive the great reward which thou hast prepared for those who have suffered for the preaching of thy Gospel.[a]

a. Ware, *Orthodox Church*, 243.

---

26. See John D. Zizioulas, *Eucharist, Bishop, Church* (Brookline, MA: Holy Cross Orthodox Press, 2002).

27. Ignatius of Antioch, *Letter to the Smyrnaeans* 8. Excerpts from this letter are presented in the appendix.

Both the bishop and the presbyter are "priests" ordained according to the priesthood of Jesus Christ (Heb. 4:14–16). The main difference between their roles is that the presbyter serves at the altar only as a representative or deputy of his bishop and cannot ordain others. Another difference is that Orthodox priests may either be married or monastic (celibate), but bishops are always celibate and must be in monastic vows.[28] A bishop may ordain presbyters, deacons, and readers and may participate with other bishops in the elevation of a presbyter to the role of bishop. Since there is no central authority in the Eastern Orthodox Church, each bishop assigned to a large geographical region (usually called an "archbishop" or "patriarch") enjoys autonomy to lead and preserve unity in the parishes under his fatherly care.

Ordination of Women

What about the ordination of women? The Orthodox Church has always viewed men and women as equally in possession of the image of God. St. Basil the Great writes that the natures of men and women "are alike of equal honor, the virtues are equal, the struggle equal, the judgment alike."[29] Many female saints are also honored as "equal to the Apostles,"[30] yet there have never been female priests or bishops in the entire history of the Orthodox Church. However, as Metropolitan Kallistos Ware affirms, "Orthodoxy certainly accepts that women can be ordained to the first of the Major Orders, the diaconate."[31] The earliest example of a female deacon is Phoebe, in Romans 16:1–2. St. Paul refers to Phoebe not as a "deaconess" but as *diakonos* (deacon)—the same term used by Paul in 1 Timothy 3:8 and Philippians 1:1. In the fourth century, St. John Chrysostom wrote many letters to his friend Olympia, who was a female deacon. Female deacons in the ancient Church were blessed inside the altar with the same rite and prayers as male deacons, with minor variations. One such variation, for example, is that during the ordination, the male deacon bends his right knee and rests his head on the

28. "Since the sixth or seventh century the bishop has been required to be celibate, and from at least the fourteenth century onwards he has had to be in monastic vows; a widower, however, can be made a bishop if he receives monastic profession." Ware, *Orthodox Church*, 284.

29. Basil of Caesarea, *Discourse* 1.18, "On the Origin of Humanity," in *On the Human Condition*, trans. Nonna Verna Harrison, Popular Patristics (Yonkers, NY: St. Vladimir's Seminary Press, 2005), 45.

30. These include Mary Magdalene, Photini, the Samaritan woman at the well, Thekla, and Helen, the mother of Constantine the Great.

31. Ware, *Orthodox Church*, 285.

The Troparion of St. Phoebe the Deacon at Cenchreae near Corinth (Commemorated on September 3)

Enlightened by grace

and taught the Faith by the chosen vessel of Christ,

you were found worthy of the diaconate;

and you carried Paul's words to Rome.

O Deaconess Phoebe, pray to Christ God that his Spirit may enlighten our

souls![a]

a. English translation by the Orthodox Church in America, https://www.oca.org/saints/lives. Used with permission.

altar, while the female deacon stands with her head bowed in respect.[32] It was particularly important to have female deacons to assist in the Baptisms of adult women for the sake of modesty, and also to distribute the Eucharist to homebound infirmed women.

Although the order of female deacon has not been eliminated, it has not been common in recent centuries for women to be ordained as deacons in the Orthodox Church. One notable exception was when the popular bishop St. Nektarios (1846–1920) ordained two nuns as deacons in 1911 to serve in the women's monastery he founded on the island of Aegina in Greece. They were ordained in the altar using the ancient Byzantine rite for deacons, and they read the Gospel during the divine services, just as a male deacon would.

Discussions on the issue of revitalizing the order of deacon for women in the Orthodox Church are ongoing in the present day.[33] More typical, although still not common, is the "tonsuring" of women to the "lower order" of reader (or chanter), which is done outside of the altar.[34] The role of the reader is to

32. Panagiotis I. Skaltsis, "The Ordination of Deaconesses in the Orthodox Liturgical Tradition," in *Deaconesses, the Ordination of Women and Orthodox Theology*, ed. Eleni Kasselouri-Hatzivassiliadi, Petros Vassiliadis, and Niki Papageorgiou (Newcastle-upon-Tyne, UK: Cambridge Scholars, 2018), 172–77. See also Kyriaki Karidoyanes FitzGerald, *Women Deacons in the Orthodox Church: Called to Holiness and Ministry* (Brookline, MA: Holy Cross Orthodox Press, 1998).

33. Ware, *Orthodox Church*, 285–87.

34. Not all Orthodox jurisdictions support the tonsuring of women as readers. This is a curious stance, since the reader is a lower order than deacon, and women have certainly been ordained to the diaconate in the two-thousand-plus-year history of the Orthodox Church.

chant the Psalms and other hymns and to read the Old Testament and Epistle readings during the divine services.

Apostolic Succession

The historic Apostolic Faith has been guarded these two-thousand-plus years as a historical transmission of the Faith—a succession of local churches led by a bishop who can trace his ordination back to one of the Apostles. This is typically referred to as "Apostolic succession." Yet the linear transmission of the Faith alone is not enough. Orthodox bishops must also maintain the Faith and worship of the Apostles without addition and without subtraction.

The Apostles, who were chosen by Christ, were also given the authority to loose and bind sins (Matt. 18:18). They were the first bishops or *episkopoi* mentioned in the New Testament, whose role was to preach, teach, and oversee the Eucharist. With missionary fervor, each of the Apostles went to various places in the world to plant and water the seeds of the Church in that place. For example, the Apostle James became the first bishop of Jerusalem. The Apostle Thomas established the Church in India, the Apostle Andrew in Greece, and the Apostle Peter in Antioch. Each second-generation bishop was ordained by the laying on of the Apostles' hands in the presence of the eucharistic community he would be serving (Acts 6:6; 13:3; 1 Tim. 4:14), a process that continues today in the Orthodox Church.

As mentioned above, Apostolic succession in the Eastern Orthodox view is not a strictly linear succession from one bishop to his successor. The eucharistic community also participates in the ordination of the new bishop who will preside over its Eucharist, since the bishop's role is to be the shepherd of his flock and the celebrant of the Eucharist for that flock. The continuity of Apostolic succession from generation to generation, therefore, involves not only the bishop "shepherd" but also the Apostolic "flock" of a particular community. Apostolic succession for the Orthodox is in actuality a succession of the entire local eucharistic community—the faithful with their bishop, continuing "in communion" with the next bishop.

Consider the succession of leadership in ancient Jerusalem. The Apostle James was the first bishop of the Church in Jerusalem. The next bishop was Simeon. However, the Apostolic succession was much more than a changing of the guard—a transition of the post from one man to the next. It was a succession of the entire eucharistic community in Jerusalem led by James, continuing as the eucharistic flock of the next bishop and shepherd, Simeon.

The relationship of the faithful in Jerusalem with their bishop, James, was refashioned by the Holy Spirit into a new relationship with the new bishop, Simeon. The Apostolic Faith continued in that community, even though the community's leader changed. Although each bishop can trace his lineage to one of the Apostles through an unbroken line, it is most proper to talk about succession of the Apostolic Faith as continuous through the Eucharist of each local church (e.g., Jerusalem, Moscow, San Francisco).

Further, the "identity" of the Orthodox Church at any location is not found in the specific person of the bishop but in the entire eucharistic community of the clergy and laity together. Metropolitan Zizioulas writes that for Apostolic continuity to take place, the baptized layperson is indispensable, because "the Church . . . relates to the apostles not only through ordination but also through baptism."[35] This is to say that Apostolic succession is most properly understood as a succession of those who have been joined to the Apostolic Body of Christ through Baptism.

In his Orthodox response to an ecumenical dialogue on ministry and ordination, Metropolitan Zizioulas clarifies that the Orthodox, unlike many Western Christians, do not understand ordination in terms of an objectified grace or power. He explains that some of those who favor Apostolic succession talk about authority and divine grace being conveyed by ordination to one person through a divine channel. Others, who oppose Apostolic succession, argue that the community is the source of the authority given in ordination. In both cases, Metropolitan Zizioulas sees evidence of an almost automatic process of causality in which the act of ordination conveys a thing (whether power, authority, or grace) either to one person or to the community. Whether the special thing is given to the one or to the community, the act of ordination is thought to convey an objectified gift.

In the Orthodox Christian Mystery of Holy Orders, by contrast, the ordained person becomes bound to a concrete community. Ordination is "an act by which the Holy Spirit establishes particular relationships within the community" and a "divine act realized as part of the eucharistic community."[36] Therefore, in summary, Orthodox Apostolic succession is not only a linear succession of bishops but a succession of the entire baptized eucharistic community in that locale led by and bound to their bishop, who has preserved the Apostolic Faith and who has maintained eucharistic communion with other Orthodox bishops and their communities.

35. John D. Zizioulas, *Being as Communion: Studies in Personhood and the Church* (Crestwood, NY: St. Vladimir's Seminary Press, 1985), 193.

36. John Zizioulas, "Is Ordination a Sacrament? An Orthodox Reply," in The Plurality of Ministries, ed. Hans Küng and Walter Kasper (New York: Herder and Herder, 1972), 34–35.

Follow the Bishop

> See that you all follow the bishop, even as Jesus Christ does the Father. (St. Ignatius of Antioch, *Letter to the Smyrnaeans* 8)

St. Ignatius was born shortly after Christ's Resurrection, and he would become the third bishop of Antioch, after the Apostle Peter and Evodius. By the time Ignatius wrote his *Letter to the Smyrnaeans* in the early second century, the Church was already being threatened by teachings and practices opposed to what the Apostles taught. The challenges that arose were not only from flawed teachings (some of these views will be discussed in chap. 5); a few of these groups had splintered off and were doing their own thing with regard to worship and the sacraments. As a bishop, Ignatius was concerned about his people unknowingly following "wolves" instead of the Good Shepherd (John 10:14). He writes in his *Letter to the Trallians* that the only way to avoid either the error of separation or the error of wrong belief is to follow the true bishops, deacons, and presbyters, since "apart from these, there is no Church."[37] Ignatius's statement was not born out of a desire for control but out of a serious concern to avoid the transmission of error and to preserve unity. Since the Church was ultimately constituted by the celebration of the Eucharist, a rite conducted by someone other than the bishop or his designated presbyters was not of the Church:

> Let no man do anything connected with the Church without the bishop. Let that be deemed a proper Eucharist, which is [administered] either by the bishop, or by one to whom he has entrusted it. Wherever the bishop shall appear, there let the multitude [of the people] also be; even as, wherever Jesus Christ is, there is the Catholic Church.[38]

In calling the Church "Catholic" here, St. Ignatius was not referring to the Roman Catholic Church (which would not exist as such until the mid-eleventh century). He was not referring to universality, either. The Greek word *katholou*, translated as "catholic," means "according to the whole." Ignatius was saying that the Church is whole and that, as the one Body of Christ, it cannot be divided. Further, Christians can rest assured that they are worshiping the true God if their congregation is led by a bishop who is a successor of the Apostles.

---

37. Ignatius of Antioch, *Letter to the Trallians* 3.1, in *The Ante-Nicene Fathers*, ed. Alexander Roberts and James Donaldson, 10 vols. (1885–1896; repr., Grand Rapids: Eerdmans, 1950–1951), 1:67. See https://www.newadvent.org/fathers/0106.htm.
38. Ignatius, *Letter to the Smyrnaeans* 8.

Even before the end of the first century, the Church confronted false teachers claiming to have received a special revelation from God. Since an individual's self-claim of apostolicity cannot be its sole guarantee of accuracy, the Church responded by showing that each of the bishop-leaders of local congregations had received their authority directly from one of the twelve Apostles. Many of St. Irenaeus's writings were directed against Gnostic teachers who taught a "secret gospel" known only to an enlightened few. Therefore, Irenaeus points out that the tradition of the Apostles was not a secret meant only for a few, but is very clear and can be grasped by anyone who wishes to behold the truth. Irenaeus argues with simple logic that if the Apostles had somehow been given hidden secrets, these too would have been handed down to their successors in the churches—but they were not![39] Additionally, Irenaeus says that the Church can enumerate every person whom the Apostles established as a bishop in the churches, and even their successors down to Irenaeus's day—and "none of [them] taught or thought of anything like [the Gnostics'] mad ideas." In *Against Heresies*, Irenaeus even presents a list detailing the specific lineage of all the bishops of Rome from St. Peter down to his day, outlining how the Apostolic Tradition was passed down from the Apostles in specific places to the successor bishops in those places, and ending with Eleutherius, who

> does now, in the twelfth place from the apostles, hold the inheritance of the episcopate. In this order, and by this succession, the ecclesiastical tradition from the apostles, and the preaching of the truth, have come down to us. And this is most abundant proof that there is one and the same vivifying faith, which has been preserved in the Church from the apostles until now, and handed down in truth.[40]

The Orthodox Bishop Today

Orthodox Christians today still "follow the bishop," as instructed by Ignatius in the early second century, not out of compulsion but out of love for Jesus Christ. In many ways the bishop's role today is the same as it was two thousand years ago. Yet the sheer pace of our world and our distance from one another (whether geographical or virtual) add new challenges to the bishop's role of preserving unity and nurturing community. Today's Orthodox bishops must also be thoroughly grounded in the Holy Tradition and yet be able to adapt and speak to contemporary culture. Much like Irenaeus, Ignatius,

39. Irenaeus, *Against Heresies* 3.
40. Irenaeus, *Against Heresies* 3.3. The full text of this chapter is presented in the appendix.

Athanasius, and a whole host of ancient bishops who struggled to keep the wolves away from their flock, Orthodox bishops and priests today are still concerned with keeping their people together in the Orthodox Faith—in communion in Christ and with one another. Although the Ecumenical Councils are in the past, contemporary challenges still need to be worked out and new ideas need to be discussed. The bishop today must also exercise oversight of administrative, legal, and business issues of a nature that St. Basil and his peers in the fourth century could not possibly have imagined.

▪ DISCUSSION QUESTIONS ▪

1. How does the designation "first among equals" for the Orthodox Patriarch of Constantinople differ from the supreme authority of the Roman pope?
2. How do you understand the role of the eucharistic community in Apostolic succession in the Orthodox Church?
3. Discuss the concerns of St. Ignatius of Antioch when he instructs his recipients to "follow the bishop."
4. What is the "royal vocation" of all people in the Orthodox Church?

— 5 —

Christology

The Word of God Is a Person

Christ is not a text, but a Living Person. (Fr. Georges Florovsky, *Bible, Church, Tradition*)

Many Christians speak about "the Word of God" as an "it," such as the Gospel that is preached or the Bible. The Word of God is most certainly intended to be preached, but in the Eastern Orthodox worldview, the Word of God is understood first and primarily as a person—Jesus Christ—and He "abides in his Body, the Church."[1] The confusion of terms is understandable since the Bible is the written Word of God and Jesus is the incarnate Logos (or Word) of God.[2]

The most magnificent "Logos theology" is found in the opening of St. John's Gospel: "In the beginning was the Word [*Logos*], and the Word [*Logos*] was with God, and the Word [*Logos*] was God" (John 1:1). The Apostle and Evangelist John "the Theologian" also declares that because the eternal Logos became a human, this Word was seen, looked at, and even touched:

We declare to you what was from the beginning, what we have heard, what we have seen with our eyes, what we have looked at and touched with our hands,

1. Georges Florovsky, *Bible, Church, Tradition: An Eastern Orthodox View*, Collected Works 1 (Belmont, MA: Nordland, 1972), 12.
2. St. Jerome did not attempt to translate the Greek word *Logos* into Latin in his translation of the works of St. Irenaeus of Lyons. See discussion in Paul Evdokimov, *The Art of the Icon: A Theology of Beauty* (Pasadena, CA: Oakwood, 1990), 31.

Orthodox Resurrectional Hymn

Let us, the faithful, praise and worship the Word,
co-eternal with the Father and the Spirit, born for our salvation from the
    Virgin;
for He willed to be lifted up on the Cross in the flesh,
to endure death, and to raise the dead by His glorious Resurrection.[a]

a. Orthodox Resurrectional Hymn Plagal Tone 1, *The Divine Liturgy* (Crestwood, NY: St. Vladimir's Seminary Press, 2005), 132–33.

concerning the word [*logos*] of life—this life was revealed, and we have seen it and testify to it, and declare to you the eternal life that was with the Father and was revealed to us. (1 John 1:1–2 NRSV)

The words of the Evangelist witness to the Incarnation of the eternal Word, the Logos—the Word of God, who was encountered with all the human senses.

So, when Orthodox Christians hear "Word of God," they think not of a text but of "a Living Person."[3] It is a most magnificent and comforting thought that the God who created the entire universe loved His creation so much that He wanted to join it in the most intimate physical and spiritual communion possible: He became one of us!

Who Is Jesus?

Who is Jesus? This question is as old as the Church itself, even predating the Cross. Jesus Himself asked His disciples, "Who do you say that I am?" (Matt. 16:13–16; Mark 8:27–29; Luke 9:18–20). Since the time of the Apostles, the Christian Faith has always affirmed that Jesus Christ is fully God and fully human, God "incarnate" (which literally means "in the flesh" in Latin). And yet the very question "Who is Jesus?" was the source of the first theological challenges to the early Church. St. John the Evangelist used the strongest word possible—**antichrist**—to describe anyone who taught falsehoods about the true nature of Jesus Christ: "Who is a liar but he who denies that Jesus is the Christ? He is antichrist who denies the Father and the Son. Whoever denies the Son does not have the Father either; he who acknowledges the Son has the Father also" (1 John 2:22–23).

3. Florovsky, *Bible, Church, Tradition*, 12.

One of the contributions of the Orthodox Church to the global church is how it has modeled ways to protect against error, especially error related to teachings about its Lord and Savior, Jesus Christ. How the ancient Church spoke about Jesus is often referred to as "classical Christology" by scholars today. "Classical" suggests that there is a foundational understanding of who Jesus is that has been handed down from the Apostles and has also been described in Scripture. The full divinity and full humanity of Christ is one of the established truths of Eastern Orthodoxy that many so-called classical Christians today take for granted. James Payton verbalizes this point: "To be sure, many Western Christians may not be aware of the controversies leading to the ancient ecumenical councils that produced the creeds that repudiate the heresies and confess the Trinity and Christology; even so, in affirming those doctrines, Western Christians embrace the teaching of those ancient doctrinal deliverances."[4] In other words, what most Christians today believe about Jesus came from the ancient councils of Eastern Orthodoxy.

Not all views of Jesus today can be considered "classical," "Orthodox," or "Apostolic." I learned this firsthand at an ecumenical workshop when one of the members objected to the phrase "Jesus Christ, our Lord and our God" in a working document. He explained that while he believed that Jesus could be Christ and Lord, he did not believe that Jesus was also God. The ensuing discussion revealed that his Protestant denomination gives individuals the option to choose whether they want to believe that Jesus is God or a created being. An individualist approach to theology raises practical as well as theological concerns. How can a congregation pray or worship together "with one accord" (e.g., Acts 2:46; 4:24) if some believe that Jesus is a created being while others believe that He is the incarnate Logos of God? After all, worshiping a created thing as God is idolatry, which the God of Moses will not allow (Exod. 20:3–5).

A young woman named Sheila gained some infamy after her interview with Robert Bellah was described in the book *Habits of the Heart*. In the interview, Sheila says, "I believe in God. I'm not a religious fanatic. I can't remember the last time I went to church. My faith has carried me a long way. It's Sheilaism. Just my own little voice."[5] "Sheilaism" has become shorthand for a system of beliefs patched together from various religious ideas as a personal creation of one's own religion. The desire to have a personal code of ethics is admirable, but in isolation such a belief system holds no substance, no power to save,

4. James Payton, *Light from the Christian East: An Introduction to the Orthodox Tradition* (Downers Grove, IL: IVP Academic, 2007), 65.
5. Robert N. Bellah et al., *Habits of the Heart: Individualism and Commitment in American Life* (Berkeley: University of California Press, 1985), 21.

and it cannot be transmitted or imparted to others without contradicting the underlying individualistic premise: "Sheilaists are isolated monads who cannot propagate their own values."[6] That is to say, every individualist religion ends with the individual: there is nothing to share or to pass on.

The particular individually selected opinion of my ecumenical colleague (that Jesus may be Lord and Savior, but not God) was not a new idea in the twenty-first century when he stated it. Elements of this same viewpoint came on the scene as early as the first Christian century. In fact, many challenges to the nature of Jesus Christ arose surprisingly early. The underlying question, for anyone who cares about following the true God, is "How do I know what to believe, given the preponderance of so many contradictory opinions?" The answer to this question lies in the significance of the history of the Orthodox Church. Despite a variety of divergent opinions, the undivided Church was able to guard against Christological (and other) errors with the guidance of the Holy Spirit, despite many struggles and across many centuries. What follows is a condensed historical view of the major challenges to the Apostles' teaching about Jesus Christ, and the essential "classical" or Orthodox theology that arose from these challenges.

Early Challenges to Christology

The first thing to know about Christian history is that doctrines and dogmas were not developed until there was a need to defend the Apostolic teachings against "false teachers" of a "different gospel." Jesus Christ warned His followers that the false prophets, like wolves, would try to steal the righteous away from faith in the true God.[7] St. Paul expressed his fear that savage wolves would come into the Church at Ephesus; he warned that some would even rise up from within their ranks "speaking perverse things, to draw away the disciples after themselves" (Acts 20:30). There were a few early sects that professed to be Christian, yet they taught a very different gospel from that of the Apostles. Their ideas about how to answer the "Who is Jesus?" question, in particular, began to generate controversy within the primitive Church.

Only Divine

The **Docetists** (from Greek *dokein*, "seeming") and Gnostics of the earliest Christian centuries believed that Jesus was only divine and just appeared to

6. Pierre Hegy, *Wake Up, Lazarus! On Catholic Renewal* (Bloomington, IN: iUniverse, 2012), 33.
7. See Matt. 7:15; 2 Cor. 11:4; Gal. 1:6–7; 2 Pet. 2:1; 1 Tim. 1:3; 6:2.

be human. Their ideas were based on the ancient Greek philosopher Plato, who taught that all matter is flawed at best and evil at worst. Although there have been many permutations of Gnosticism and Docetism, fundamental to their various forms is the idea that true reality must necessarily be invisible, immaterial, and preexistent, and thus divine. In the view of Gnostics and Docetists, all material things, such as the human person, plants, animals, minerals—literally everyone and everything—are not only flawed but are the result of corruption and evil in the primordial world. Therefore, it is simply unthinkable that Jesus, as a divine being, could have undergone a bodily incarnation since the human body is composed of matter and thus (according to Gnostic views) it must also be corrupt. Some Gnostic writings speak of Jesus's divinity passing through Mary's humanity like "water through pipes," so that His pure divinity would not be contaminated by her polluted humanity. In other forms of Gnosticism, Jesus was the teacher who came to provide secret enlightened understanding or *gnōsis* to a select few.[8]

The background of these early challenges to Christ's humanity explains why John the Evangelist denounces in the strongest possible terms those who did not believe that Jesus was fully human: "For many deceivers have gone out into the world who do not confess Jesus Christ as coming in the flesh. This is a deceiver and an antichrist" (2 John 7). Remember, this is the Gospel writer who boldly proclaims that this Word/Logos was seen and even touched by His followers (1 John 1:1). The Apostles knew that this man was God and that God became human out of love for His creation. To teach otherwise was simply not true, and worse, it was an expressly "anti-Christian" belief.

Only Human

If Docetists and Gnostics imagined Jesus to be more divine than human, or only divine, the other side of the coin would be the first-century Ebionites, who imagined Jesus to be a mere mortal. The Ebionites were early Jewish followers of Jesus who believed that Jesus was born entirely human as the biological child of Joseph and Mary, with no virgin birth. The Ebionites did believe that Jesus was Israel's Messiah, but they believed that God chose this human man to be adopted into the Godhead as the Son of God, which most likely happened at His Baptism. (This belief is also known as **Adoptionism**.) They denied Jesus's preexistence, His Incarnation, and His Resurrection after death. These denials ignored the testimony of their contemporaries—the Apostles—who had a firsthand testimony of

---

8. Irenaeus discusses these Gnostic views in *Against Heresies*.

Jesus as God incarnate.[9] Although the Ebionite sect soon faded away, its emphasis on the human-only Jesus took root and has sprouted again and again throughout history, first in the fourth-century Arian controversy and later in the Enlightenment of the Christian West. It ultimately came to full bloom in the twentieth century with liberal Protestantism.

Nothing New under the Sun

The prophetic wisdom of King Solomon reminds us that "there is nothing new under the sun" (Eccles. 1:9). The seeds of all of today's heresies were already present in the earliest generations of the Church. The Gnostic religion is also still in existence today. You might ask, "Why would this be a problem? Isn't it a good thing to emphasize Christ's divinity?" Of course it is, but the problem is always in the imbalance. Leaning too heavily toward the divinity of Christ is problematic for many reasons—for instance, it gives rise to the kind of congregation that worships a divine being that cannot totally relate to His creation. A God that cannot relate to humanity (such as the "unmoved mover" of Aristotle or an impersonal divine "force" like that of the "New Age" Gnostics) is not the covenanting God of the Old Testament or the merciful and compassionate Savior of the New Testament who wept at the death of His friend (John 11:35).

On the other hand, if Jesus is only human, the logic fails rather quickly in the other direction: a mere human being cannot save humanity. The **heresy** of Jesus as a "created being" is still actively preached by Jehovah's Witnesses in the present day, and, as mentioned earlier, some Protestant denominations allow it as an optional belief. The Orthodox Church has followed the Apostles in teaching that the God of the Bible loves His creation so much that He condescended to take on the human condition fully, and yet He paradoxically remained fully God (John 3:16). One might then ask, "How can God become human and remain God?" This is one of the many apophatic paradoxes of Orthodox Christianity, complicated by the limits of human understanding to fully comprehend God's ways. The Orthodox Church is absolutely committed to the dogma that Jesus Christ is fully divine and fully human because it has been revealed to the entire Church by the Holy Spirit to be true. Although the Church has been able to explain *why* it is necessary for Jesus to be fully human and fully divine, finite human reasoning can never conceive *how* it is so. Eastern Orthodoxy is comfortable remaining in the state of unknowing

9. Alister E. McGrath, *Historical Theology: An Introduction to the History of Christian Thought* (Oxford: Wiley-Blackwell, 2012), 41.

that Vladimir Lossky describes as "an attitude of mind which refuses to form concepts about God."[10]

The Rule of Truth

> Error, indeed, is never set forth in its naked deformity, lest, being thus exposed, it should at once be detected. But it is craftily decked out in an attractive dress. (St. Irenaeus, *Against Heresies* 1.preface 2)

It is a most fascinating aspect of the historical narrative of the early Church that the earliest Christian communities had no theological texts and no New Testament in the way that we do today. It is rather amazing, actually, that they were able to handle so many serious theological challenges in order to arrive at the dogmas that most Christians today affirm and take for granted. Without concrete formal doctrines, how could a presbyter or a bishop—or any believer, for that matter—know what was a correct teaching about Jesus Christ? Should they just have believed whatever they wanted (Sheilaism), since not even the New Testament had been formalized yet? How were the faithful able to identify "wolves" (John 10:12) who were teaching a gospel different from what Jesus or the Apostles preached, if there was no "official" or formal support for their views?

These are valid questions, which I hope to continue to answer by the example of the Apostolic Church and later Church Fathers. It may seem on the surface that what should have happened in the first few hundred years of Christianity is what has happened in the past few hundred years: the multiplication of diverse, independent congregations growing out of disparate teachings. Nevertheless, despite the lack of a formal or concrete standard, what actually happened is that the Orthodox Church maintained the doctrinal orthodoxy of the Apostles' teachings, as well as the unity of practice of the Christian Faith as one undivided Church.

We have already seen that St. Irenaeus, the second-century bishop of Lyons, was one of the Church Fathers who was instrumental in fending off false teachings, especially those of Gnosticism, which taught that only a select few had *gnōsis*, or knowledge of the true faith, which was hidden from others. In *Against Heresies*, Irenaeus writes that the heretics boast of having "perfect knowledge," but that their system is nevertheless flawed at its core, being novel teaching that "neither the prophets announced, nor the Lord taught, nor the

---

10. Vladimir Lossky, *The Mystical Theology of the Eastern Church*, trans. The Fellowship of St. Alban and St. Sergius (Crestwood, NY: St. Vladimir's Seminary Press, 1976), 38–39.

apostles delivered."[11] What is even more dangerous, he says, is that the heretics try to show credibility by weaving in biblical texts with their "peculiar assertions" (contemporary scholarship would call it "proof texting"). As the quotation at the beginning of this section asserts, the naked deformity of error is always hidden in attractive dress. Irenaeus says that "by transferring passages, and dressing them up anew, and making one thing out of another, they succeed in deluding many through their wicked art in adapting the oracles of the Lord to their opinions."[12] Irenaeus expresses this same thought again and again in different ways in every section of his work—evidence of his primary concern as a bishop and shepherd. The Gnostic teachers "succeed in deluding many" and "they also overthrow the faith of many, by drawing them away, under a pretence of superior knowledge." They "cunningly allure the simple-minded to inquire into their system."[13] Salvation was at risk because error was taking root, and Irenaeus needed to protect his people—and all people—from the wolves.

According to Irenaeus, the only way one could be assured of belonging to the true Church was to be led by the local bishop, who had an unbroken lineage from the Apostles and maintained the same "rule of faith" or "canon of truth" as the "Way" of the Apostles.[14] If a person was in communion with the bishop, and the bishops were all connected to one another in the Apostolic Christian Faith, then the person was in communion with the one true Church. Yet the rule of truth (or faith) that Irenaeus and others described was not actually a "rule" in the obvious sense, corresponding to how we might think of the "rule of law" today.

Scholars sometimes identify the rule of truth with creeds that were recited by early Christians at Baptism to summarize the Christian beliefs. But for Irenaeus, the rule of truth was actually the gift of discernment received from the Holy Spirit in Christian Baptism. Irenaeus observes that even though the heretical teachers may quote expressions from Scripture and twist them to fit their own misguided purposes, baptized Christians will be able to recognize the error because they have received the rule of the truth in their hearts:

> In like manner he also who retains unchangeable in his heart the rule of the truth which he received by means of baptism, will doubtless recognize the names, the expressions, and the parables taken from the Scriptures, but will by no means acknowledge the blasphemous use which these men make of them.[15]

11. Irenaeus, *Against Heresies* 8.1. See https://www.newadvent.org/fathers/0103108.htm.
12. Irenaeus, *Against Heresies* 1.8.1.
13. Irenaeus, *Against Heresies* 1.preface 1.
14. See "the Way" in Acts 9:2; 19:9, 23; 22:4; 24:14, 22.
15. Irenaeus, *Against Heresies* 1.9.4.

Irenaeus's distinction between the true use and the false use of Scripture may seem on the surface to rely on a fine line of demarcation, since all theology arises from a personal experience of the Holy Spirit. Yet an individual's own impression might not be accurate to the truth. For a teaching to become honored within the rule of truth/faith, it must meet an important criterion: it must be consistent with the shared or corporate liturgical experience of God in the Church. Only because revelation is shared can it be interpreted and formalized by the community of faith in the Body of Christ.

Admittedly, there is something seductively attractive in the heretical notion (like that of the early Gnostics) that every "enlightened" human can ascend to be pure spirit. The allure of false views is why the Church considered heresy to be so dangerous. Unfortunately, the same danger is still present today. Consider Eckhart Tolle's *A New Earth*, which has sold many millions of copies since it was published in 2005. The study videos Tolle produced with television talk-show host Oprah Winfrey have been viewed more than thirty-five million times. Tolle occasionally quotes Scripture, but never in its proper context. For example, he says that the "new heaven and new earth" of Revelation 21:1 is not a future reality, but something that is "arising within you at this moment" because Jesus told His disciples, "Heaven is right here in the midst of you."[16] There also is no need for God, since each human possesses the potential to be ultimate truth: "Yes, you *are* the Truth. If you look for it elsewhere you will be deceived every time. The very Being that you are is Truth. Jesus tried to convey that when he said 'I am the way and the truth and the life.'"[17] The pattern that Irenaeus warned about is still present, even today, when people set themselves up as teachers and draw many away from the true Faith—and the true God—under a pretense of superior knowledge.

Error and Heresy

In spite of the Spirit-led ideal of being in "full accord" with one another, human beings still seem to have trouble following God's will. Sometimes the cause is error, sometimes laziness, and sometimes willful disobedience. There is a significant difference between how the Church has dealt with mistaken ideas about God, which can be corrected, and how it has dealt with willful defiance, which by its very nature cannot be corrected.

16. Eckhart Tolle, *A New Earth: Awakening to Your Life's Purpose* (New York: Penguin, 2005), 308–9.

17. Tolle, *New Earth*, 71.

There is a great deal of conceptual latitude in the apophatic nature of Orthodox theology in the refusal to state definitive conclusions about the eternal nature of God. The speculations of finite humans will never reach anything close to understanding the infinite God. But the fact that human language is limited does not mean that all statements about God are valid. If one has a wrong view of God or of the Church, one's salvation may be at stake and one also risks contaminating others with the same errors. This is why Metropolitan John Zizioulas cautions that "orthodoxy concerning the being of God is not a luxury for the Church and for man: it is an existential necessity."[18] If one's view of God is wrong, one's relationship with God will be flawed, and one's interpersonal relationships will not be according to the will of the true God, since true peace comes only from the true God.

Wrong suppositions are usually tolerable, unless truth and facts are essential for safety or health—or salvation. Consider, by way of example, our understanding of this planet on which we reside. At least by the third century BC, Greek astronomers had established the idea of a spherical earth as a physical given.[19] And yet, just a few years ago, the website of The Flat Earth Society proudly announced that a young rapper had joined their cause. The rapper took to Twitter to share his "revelation" that the earth must be flat because he could still see the horizon at eye level from a tall building. He even started a GoFundMe account to purchase a satellite that could finally prove that the earth is flat. A well-known astrophysicist, Neil deGrasse Tyson, saw the rapper's many tweets and could not resist responding. A debate ensued, and in one post the scientist wrote, "Flat Earth is a problem only when people in charge think that way. No law stops you from regressively basking in it."[20] Surprising as it may seem that anyone still believes that the earth is flat, Tyson said it should not actually matter that the rapper believes this, as long as he is not in charge. It *would* matter, however, if he needed to compute a long-distance flight path, which is always shown as being curved. Even the architects of the massive Mall of America in Minnesota needed to account for the earth's curvature. We would similarly hope that our medical professionals have accurate understandings of illnesses and cures and are not "regressively basking" in false assumptions. It is a fact that the boundary between truth

18. John D. Zizioulas, *Being as Communion: Studies in Personhood and the Church* (Crestwood, NY: St. Vladimir's Seminary Press, 1985), 15.

19. Stephen J. Gould, "The Late Birth of a Flat Earth," in *Dinosaur in a Haystack: Reflections in Natural History* (New York: Three Rivers, 1997), 38–50.

20. Quoted in Laura Wagner, "Neil DeGrasse Tyson Gets into a Rap Battle with B.o.B over Flat Earth Theory," NPR, January 26, 2016, https://www.npr.org/sections/thetwo-way/2016/01/26/464474518/neil-degrasse-tyson-gets-into-a-rap-battle-with-b-o-b-over-flat-earth-theory.

and falsehood can also be the boundary between peril and safety, or between sickness and health. For theology, and especially with regard to ideas about God, the boundary between truth and falsehood is not only practical; it is also spiritual, cosmic, and eternal.

The early Church did not consider every disagreement to be a choice between truth and heresy, however. Not every wrong teaching was at the level of "heresy," but there were still nonnegotiable truths that had to be gotten right. An important distinction is still made between error and heresy. "Heresy" is intentional false teaching. The word sounds very similar in Greek (*airesis*) and refers to a choice of beliefs. A heretical teaching arises out of a decision to deviate from revelation in favor of one's own insights. In the Christian context, heresy means an intentional or formal preference to deny or compromise a core dogma of the Christian Faith even when one is faced with a preponderance of evidence that the resulting belief is not correct. Heresy is certainly not about asking difficult questions. It is not the same thing as being ignorant about something, or having ideas or practices that later may be proved to be in error. Heresy is much more serious than just missing the mark, since heresies are not only the wrong answers to the most important questions, but are also evidence of a mind closed to correction by the Holy Spirit.

The Apostles were not afraid to call out heresy when it infiltrated the Church. St. Paul warned the faithful at Galatia that anyone who preached another gospel should be "under God's curse" (Gal. 1:9 NIV)—in Greek, **anathema**. The Apostle Peter also warned against "false teachers among you" who "will secretly introduce destructive heresies, even denying the sovereign Lord who bought them—bringing swift destruction on themselves" (2 Pet. 2:1 NIV). St. Paul tells Timothy that the false teachers (Hymenaeus and Philetus) have strayed so far from the truth that they have turned to "profane and idle babblings" (2 Tim. 2:16). Paul cautions Timothy to be very careful to preach the Word of Truth without error and explains that the destructive messages of these false teachers need to be stopped and removed from the Church because they are spreading like cancer and have already taken people away from their faith.

In the early second century, Irenaeus told a colorful story about John the Evangelist, who was said to have seen a known heretical teacher, Cerinthus (a Gnostic), in a bathhouse in Ephesus. The Evangelist ran out screaming, "Let us fly, lest even the bathhouse fall down because Cerinthus, the enemy of the truth, is within."[21] According to Professor John Behr of the University

---

21. Irenaeus, *Against Heresies* 3.11.1, quoted in John Behr, *John the Theologian and His Paschal Gospel: A Prologue to Theology* (Oxford: Oxford University Press, 2019), 66–67.

of Aberdeen, there is evidence that the Evangelist wrote his Gospel with the specific intention of combating the errors of Cerinthus in order to preserve the "rule of truth."[22] The harsh and even dire warnings of Saints Peter, Paul, and John (and others) were not spoken out of cruelty or to limit someone else's free speech, but out of concern for the gravity of misleading the faithful and taking people away from the true Christian Faith.

Christology and the Ecumenical Councils

Payton writes that "whether all Christians are conscious of it or not, the doctrinal positions of all Christianity, Western and Eastern alike, affirm and build on the doctrinal decrees promulgated by the ancient ecumenical councils."[23] Not only are most Christians unaware of their debt to the ancient Church in this regard, but the seven Ecumenical Councils are usually never considered at all, despite their importance in contemporary Christianity. What follows is a summary of some of the major Christological controversies and the councils that addressed them, beginning with the challenge from Arianism.

The Arian Controversy

The practice of Christianity was made legal by Emperor Constantine the Great in the year 313. The emperor's action ended the state-led persecutions and martyrdoms of Christians undertaken by many of his predecessors. With new freedoms, Christians could openly discuss theology without fear of persecution. In this climate, an Egyptian priest named Arius began to gain popularity, preaching the misguided idea that Jesus was a created being. Arius thought (and taught) that there must have been a time when the Son of God did not exist, since a father must logically precede his son.[24]

Theological ideas are not often openly discussed in public today, outside of families, churches, seminaries, or ecumenical meetings. This was not the case after Christianity became legal in the early fourth century, when the attention and interest of the public were aroused by all the important theological issues of the day. The marketplaces (and even the bars!) were often disrupted by heated debates about whether Jesus was divine or merely a created being. Christians would even sever friendships with those on the other side of the

22. Behr, *John the Theologian*, 67.
23. Payton, *Light from the Christian East*, 65.
24. Athanasius, *The Orations of Athanasius against the Arians*, ed. William Bright (Oxford: Clarendon, 1884; repr., Cambridge: Cambridge University Press, 2014).

issue. Consider this scene described in a letter written by St. Gregory of Nyssa in the fourth century:

> It is a city full of earnest theological disputes, everyone talking and declaiming in the squares, in the market places, at the cross-roads, in the alley ways. If you ask anyone for change of silver, he will debate with you whether the Son is begotten or unbegotten. If you ask for the price of a loaf, you will receive the answer "The Father is greater, the Son is less." If you ask whether the bath is prepared, you will be solemnly told that "There was nothing before the Son was created."[25]

In many ways, Arius was an impressive and crafty promoter who forged a grassroots publicity campaign to bring the entire Christian populace over to his ideas about Jesus. He even drafted songs with the lyric "There was [a time] when he was not" to the tunes of popular drinking songs, in order to subtly indoctrinate people to the idea that the Son had not been eternally with His Father. According to a fourth-century historian, Philostorgius,

> Arius, after his secession from the Church, composed several songs to be sung by sailors, and by millers, and by travelers along the high road, and others of the same kind, which he adapted to certain tunes, as he thought suitable in each separate case, and thus by degrees seduced the minds of the unlearned by the attractiveness of his songs to the adoption of his own impiety.[26]

Arianism clearly was gaining popularity among average Christians and even many of the clergy. The choices were binary: either Jesus was divine or He was not. At that time in Church history, a Christian would either be "Arian" (believing that Jesus was created) or "Orthodox" (believing that Jesus is both divine and human). Emperor Constantine the Great knew that the Arian issue was threatening to divide both the Church and the Byzantine Empire. So he extended an invitation to all the known bishops of the Christian Church—East and West—to gather in Nicaea, in Asia Minor, in AD 325. Three hundred and eighteen bishops accepted his invitation.

As impossible as it may be to contemplate *how* God became incarnate in Jesus Christ, the logic of *why* God became incarnate is actually fairly basic. St. Athanasius of Alexandria, in the fourth century, used very simple language and incontrovertible logic to illustrate how Jesus could not be the Savior of

---

25. Gregory of Nyssa, *Oratio de deitate Filii et Sancti Spiritus* 4, quoted in *Gregory of Nyssa: The Letters*, ed. Anna M. Silvas (Leiden: Brill, 2007), 51.

26. Philostorgius, *Epitome* 2.2, in *The Ecclesiastical History of Philostorgius*, trans. E. Walford (London: Henry G. Bonn, 1855), 434.

fallen humanity unless He was divine. Athanasius argues that it would not be possible for even a "special" created being to save all humanity, since a creature cannot save another creature. He argues that if the mediator between ourselves and the Father is not divine, we can never hope to reestablish fellowship with God. What is more, since the image of God in humans was damaged, it could not be restored except by Jesus, "the image of the Father":

> But how could this have occurred except by the coming of the very image of God, our Savior Jesus Christ? For neither by human beings was it possible, since they were created "in the image"; but neither by angels, for they were not even images. So the Word of God came himself, in order that he being the image of the Father (cf. Col. 1.15), the human being "in the image" might be recreated.[27]

The brilliance of Athanasius's argument is that he approaches the problem from both sides. Yes, the Savior of humanity has to be divine. Yet, from the other side of the argument, if this Savior did not also take on the entire human condition by becoming fully human, how could He possibly heal it? He could not. So Athanasius insists that Jesus's humanity was just as important as His divinity. The Savior must be both divine and human—which is exactly what the Apostles believed and taught.

Athanasius was only a deacon at the time of the First Council at Nicaea (he later became Archbishop of Alexandria), but he nevertheless provided helpful explications of all the logical flaws in the Arian teachings. First of all, he reminded everyone that the language Scripture uses to speak about the Trinity is language of God's self-differentiation. We should not think of God as a biological father, but we should understand that the Father and the Son are differentiated by their relationship. Athanasius also turned the tables on Arius's main speculation that "there was a time when the son was not" by pointing out that the Father would not be the eternal Father without an eternal Son.[28] Further, since both the Father and the Son are eternal, their relations with one another are not time-bound, and it is therefore illogical to suggest that one existed before the other. Christ's being is in the Father, who is without beginning. Therefore, "the offspring is the Son, who did not begin at a certain beginning but is eternal."[29]

Athanasius also made an argument from worship, pointing out that the New Testament and the liturgical tradition of the Church had always worshiped

27. Athanasius, *On the Incarnation* 13, trans. John Behr, Popular Patristics 44B (Crestwood, NY: St. Vladimir's Seminary Press, 2011), 63.

28. Athanasius, *Orations against the Arians* 2.29, in *Athanasius*, by Khaled Anatolios (London: Routledge, 2004), 165.

29. Athanasius, *Orations against the Arians* 2.58, in Anatolios, *Athanasius*, 122.

Jesus Christ as Savior. If Jesus is not God, then Christians (including Arius, who was a priest) are guilty of paganism by worshiping a created being. Arius did not seem to have any problem worshiping Jesus as a created being, so Athanasius reminded the Arians of St. Paul's warning in Romans: "Although they knew God, they did not glorify Him as God," and they "exchanged the truth of God for the lie, and worshiped and served the creature rather than the Creator, who is blessed forever" (Rom. 1:21, 25).[30] For Athanasius, any distorted view of God is equivalent to idolatry, since the wrong god is being worshiped instead of the true God.

There could be no compromise at the Nicene Council. Either the Orthodox view of Christ's divinity would be affirmed, or the Arian view of Christ as a created being would ascend. Would "majority rules" be an appropriate model for such an important theological dogma? In fact, had there been a democratic vote at the beginning of the council, the Arians would very likely have prevailed. But the Church at that time had not forgotten the all-important principle of conciliarity established by James, the bishop of Jerusalem, in the first century, when he convened a council of the Apostles and faithful elders to wait on the Spirit's guidance on the question of Gentile converts (Acts 15). Since communion in the Body of Christ is the fabric of the Christian Church's unity, even the most heated of disputes needed to end up with total, or near total, agreement.

The Fathers of all the Ecumenical Councils carefully, prayerfully, and soberly labored under the guidance of the Holy Spirit to find acceptable ways to put eternal realities into finite human language without stepping into error. It was believed that since the Holy Spirit is one, the Spirit would guide all Christian bishops who assembled at the council to the same truth. When they all finally agreed—"It seemed good to the Holy Spirit, and to us" (Acts 15:28)—the Spirit-directed decision would be what the Church would teach from that point forward.

The First Ecumenical Council at Nicaea was notable not only because it was the first, but also because of the gravity of its main focus, which was the divinity of Jesus Christ. The Fathers of the First Ecumenical Council issued several statements regarding a variety of issues related to Church order, but the council's main "claim to fame" is the declaration, in the strongest possible language of denunciation, that anyone who taught the false beliefs of Arianism was anathema:

> But as for those who say, There was when He was not, and, Before being born He was not, and that He came into existence out of nothing, or who assert

30. Athanasius, *Orations against the Arians* 2.81, in Anatolios, *Athanasius*, 174.

that the Son of God is of a different hypostasis or substance, or is subject to alteration or change—these the Catholic and Apostolic Church anathematizes.[31]

By the way, in the novel *The Da Vinci Code*, Dan Brown states incorrectly that the vote on the divinity of Christ at the Nicene Council was "relatively close."[32] It was not! Of the 318 bishops who attended, all but two sided with the Orthodox view, supporting Christ's full divinity in opposition to Arius.

Is Mary the "Theotokos"?

Mary, the mother of Jesus, is called **Theotokos** in the Orthodox Church. *Theotokos* in Greek literally means "God-bearer." Although this topic may seem unrelated to Christology, this is not a detour! Not everyone in the Patristic era thought it was proper to describe Mary as Theotokos, and the historical debates surrounding the use of that term to describe Mary had much more to do with Jesus Christ than with His mother.

After the Arian heresy was defeated and Christ's divinity affirmed at the First Ecumenical Council at Nicaea in AD 325, the next wave of Christological controversies developed around how best to speak about Christ's two natures. How could Jesus be both God and human at the same time? Did the two natures of Christ exist alongside each other, like two boards of wood glued together? Did one of the natures overshadow or obliterate the other? Jesus had a human body, but did He also have a human will? Or had the divine will overtaken the human will and nature? And finally, did Mary give birth to one who is God? These and many similar questions consumed the religious dialogue of the Byzantine Empire in the fourth through sixth centuries.[33]

Enter Alexandria and Antioch, two ancient centers of Christian thought. Both of these centers gave rise to distinctive ideas and nuanced theological writings. For example, Alexandria leaned toward an emphasis on Jesus Christ's divine nature and on salvation as participation in His divine nature. St. Athanasius of Alexandria points out that Jesus was always divine: "So he was not a

---

31. "Declaration of the First Ecumenical Council at Nicaea," in J. N. D. Kelly, *Early Christian Creeds*, 3rd ed. (Abingdon, UK: Routledge, 2014), 216.

32. Dan Brown, *The Da Vinci Code* (New York: Anchor, 2006), 253.

33. For further reading on the people and theological details surrounding the Christological controversies, see Richard A. Norris Jr., ed., *The Christological Controversies* (Philadelphia: Fortress, 1980); Frances M. Young with Andrew Teal, *From Nicaea to Chalcedon: A Guide to the Literature and Its Background*, 2nd ed. (Grand Rapids: Baker Academic, 2010); and Thomas P. Rausch, *Who Is Jesus? An Introduction to Christology* (Collegeville, MN: Liturgical Press, 2003).

human being and later became God. But, being God, he later became a human being in order that we may be divinized."[34] Cyril of Alexandria (378–444) emphasizes how humanity shares in God's nature: "He took what was ours to be his very own so that we might have all that was his."[35]

The writers from Antioch leaned in the other direction, emphasizing the example of Jesus's human nature as a role model for us to follow. Although the teachers in Antioch did not discount Christ's divine nature, they found great value in Christ's moral teaching and discipleship. The Antiochian writers often spoke more about the new obedience to God exemplified in Jesus Christ and less about humanity's participation in the divine nature (the common theme in Alexandria). For example, St. John Chrysostom's sermons and biblical commentaries always pointed out the lesson to be learned by following Christ: "Hearing therefore these things, let us fortify ourselves on all sides, regarding His instructions, and striking our roots deep."[36]

As it happened, heresies developed in both thought centers from ideas that leaned too far in the direction of emphasizing one of Christ's natures over the other. The overemphasis on Christ's divinity in the Alexandrian tradition by a bishop named Apollinaris produced the heresy of Apollinarianism. The overemphasis on Christ's human nature in Antioch by a bishop named Nestorius produced the opposite heresy of Nestorianism.

Apollinaris wanted to emphasize the unity of the two natures of Christ, but he was very concerned that somehow the weaknesses of human nature would have corrupted the divinity of Christ, thereby compromising Christ's sinlessness. So Apollinaris imagined that the divine Logos must have taken the place of the human soul and mind of Jesus. Apollinarians taught that Jesus had no real human nature or mind, but this notion fails because Jesus could not have been a genuine human without a genuine human soul.

Other heresies coming out of Alexandria were similar in their exaggerated emphasis on the divine over the human. Eutyches taught that the Logos entirely overtook the human nature of Christ. The Eutychian heresy was also called "Monophysitism" (which literally means "one nature"). The Orthodox response to Monophysitism and any related views that minimized or eliminated Christ's human nature was given simply and profoundly by St. Gregory

---

34. Athanasius, *Orations against the Arians* 1.39, in Anatolios, *Athanasius*, 96.

35. Cyril of Alexandria, *On the Unity of Christ*, trans. John Anthony McGuckin, Popular Patristics (Crestwood, NY: St. Vladimir's Seminary Press, 2015), 59.

36. John Chrysostom, *Homily XLIV on Matthew 12:46–49*, in *A Select Library of Nicene and Post-Nicene Fathers of the Christian Church*, 1st series, ed. Philip Schaff, 14 vols. (1887–1900; repr., Grand Rapids: Eerdmans, 1956), 10:283. See https://www.newadvent.org/fathers/200144.htm.

the Theologian (of Nazianzus): "The unassumed is the unhealed."[37] In other words, human nature could not have been redeemed if only part of human nature had been assumed by the Logos. Jesus Christ must therefore be fully God and fully human.

How did the two natures relate to each other? The Antiochian bishop Nestorius imagined that each nature existed next to the other nature as a "perfect conjunction." The Alexandrians, especially Cyril, accused Nestorius of speaking of two sons, one human and one divine, existing alongside each other, perhaps like two wooden boards fused together, where there is no interaction between the two. Cyril pointed out that Nestorius's "perfect conjunction" was not a unity at all. Cyril insisted that although the relationship between Christ's two natures cannot be fully understood by humans, Christ must always be described as one person who is fully God and fully human. Cyril used the term "hypostatic union" to describe this genuine unity of two perfect natures, and this would become the standard Orthodox terminology. The hypostatic union of Christ's two natures cannot be broken or destroyed, not even in death (a point that has vital implications for how Orthodoxy sees the Crucifixion and Resurrection).[38]

And here is where "Theotokos" comes back into the picture. It was this same Nestorius who strongly objected to the Alexandrians' use of the term *Theotokos* to refer to the Virgin Mary. Nestorius preferred the term *Christotokos* (Christ-bearer), since he did not believe that the son of Mary is completely and fully God, but rather has something like a God part alongside a human part. St. Cyril of Alexandria refutes this idea, writing simply and logically, "I am amazed that there are some who are extremely doubtful whether the holy Virgin should be called mother of God [Theotokos] or not. For if our Lord Jesus Christ is God, then surely the holy Virgin who gave Him birth must be God's mother."[39] Done!

Finally Settled

The Council of Ephesus in 431 settled the issue of Theotokos once and for all and declared that Mary is indeed "Theotokos" because her son, Jesus, is the one person who is fully God and fully human. That Mary has been declared to be "God-bearer" or "Theotokos" is also the only dogma related to Mary in the

37. Gregory of Nazianzus, *Letter 101*, to Cledonius, §32, quoted in Kallistos Ware, *The Orthodox Way* (Crestwood, NY: St. Vladimir's Seminary Press, 1979), 75.
38. See the section "The Cross and Resurrection" in chap. 6.
39. Cyril of Alexandria, "Epistle 1, to the Monks of Egypt," in *Ancient Christian Doctrine*, vol. 2, *We Believe in One Lord Jesus Christ*, ed. John Anthony McGuckin (Downers Grove, IL: InterVarsity, 2014), 129.

Orthodox Church. Mary is venerated in the Orthodox Church solely because she is the Mother of God "according to the flesh." The Council of Ephesus would become known as the Third Ecumenical Council, but the issue of the two natures of Christ would still take one more council to finally be settled.

It was the Fourth Ecumenical Council, held in Chalcedon in Asia Minor by Emperor Marcian and Empress Pulcheria, that settled the Christological controversy. With more than six hundred bishops in attendance, the council affirmed Cyril of Alexandria's notion of the "hypostatic union" of the two undivided natures of Christ and rejected both Nestorianism and Eutychianism. It also reaffirmed the decision of the Council of Ephesus that the Virgin Mary is truly Theotokos, since the one born from her is the uncreated, divine Son of God and one of the Holy Trinity. In His human birth, the Logos of God became a real man in every way, but without sin. The Council of Chalcedon also issued its own statement declaring that Jesus of Nazareth is one person (*hypostasis*) in two natures—human and divine—united "without change, without confusion, without division, without separation." He is completely God and completely human. As God, He is "of same essence" (*homoousios*) as God the Father and the Holy Spirit. And as man, He is "of same essence" (*homoousios*) as all human beings.[40]

James Payton describes the decrees of the Ecumenical Councils of Eastern Orthodoxy as being more like "No Trespassing" signs to defend against error, rather than as a basis for further doctrinal developments: "For Orthodoxy, the ecumenical councils were manifestations of a Spirit-inspired unity in the faith, not legal institutions for defining doctrine. The councils met to discern how best to protect the faith, not to explain it."[41] Chalcedon put up a "No Trespassing" sign to Monophysitism by declaring that Christ's two natures are "without confusion and without change." A human did not become God, nor did God pretend to be human. The "No Trespassing" sign for Nestorianism was the statement that Christ's two natures are "without division and without separation." Thus, the two natures do not exist separately or alongside one another, but are a union.

Patristics scholar Frances Young has provided a persuasive insight into the logical problem of the two natures. Young argues that in any discussion about two created things, one will always dominate or displace the other, or the two will be side by side, or they will form a new hybrid. The wrong views of the nature of Christ went far afield because they could not

40. Henry Bettenson, ed., *Documents of the Christian Church*, 4th ed. (New York: Oxford University Press, 2011), 54.
41. Payton, *Light from the Christian East*, 67.

escape the human logic of comparing created things. But God is beyond creation and is everywhere. God is not limited by the limited categories of human thought. "God and something created are not mutually exclusive—they can, as it were, occupy the same space."[42] The carefully constructed parameters of the Council of Chalcedon did not provide specific insights into the mystery of how the two natures of Christ relate to each other. The language of the councils did, however, provide the Church with the theological boundaries—the "No Trespassing" signs—to protect against false teachings. Ultimately, Young concludes, "Chalcedon forces us to go on wrestling with the mystery."[43]

Singing Theology

One of the unique aspects of Orthodox life and worship, as compared to most Western Christian traditions, is that the majority of worship is sung and chanted as a responsive prayer between clergy and laypeople. There is nothing in Orthodox liturgical worship like the praise music most Western Christians have experienced in the past few decades, or even the "old hymns" of Protestant denominations in the nineteenth and twentieth centuries. Orthodox hymns are highly theological in the sense that they are directed to God and proclaim scriptural truths about events in the Bible or about the lives of the saints, and especially dogmas about the Holy Trinity—in the form of praises, **doxology**, and thanksgiving. Orthodox hymns also do not rhyme! They are

"The Hymn of the Evening" (Second Century) Sung at Vespers

O Gladsome Light of the holy glory of the Immortal Father, heavenly, holy, blessed Jesus Christ. Now we have come to the setting of the sun and behold the light of evening. We praise God: Father, Son, and Holy Spirit. For it is right at all times to worship Thee with voices of praise, O Son of God and Giver of Life, therefore all the world glorifies Thee.[a]

a. English translation by the Orthodox Church in America, https://www.oca.org/orthodoxy/the -orthodox-faith/worship/the-daily-cycles-of-prayer/vespers.

42. Frances Young, "The Council of Chalcedon 1550 Years Later," *Touchstone*, January 2001, 5–14.
43. Young, "Council of Chalcedon," 14.

traditionally chanted in two parts: a melody and an *eison* (drone note), although four-part polyphonic music is also found in some Orthodox churches.

Orthodox hymns are nearly always chanted from the perspective of the corporate Body of Christ ("Save us, O Son of God, risen from the dead, we sing to You: Alleluia!")[44] and not from an individual perspective ("I'm so glad You're in my life").[45] The earliest Christian hymns were taken from the Psalms, and many of today's Orthodox hymns originated in the earliest centuries—some even from the second century. For example, "The Hymn of the Evening," which is still sung at every Orthodox **Vespers** service today, was called "ancient" by St. Basil the Great in the fourth century.

Another theologically rich hymn came out of the Fifth Ecumenical Council in Constantinople in AD 533 and has been attributed to the emperor Justinian the Great. Justinian called this council in the hope that the false teachings of Nestorius and Eutyches would finally be quashed. You might remember that Nestorius was accused of teaching that Jesus was really two sons alongside each other: one the human Christ, and one the divine Logos. Eutyches promoted the heresy that Jesus's human nature was overtaken by His divine nature. When Emperor Justinian confessed the Orthodox Faith in the hymn "Only Begotten Son" (also known as the "Hymn of Justinian"), he endeavored to overturn the errors of these two (and other) Christological challenges by stating the Church's conciliar and true view of Jesus Christ.

This hymn is an ideal example of how the declarations of an Ecumenical Council were not intended to be merely "high theology" for the Church hierarchy, but were expected to be proclaimed and lived by all the Orthodox faithful. The sixth-century "Hymn of Justinian" is still chanted at every Divine Liturgy today, in every Orthodox Church, in every place, in every culture:

> Only begotten Son and Logos of God, being immortal, You condescended for our salvation to take flesh from the holy Theotokos, and ever virgin Mary, and without change became man. Christ our God, You were crucified, but trampled down death by death. Being One with the Holy Trinity, glorified with the Father and the Holy Spirit: save us.[46]

While typical worshipers in the Orthodox Divine Liturgy may not be theological scholars, many have memorized this hymn (and many other Orthodox hymns) and can therefore convey the conciliar theological dogmas of the

44. Hymn of the Second Antiphon of the Divine Liturgy.
45. Rick Doyle Founds, "Lord, I Lift Your Name on High," © 1989 Maranatha! Music.
46. Greek Orthodox Archdiocese of America, *The Divine Liturgy of St. John Chrysostom* (Brookline, MA: Holy Cross Orthodox Press, 2015), 9–10.

ancient Church. In fact, they sing Christology, even though most are not aware that the words were crafted to condemn the early Christological heresies. For example, against Nestorius, this hymn proclaims that the Virgin Mary is Theotokos because she gave birth to the one who is truly God. Against Eutyches, who denied Jesus's human nature, it emphatically states that Jesus "condescended . . . to take flesh" from the Theotokos and became man, but without change to His divine nature. Against Arius, who taught that Jesus was a created being, it proclaims Jesus as "immortal" and "Logos." Against the Pneumatomachians (Spirit fighters), it glorifies the Holy Spirit together with the Father and the Son as "One with the Holy Trinity." Further, it reminds us why Jesus did all these things: "for our salvation."

▪ Discussion Questions ▪

1. What do you think are the essential beliefs about Jesus Christ that must be held if one is to be considered Christian?

2. Describe how St. Irenaeus understood the "rule of the truth" (or the "canon of truth" or the "rule of faith").

3. If the ancient Church had decided that Mary should *not* be called "Theotokos," what would that have said about its views about the nature of Jesus?

4. What value do you see in the way dogmatic statements came out of the Ecumenical Councils discussed in this chapter? Do you think the councils were necessary? Or could these issues have been settled another way?

Who Are We?
What Are We to Do?

Created for Communion

The psalmist David, pondering his own existence, asks the Lord, "What are human beings that you are mindful of them, mortals that you care for them?" (Ps. 8:4 NRSV). Who has not asked, like King David—perhaps in a reflective moment by a mountain stream or after a bad day at work or school—"Why am I here? What is the meaning, purpose, and calling of my life?" According to a Judeo-Christian worldview, human creation is unique from the creation of other creatures in some magnificent way. But how? The creation narratives do not give us a specific answer, but they do point in a direction in which an answer lies:

> Then God said, "Let us make humankind in our image, according to our like-ness; and let them have dominion over the fish of the sea, and over the birds of the air, and over the cattle, and over all the wild animals of the earth, and over every creeping thing that creeps upon the earth."
>
> > So God created humankind in his image,
> > in the image of God he created them;
> > male and female he created them. (Gen. 1:26–27 NRSV)

It is a foundational principle in Judeo-Christian theology that being cre-ated in the image and according to the likeness of God means that humans have been given a special standing in the created world. Unlike that of other creatures, the *being* of humanity shares a certain similarity to the *being* of God. With its typical apophatic reserve, however, Eastern Orthodoxy does not attempt to specify exactly how the image of God resides in humans. As Fr. Emmanuel Clapsis points out, the biblical narrative "is silent about any qualities of human nature that might account for this special standing of God's image and likeness."[1] There is no well-defined theological anthropology in Eastern Orthodoxy, since anthropology was never a topic for debate in the dogmatic history of the Church.[2] Genesis 1:26–27 nevertheless remains as the primary scriptural key to insights about who we are as humans and our role in the created universe. One viewpoint within Orthodox thought is that these majestic statements clearly define human nature in relation to God, such that humankind was not created to be independent of God.

Alfons Brüning, who teaches at the Institute of Eastern Christian Studies in the Netherlands, observes that a stereotypical interpretation of this passage in the West is that the "image" refers to the "dignity and rights belonging to every single *individual*."[3] But the Orthodox cannot bypass a vital clue in the opening address of this brief divine conversation: "Let us." Whatever else constitutes the image of God, these words convey that the divine-human relationship exists within the communal nature of the Holy Trinity. What is also apparent to biblical scholars, but often missed in English translations, is that the Hebrew *ha'adam* (and in the Septuagint, the Greek *anthrōpon*) of Genesis 1:26–27 refers not to one particular individual but to human creation generally. Fr. Clapsis puts it like this: "All the divine gifts that God has bestowed on *adam* in creation must be applied to the whole human nature. The multiple existences of persons in the race of *adam* do not destroy the unity of humanity."[4] The majesty of the image of God cannot be thought of as being given individually, since nothing in the cosmos of God's creation is individual. As Metropolitan Zizioulas often reminds his readers, "There is no true being without communion. Nothing exists as an 'individual,' conceivable in itself" because the source of being is not an

1. Emmanuel Clapsis, "Elements of Theological Anthropology" (transcript of "Exploring the Mind-Body-Soul Connection: Spirituality in Illness and Healing," Conference of the Orthodox Christian Association of Medicine, Psychology, and Religion, Holy Cross Greek Orthodox School of Theology, Brookline, MA, November 6–8, 2014). Rev. Dr. Emmanuel Clapsis is the Archbishop Iakovos Professor of Orthodox Theology at Holy Cross Greek Orthodox School of Theology.

2. Very few treatises from the ancient Christian world were written on the implications of human creation. Gregory of Nyssa's *On the Making of Man* is a notable exception.

3. Alfons Brüning, "Can Theosis Save 'Human Dignity'? Chapters in Theological Anthropology East and West," *Journal of Eastern Christian Studies* 71, nos. 3–4 (2019): 179.

4. Clapsis, "Elements of Theological Anthropology."

individual but a Trinity of communion.[5] That is to say, human beings have been created for communion.

What Are We to Do?

Another very important question to ponder is this: "Since we have been given the image of God, what are we to do?" The broader Christian Gospel provides the response to this question: "For we are His workmanship, created in Christ Jesus for good works, which God prepared beforehand that we should walk in them" (Eph. 2:10). God has created us to do something!

From at least the late second century and St. Irenaeus, ancient Christian commentators understood "in the image" and "according to the likeness" to be two distinct aspects of human nature. The "image" is the natural resemblance to God (however it might be understood) as a static potential given to all human beings. The "likeness" is the dynamic process of one's life in movement toward God. Many other Eastern Christian teachers, including Diadochos of Photiki (fifth century), Maximus the Confessor (seventh century), John of Damascus (eighth century), and Gregory Palamas (fourteenth century), explicitly articulated a similar distinction in the two terms "image" and "likeness," with the latter being the goal of the life lived in the image of the Trinity. Orthodox Christianity also affirms that the purpose of Christian life is to "grow up in all things into Him who is the head—Christ" (Eph. 4:15).

The Greek Fathers saw clearly from the Genesis account that the natural state of humanity is union with God and that separation from God is an *abnormal* state. If a person does not participate in God's life, there is something *in*human about that person—something is "missing" in the person's very nature as a human being.[6] It is no coincidence that the Bible uses the same language of "image" and "likeness" to describe both the creation of humanity in Genesis and the *new creation* possible in Christ: "[You] have clothed yourselves with the new self, which is being renewed in knowledge according to the image of its creator" (Col. 3:10 NRSV).

The Orthodox understanding of salvation is consistently defined not only in terms of the corporate, communal Body of Christ, but also as a process. This process is often said to be a movement from the divine "image" to the divine "likeness." Having been created in the image of Christ, there is a hope and an expectation for humans to grow in likeness to Christ: "We all,

5. John D. Zizioulas, *Being as Communion: Studies in Personhood and the Church* (Crestwood, NY: St. Vladimir's Seminary Press, 1985), 18.

6. Jordan Bajis, *Common Ground: An Introduction to Eastern Christianity for the American Christian* (Minneapolis: Light and Life Publishing, 1991), 240.

with unveiled face, beholding as in a mirror the glory of the Lord, are being transformed into the same image from glory to glory, just as by the Spirit of the Lord" (2 Cor. 3:18).[7] The natural participation of humans in God is not a "static givenness" but a challenge and a calling.[8]

Humanity's **free will** is another foundation of Orthodox theological anthropology and soteriology. Oxford professor Richard Swinburne, writing just a few years after he joined the Orthodox Church, argues that the weight of the Christian tradition from the beginning has supported free will as the central notion of what it means to be made "in the image of God." Swinburne quotes several of the Eastern Fathers, including Gregory of Nyssa, John of Damascus, and Gregory Palamas, to support his statement that "the glory of humans is not just their very serious free will, but the responsibility for so much which that free will involves."[9]

Gift and Task

The Orthodox understanding of the relationship between "image" and "likeness" has often been expressed by the concepts of "gift" and "task." Fr. John Meyendorff affirms that "divine life is a gift, but also a task which is to be accomplished by a free human effort."[10] The image of God denotes a potential for life in God. The likeness of God is the calling of Christians to follow Christ toward the realization of that potential. Fr. Christoforos Stavropoulos depicts this idea with an analogy to seeds, growth, and a garden: "Within each human being, God sows all those seedlike gifts which make us his image and lead us toward his likeness, insomuch as we cultivate these gifts."[11] Metropolitan Kallistos Ware suggests that the *image* can be understood as the tools one possesses at the beginning of a journey. The *likeness* is what one hopes to reach at the end of the journey.[12] Both ideas are consistent with the Eastern Orthodox understanding of salvation as a process. In a similar way, St. Paul likens the Christian life to an athletic endeavor with a goal: "I have

7. Other New Testament references include 1 Cor. 15:49; 2 Cor. 3:10; 4:4; Col. 1:15; 3:10; Rom. 8:29; Eph. 4:22–24; Phil. 3:21.

8. John Meyendorff, *Byzantine Theology: Historical Trends and Doctrinal Themes*, 2nd ed. (New York: Fordham University Press, 1983), 138.

9. Richard Swinburne, *Providence and the Problem of Evil* (New York: Oxford University Press, 1998), 106.

10. Meyendorff, *Byzantine Theology*, 138–39.

11. Christoforos Stavropoulos, "Partakers of the Divine Nature," in *Eastern Orthodox Theology: A Contemporary Reader*, ed. Daniel B. Clendenin (Grand Rapids: Baker Academic, 1995), 186.

12. Kallistos Ware, *The Orthodox Way* (Crestwood, NY: St. Vladimir's Seminary Press, 1979), 41.

fought the good fight, I have finished the race, I have kept the faith" (2 Tim. 4:7) for the purpose of receiving "an imperishable crown" (1 Cor. 9:25).

Tragedy in the Garden

> The world is a fallen world because it has fallen away from the awareness that God is all in all. (Fr. Alexander Schmemann)[13]

Perhaps the deepest and widest chasm between Eastern Orthodox theology and Western Christian theology is seen in their respective views on "the Fall." Genesis 3 describes the temptation and sin of Adam and Eve, as well as the subsequent curse and their banishment from the garden of Eden. The common term used in the West to describe the Fall of Adam and Eve is "original sin"—a phrase that likely originated with Augustine in the fourth century. However, in the earlier Greek Fathers and for the Eastern Orthodox today, one will often find the terms **ancestral sin** and **primal curse** used to distinguish the Eastern Christian view from the Western idea of the inherited guilt of Adam. Before elaborating on the Orthodox understanding, it is important first to clarify what is *not* the consensus Orthodox view.

The West: Guilty!

The first major difference between the Eastern and Western views of the original sin is that in the West, following Augustine, the original sin transmits guilt. Whether because of his self-admitted lack of fluency in Greek, or perhaps because he used a flawed Latin translation of the New Testament,[14] most scholars today believe that Augustine misread Romans 5:12: "Therefore, just as through one man sin entered the world, and death through sin, and thus death spread to all men, because all sinned . . ." Augustine translated the Greek words for "because" as "in whom," which drastically changes St. Paul's intended meaning. Instead of death entering *because* of sin (as is clear in the Greek), Augustine taught that the sin itself was transmitted *from* Adam "to all men," who bear guilt. For Augustine, every individual human person after Adam is personally guilty of Adam's sin, which is transmitted biologically through procreation.[15]

---

13. Alexander Schmemann, *For the Life of the World: Sacraments and Orthodoxy* (Crestwood, NY: St. Vladimir's Seminary Press, 1998), 16.

14. John Meyendorff has shown that it was the flawed Latin Vulgate translation that caused Augustine to interpret Rom. 5:12 incorrectly. See John Meyendorff, *Byzantine Theology*, 144–46.

15. Augustine conflated Rom. 5:12 with 1 Cor. 15:22 and concluded that sin was passed biologically from Adam to all his descendants through human procreation.

Today's Roman Catholic Catechism follows Augustine and the later Roman Catholic Council of Trent (1511–1512) in teaching that "all men are implicated in Adam's sin . . . transmitted by propagation to all mankind."[16]

Because he believed in the actual transmission of sin and its guilt, Augustine held that human nature after the Fall was "corrupted at its root" and that the image of God was all but obliterated.[17] He argued that even infants enter human life eternally damned, having inherited the guilt of Adam's sin from their parents, regardless of whether their parents had been baptized to remove their own guilt.[18] The Protestant Reformers who followed Augustine—especially Martin Luther and John Calvin—followed his thinking on inherited guilt and the corrupted human nature.[19] Calvin, for instance, writes that because of the guilt we have inherited from Adam, human nature is "destitute of all good," "totally vitiated and depraved," "utterly defiled and polluted."[20] Through Augustine and the Reformers, "western Christianity shares the general conviction that God has imputed the sin of Adam to all his descendants and that they all are guilty of that sin."[21] It follows in this Western idea that every human has incurred an individual debt to God by being present in Adam's sin.

The East: Fallen, Yet Still Good

In Eastern Orthodoxy, sin is a fault of persons, not of nature. Orthodox Christianity has never taught that we are guilty of Adam's sin, either individually or as a species, mainly because neither Jesus Christ nor His Apostles

16. United States Catholic Conference, *Catechism of the Catholic Church: With Modifications from the Editio Typica* (New York: Doubleday, 2003), 114.

17. The total destruction of the image of God became more explicit in Augustine's later writings, especially in his *Literal Interpretation of Genesis*, written in the period of 400–412. See Matthew Puffer, "Human Dignity after Augustine's *Imago Dei*: On the Sources and Uses of Two Ethical Terms," *Journal of the Society of Christian Ethics* 37, no. 1 (Spring/Summer 2017): 74.

18. "Infants, although born from the goodness of marriage, were yet made guilty by the evil of conception; and though the guilt is cleansed by baptism, the infection of concupiscence (sexual sin) remains in their flesh, to be transmitted to their own offspring." Augustine, *De nuptiis et concupiscentia* 1.32.37, in *Augustine through the Ages: An Encyclopedia*, ed. Allan D. Fitzgerald (Grand Rapids: Eerdmans, 1999), 45. See also Augustine, *Enchiridion* 46–47; Augustine, *De peccatorum meritis et remissione* 1.13, 34; 3.11; Kenneth Wilson, *Augustine's Conversion from Traditional Free Choice to "Non-free Free Will": A Comprehensive Methodology* (Tübingen: Mohr Siebeck, 2018).

19. Jairzinho Lopes Pereira, *Augustine of Hippo and Martin Luther on Original Sin and Justification of the Sinner* (Göttingen: Vandenhoeck & Ruprecht, 2013), 200.

20. John Calvin, *Institutes*, trans. John Allen (Philadelphia: Presbyterian Board of Publication, 1921), 229, 230, 680.

21. James Payton, *Light from the Christian East: An Introduction to the Orthodox Tradition* (Downers Grove, IL: IVP Academic, 2007), 111.

taught this. Adam alone is guilty of Adam's sin, just as each of us is guilty of our own sin. In further contrast to the Western view, the Orthodox would never speak of created human nature as "destitute of all good" or "depraved." Our nature is a gift from God, and it is good because God said it was good (Gen. 1:31). Gregory of Nyssa argues that because God is the "fullness of good," the image in humanity "finds its resemblance to the Archetype in being filled with all good."[22] Even though the image of God is tarnished, human creation is still good, even in an imperfect form. So the beauty and goodness in human creation continues "so long as it partakes as far as is possible in its likeness to the archetype."[23]

St. Irenaeus believed that although Adam and Eve were immature and vulnerable, they had no excuse for sinning, and that although the image of God was tarnished, it was not lost. What was lost was communion with God.[24] Russian Professor of Theology Paul Evdokimov represents the consensus of Patristic witness in stating that "the Fall severely inhibits the image of God, but does not corrupt it."[25] For Gregory of Nyssa, the image has not been lost, but something like an "ugly mask" now covers "the beauty of the image."[26] Humans still have free will, and in that free will we are able to exercise personal volition to turn toward God or to freely turn against God—as did our primal ancestors. Neither choice has been preordained. Orthodox Christianity teaches that following God's will is a choice available to everyone, even after the Fall, since free will is still active.

Loss of Communion, Inheritance of Mortality

Adam and Eve, representing all humankind, made an unfortunate choice to turn away from God, which led them to the unnatural state of separation from God. In the Orthodox view of the ancestral sin, our ancestors' willful separation from the God of life separated all creation from the source of life itself. Consequently, communion with the Creator has been lost, and all

22. Gregory of Nyssa, *On the Making of Man* 16.10, in *A Select Library of Nicene and Post-Nicene Fathers of the Christian Church*, 2nd series, ed. Philip Schaff and Henry Wace, 14 vols. (1890–1900; repr., Grand Rapids: Eerdmans, 1952), 5:405. See https://www.newadvent.org/fathers/2914.htm.

23. Gregory of Nyssa, *On the Making of Man* 12.9, in *A Select Library of Nicene and Post-Nicene Fathers of the Christian Church*, 2nd series, ed. Philip Schaff and Henry Wace, 14 vols. (1890–1900; repr., Grand Rapids: Eerdmans, 1952), 5:399. See https://www.newadvent.org/fathers/2914.htm.

24. Irenaeus, *Against Heresies*, as discussed in Thomas G. Weinandy, "St. Irenaeus and the *Imago Dei*: The Importance of Being Human," *Logos* 6, no. 4 (Fall 2003): 26.

25. Paul Evdokimov, *Orthodoxy* (New York: New City, 2011), 96.

26. Gregory of Nyssa, *On the Making of Man* 18.

creation has become subject to destructive enemies: death, decay, and evil. We have thus contracted something like a disease—the disease of death and decay—and we are desperately subject to a world in which the Evil One presently has a stronghold.

Fr. Meyendorff summarizes the consensus view within the Greek Patristic and Byzantine traditions: What we have inherited from the Fall is "essentially of mortality rather than of sinfulness, sinfulness being merely a consequence of mortality."[27] Meyendorff is saying here that although neither Adam's sin nor guilt have been transmitted to us, our personal sinfulness arises as a result of humanity's inherited mortality and corruptibility. Salvation is thus seen as a healing and renewal of the human nature that has been assaulted by Satan. Death, not guilt, is the primary consequence of the Fall, but it has been overturned by Jesus Christ! Consider one of the hymns sung to Christ the "Giver of Life" at the Matins (or Orthros) service of the Orthodox Church:

> You have raised the dead with you and have shattered the gates of **Hades** and destroyed the power of death. Therefore, we praise you with love; you who arose and demolished the power of the deadly enemy. You . . . delivered the world from the arrows of the serpent, and freed us from the errors of the enemy, O mighty One. Therefore in faith we praise your resurrection by which you saved us as God of all.[28]

Jesus Christ, the "God of all," has destroyed the gates of Hades and the power of death and rescued us from the power of the Evil One.

Expelled from Paradise

We've got to get ourselves back to the garden. (Joni Mitchell, "Woodstock")

The most unfortunate consequence of the ancestral sin is that humanity was expelled from the garden of Eden. The Eastern Orthodox refer to Adam and Eve's "Expulsion from Paradise" as leaving their home—the place where they belonged, the place of communion with God. Their actions separated them from God and brought spiritual darkness and physical death to all creation. Even in humanity's fallen state, however, those created in the image of God still long to return to that garden and to communion with the Creator.

When the folk singer and songwriter Joni Mitchell wrote the lyric "We've got to get ourselves back to the garden" about the 1969 Woodstock music

27. Meyendorff, *Byzantine Theology*, 144.
28. The Oikos of the Sixth Tone, in *The Service of the Sunday Orthros*, trans. N. Michael Vaporis (Brookline, MA: Holy Cross Orthodox Press, 1994), 56.

festival, she was actually referring to the garden of Eden. She was trying to express what she felt and believed was a common human instinct: the desire to return to a place of genuine peace and goodness. The return to Paradise is a common theme of repentance and the hope of salvation in Eastern Ortho-doxy, since it is the longing of human creation in the image of God to "get ourselves back to the garden":

> I am an image of Your ineffable glory, though I bear the scars of my transgres-sions. Take pity on me, the work of Your hands, Master, and cleanse me by Your compassion. Grant me the desired homeland for which I long, making me again a citizen of Paradise.[29]

Orthodox Christianity also teaches that God did not reject His disobedient creation. The Expulsion from Paradise is commemorated in the Orthodox Church every year on the day called "The Sunday of Forgiveness." Adam's longing to return to Paradise is the theme of several of the hymns sung at the Vespers service on the preceding evening. One of the poetic hymns of forgive-ness at Vespers is presented as the humble plea of Adam to Paradise, with a merciful response from the all-compassionate Savior:

> Through eating Adam was cast out of Paradise. And so, as he sat in front of it, he wept, lamenting with a pitiful voice and saying, "Woe is me, what have I suffered, wretch that I am! I transgressed one commandment of the Master, and now I am deprived of every good thing. Most holy Paradise, planted because of me and shut because of Eve, pray to him who made you and fashioned me, that once more I be filled with your flowers." Then the Saviour said to him, "I do not want the creature which I fashioned to perish, but to be saved and come to knowledge of the truth, because the one who comes to me I will in no way cast out."[30]

Growing in Likeness

When reciting the Nicene Creed, Christians proclaim that they believe Jesus became incarnate, was crucified, died, and rose "for us and for our salvation." There are no details, however, about how that salvation is to be worked out. As with many other Eastern Orthodox concepts, there is no dogmatic position,

29. Verse from the funeral and memorial services, *The Divine Liturgy of St. John Chrysos-tom*, 113. English translation from *Divine Liturgy*, priest ed. (New York: Greek Orthodox Archdiocese of America, 2015).
30. Glory Hymn from the Octoechos, on Forgiveness Sunday. The entire service is available at "Triodion," http://newbyz.org/lastriodion.html.

fixed doctrine, or any official pronouncement on the doctrine of salvation. "The tradition of the Church concerning our reunion with God in Christ, our redemption or salvation or justification by God in Christ, has not been challenged in the East. It is for this reason that one does not find any fixed doctrine even among the ancient Fathers, but only a common tradition."[31] This "common tradition" in the Orthodox Church presents salvation primarily in terms of freedom from death through union with Christ.

There are five main themes or truths that work together in the common tradition of salvation in the Orthodox Christian East (the first three of which have already been discussed): (1) human nature is good (not depraved); (2) humanity has inherited the consequences of original sin—death and decay (not Adam's guilt); (3) free will remains active (even after the ancestral sin); (4) salvation is a process (not a moment); and (5) salvation is a free gift, but the gift must be exercised: "Faith without works is dead" (James 2:26).

Each of these themes of salvation is related to the other themes. For example, themes 3 and 5 are related, since although Orthodox Christians understand salvation to be a free gift of God that cannot be earned, the gift should be received with a freely offered response of active faith. We can exercise our God-given liberty by moving closer to God, or we can exercise our free will by moving farther away from God. God does not decide either option for us. As Metropolitan Ware points out, "God wanted sons and daughters, not slaves. The Orthodox Church rejects any doctrine of grace which might seem to infringe upon human freedom."[32] The Orthodox understand that salvation is a gift from a loving God, but that it is also possible for the gift to be refused.

As already mentioned, Irenaeus and many others made a distinction between the static gift of God's image and our dynamic calling to grow in likeness, or similitude, to Christ. The Orthodox understand that growing in likeness to Christ is not a human work to earn salvation, but is the essence of what it means to be a Christian. The testimony of Scripture confirms that salvation must include the conforming of one's life to Christ in order to become adopted as children of God (Rom. 8:14–17; John 1:12–13; Gal. 4:4–5).

One Size Does Not Fit All

Isaiah the Prophet refers to salvation as a "garment" (Isa. 61:10). As with most garments, one size does not fit all with salvation, because each human

---

31. Savas Agourides, "Salvation according to the Orthodox Tradition," *Ecumenical Review* 21, no. 3 (July 1969): 190.

32. Timothy Ware, *The Orthodox Church: An Introduction to Eastern Christianity*, 3rd ed. (London: Penguin, 2015), 215.

person is unique. God calls each person to respond uniquely to the Gospel message with the unique gifts of grace each has received. The thief on the cross, for example, is immediately granted his desire to be with the Lord in Paradise without sacramental Baptism or any other action (Luke 23:43). The rich young man who asks Jesus what is needed to inherit eternal life is given a very different prescription for salvation. Jesus answers, "If you want to be perfect, go, sell your possessions and give to the poor. . . . Then come, follow me" (Matt. 19:21 NIV). Jesus perceives in this young man's life the stumbling blocks keeping him from inheriting eternal life, and Jesus is very clear in His specific instructions for salvation: Sell. Give. Follow.

These examples from the New Testament support the Orthodox belief that the fullness of the Christian life can only be found by first taking care of whatever is holding one back from growing in Christlikeness. For some the stumbling block is money, but it may be pride or covetousness for others. The instructions given by Christ about how to attain eternal life are nothing if not calls to action: "repent," "forgive," "trust," "cleanse," "give," "follow," and so forth. The Orthodox believe that action is an essential response to the gift of salvation. According to Fr. Anton Vrame, the needed response to Christ is "growth in personhood" because the "development of one's humanity is consistent with growth toward God-likeness."[33]

The grace of the Holy Spirit has been given to each member of Christ's Body, but it has been given uniquely for each person. The following hymn is from the evening service on Monday of **Holy Week** (the week leading up to Easter). The hymn reminds us that all Christians are called to be faithful stewards of this grace, and are to increase our talents and gifts by using them rather than hiding them away for safekeeping:

Come, O believers, let us labor with zeal for the Master. Since He distributes His wealth to His servants, let each of us correspondingly increase the talent of grace that we received. Let one acquire wisdom by means of good deeds. Let another celebrate the liturgy with splendor. Let the believer communicate the word to the uninitiated, and let another disperse his wealth to the poor. And so let us increase that which was lent to us, so that as faithful stewards of grace we may be counted worthy of the Master's joy. O count us worthy of this joy, Christ God, since You love humanity.[34]

33. Anton C. Vrame, *The Educating Icon: Teaching Wisdom and Holiness in the Orthodox Way* (Brookline, MA: Holy Cross Orthodox Press, 1999), 71.

34. The *Aposticha* hymn of Holy Monday evening. Translation copyright © 2018 by Fr. Seraphim Dedes, accessed July 1, 2020, https://www.agesinitiatives.com/dcs/public/dcs/h/b/tr/d066/ma/en/index.html.

Note that the hymn poetically affirms that each believer should work with zeal for Christ, using the unique talent of grace that he or she has been given. Grace is the key to any labor of faith. The Orthodox are in complete agreement with Luther in his insistence that no human can ever do enough to be saved by works alone. Yet Orthodoxy also teaches that God sees one's efforts motivated by faith and blesses those efforts with His grace. In this way salvation is a cooperative effort between the human person and God.

Synergy

The Orthodox refer to this cooperation with God as "synergy." Synergy is the process of salvation in which Christians cooperate with the Holy Spirit in conforming their will to God's will in Jesus Christ (Rom. 8:28; 2 Cor. 6:1). The principle of synergy or cooperation with God reminds us that we are not alone. God is a personal God who loves His creation and has not abandoned it. We can do nothing without God's help, but we are expected to be "fellow workers" (Greek: *synergoi*) with God (1 Cor. 3:9).

In Eastern Orthodoxy, synergy also means harmony between human free will and God's will. The Orthodox consider the supreme example of synergy, or cooperation between God's purpose and human freedom, to be Mary, the Mother of God.[35] Mary freely assented to God's will: "Let it be to me according to your word" (Luke 1:38). God respects human choice and would not have forced His Son to become incarnate through her.

This is a good place to consider for a moment the person of Mary. You will recall from chapter 5 that the Orthodox have referred to Mary as "Theotokos" or "God-bearer" since at least the early fourth century, because the

The "Magnificat" Hymn to the Virgin Mary Sung at Every Orthodox Divine Liturgy

It is truly right to bless you, Theotokos, ever blessed, most pure, and Mother of our God. More honorable than the Cherubim, and beyond compare more glorious than the Seraphim, without corruption you gave birth to God the Logos. We magnify you, the true Theotokos.[a]

a. *The Divine Liturgy of St. John Chrysostom*. English translation from *Divine Liturgy*, priest ed. (New York: Greek Orthodox Archdiocese of America, 2015), 57.

35. Ware, *Orthodox Church*, 251.

child she bore was (and is) truly God. A Protestant student in one of my historical theology classes recently asked whether the Orthodox worship Mary as Roman Catholics do. The answer, of course, is no! The Orthodox do not worship Mary, but neither do Roman Catholics.

Nevertheless, most Orthodox teachers would be concerned about the Roman Catholic doctrine of the Immaculate Conception of Mary, which Pope Pius IX in 1854 declared to be an essential dogma for Roman Catholics. The Immaculate Conception of Mary attempts to solve the problem of Mary's birth, given Augustine of Hippo's teaching that procreation passes along inherited guilt to every child. The Immaculate Conception of Mary means that, of all the parents who have ever conceived children, Mary's parents were the only couple in history who did not transmit original sin and guilt to their child. In this view Mary is also an ontologically unique person, different from every other human being, since she is the only human child who was not "made guilty by the evil of conception" (to use Augustine's phrase).[36] Theologically speaking, this nineteenth-century Roman Catholic dogma also adds an element of divine determinism that seems to devalue Mary's yes in response to the Angel Gabriel's announcement.

In contrast, Orthodoxy understands Mary to have been conceived just as every other human person is. Eastern Orthodoxy definitely—and even lavishly—honors Mary for her freely offered submission to the will of God, and especially because she was the only human to literally carry in her womb "the Lord Who founded the earth."[37] Mary is hailed in most liturgical services as being "more honorable than the Cherubim, and beyond compare more glorious than the Seraphim." No other saint—male or female—is so honored. The profound and poetic verses of "The Akathist Hymn" offer praises to Mary for being "the spacious and wondrous dwelling place of the Word" and for nursing "the One Who by His divine command gives food to all."[38] An icon of the Theotokos holding her Son is also the centerpiece icon behind the altar in most Orthodox sanctuaries. Mary's acceptance of God's will in her life—"Let it be to me according to your word" (Luke 1:38)—is an example for all people in the Church to offer themselves without reservation to God. In other words, the superlative role model for Christians is a woman.

---

36. Augustine, *De nuptiis et concupiscentia* 1.32.37.
37. Ode 4 of "The Akathist Hymn." This hymn is a devotional poem consisting of praises to the Mother of God; it was composed during the sixth century and is sung each Friday during Great Lent.
38. "The Akathist Hymn," odes 5, 8.

Being Saved

Work out your own salvation with fear and trembling. (Phil. 2:12)

Are you saved? Many devout Protestant Christians remember the exact day that they believe they were saved. Often, it was the day on which they prayed for Jesus to come into their lives.[39] It might surprise some readers to learn that Orthodox Christians will not state that they have been saved, for two important reasons. The first reason is that only God can declare who is saved. Orthodox Christians indeed hope to be saved, and even work toward salvation, but out of humility do not claim for themselves something that they believe only the Lord can declare. The second reason is that in the Eastern Orthodox understanding, salvation is not a moment. For the Orthodox, salvation is understood as a process that continues throughout one's life and even into the next life. An Orthodox Christian would more typically say, "I am being saved," in solidarity with St. Paul's instruction to the Philippians to "work out your own salvation with fear and trembling" (Phil. 2:12). "I am being saved" not only acknowledges the dynamic and continuous nature of salvation but also supports the synergy of divine and human cooperation.

St. Paul also says that salvation is not a prize to be seized but something to be hoped for while "reaching forward" to what lies ahead (Phil. 3:11–14). Several early Church Fathers, especially St. Gregory of Nyssa, used the same notion of "reaching forward in expectation" to teach that eternal life, begun in this life, is an infinite progress of increasing communion with God. Because God is infinite and we are not, Gregory said that the soul will never tire of moving closer to divine love.[40]

When salvation is understood as an unending movement in response to the love of God, there can be no specific "moment" of achieving salvation. If a mountain is infinitely high, a climber may reach each successively higher ledge or peak but will never reach the top. In his work *De perfectione*, Gregory explains that there should be no frustration in not ever achieving an ultimate end, because every achievement toward growing in communion with God marks another beginning. No one should think he or she has reached the summit of perfection, since perfection consists "in never stopping to grow

---

39. The content, form, and meaning of such a prayer and the expected subsequent action vary, but the basic idea held by many Protestants is that salvation occurs through this verbal commitment to Jesus.

40. Lucas Francisco Mateo Seco, "Epektasis," in *The Brill Dictionary of Gregory of Nyssa*, ed. Lucas Francisco Mateo Seco and Giulio Maspero, trans. Seth Cherney (Leiden: Brill, 2010), 263–69.

towards the better."[41] In other words, because of the infinite nature of God's love, mercy, and goodness, there will always be more love, mercy, and goodness ahead to experience.

Theosis

You are gods, and all of you are children of the Most High. (Ps. 82:6)

When a Bible passage seems particularly unusual or hard to understand, we might give ourselves permission to pass over it. "You are gods, and all of you are children of the Most High" from Psalm 82 may be one of those passages. However, since it appears both in the Psalms and again in the Gospel of John, and since in both cases it is God who is speaking, it is probably a good idea to pay attention. Eastern Orthodox Christianity has paid attention. These and other explicit statements are consistent with the consensus of Apostolic and Patristic thought that our fallen human nature is not only restored in Christ but has been completely transformed in Christ as a "new creation."[42] The forming of human children to be equivalent to "gods" is only possible "because Christ has enabled believers to share in the divine life which he made incarnate."[43]

Salvation understood as sharing in God's nature is explicit in many places in the Bible, such as 2 Peter 1:3–4, which says that Jesus, through His divine power, has given us "all things that pertain to life and godliness" and that through these we "may be partakers of the divine nature." Being partakers of the divine nature is a great gift to humanity, but it is not an idea exclusive to the Christian East. Sharing in God's nature is the key idea in Paul's discussions of Christians as members of Christ's Body and of Christians being adopted as "sons of God" through Baptism.[44] Martin Luther also spoke of salvation as "union with God" in some of his early sixteenth-century writings.[45]

41. Gregory of Nyssa, *De perfectione*, quoted in Seco, "Epektasis," 264.
42. "Therefore, if anyone is in Christ, he is a new creation; old things have passed away; behold, all things have become new" (2 Cor. 5:17).
43. Norman Russell, *Fellow Workers with God: Orthodox Thinking on Theosis*, Foundation Series 5 (Yonkers, NY: St. Vladimir's Seminary Press, 2009), 24.
44. Biblical references to "sons of God" include Rom. 8:14, 19, 23; 9:26; Gal. 3:26; 4:5–6. References to "members of Christ's Body" include Rom. 12:5; 1 Cor. 12:12, 27.
45. See Tuomo Mannermaa, "Theosis as a Subject of Finnish Luther Research," *Pro Ecclesia: A Journal of Catholic and Evangelical Theology* 4, no. 1 (1995): 37–48. See also Veli-Matti Kärkkäinen, "Salvation as Justification and Theosis: The Contribution of the New Finnish Luther Interpretation to Our Ecumenical Future," *Dialog: A Journal of Theology* 45, no. 1 (2006): 74–82.

Eastern Orthodoxy holds to the Patristic teaching that Jesus shared in our nature so that we can share in His divine nature. Irenaeus wrote that the Word of God became what we are so that "He might bring us to be even what He is Himself."[46] Athanasius would say something very similar later in the fourth century: Jesus "was incarnate that we might be made god."[47] The idea of participation in the divine nature was not new, but it did not have a formal name until the fourth century, when Gregory the Theologian described it as *Theosis* ("becoming God-like" or "union with God") in a speech in AD 363.[48] Due to its rich Patristic and biblical heritage, theosis has become the main way of speaking about salvation in the Orthodox Church, as the process of growing in holiness and increasing in communion with God.

Some also refer to theosis as **deification**—a term that can be highly misleading and sometimes even alarming. Theosis is not pantheism, in which creation is equivalent to God. Nor is theosis borrowed from the Eastern religions in which the individual human life is expected to ultimately become absorbed into one impersonal cosmic reality. Nor does participation in the divine nature suggest that a created being can actually become divine (as in the heresy of Adoptionism, mentioned in chap. 5). Metropolitan Ware clarifies the alternative view of Orthodoxy, in which the human uniqueness is retained: "Orthodox mystical theology has always insisted that we humans, however closely linked to God, retain our full personal integrity. The human person, when deified, remains distinct (though not separate) from God."[49]

A word picture may help to clarify this. St. Cyril of Alexandria offered an analogy of what happens to iron when it is heated by fire. "When iron is brought into contact with fire, it becomes full of its activity. . . . While it is by nature iron, it exerts the power of fire."[50] St. John of Damascus spoke of the process of theosis with a similar analogy. The heated iron is still iron; but iron that has been heated to red hot, as opposed to iron that is still cold,

46. Irenaeus, *Against Heresies* 5 preface, in *The Ante-Nicene Fathers*, ed. Alexander Roberts and James Donaldson, 10 vols. (1885–1896; repr., Grand Rapids: Eerdmans, 1950–1951), 1:526; see https://www.newadvent.org/fathers/0103500.htm. Other second-century Fathers who reflected on salvation as participation in God's nature include Clement of Alexandria and Hippolytus of Rome.

47. Athanasius, *On the Incarnation* 54, trans. John Behr, Popular Patristics 44B (Crestwood, NY: St. Vladimir's Seminary Press, 2011), 107.

48. Gregory of Nazianzus, *Oration* 4.71. See Russell, *Fellow Workers with God*, 22.

49. Ware, *Orthodox Church*, 226.

50. Cyril of Alexandria, "Sermon CXLII," in *Commentary on the Gospel of St. Luke*, trans. R. Payne Smith (Oxford: Oxford University Press, 1859), 667.

can be molded. This is analogous to how the saints can share in the power of God but "do not lose their identities as individuals by striving to become one with God."[51]

All Creation Rejoices

In the Orthodox Christian worldview, the consequences of the ancestral sin were not experienced only in the human species. Nonhuman creation also dies now, and all creation awaits its ultimate renewal in Jesus Christ. St. Paul declares that creation groans and labors with birth pangs (Rom. 8:22) and that creation, too, "will be delivered from the bondage of corruption into the glorious liberty of the children of God" (Rom. 8:21). Even the sun, moon, stars, water, and heavens praise the Lord (Ps. 148). This is not just poetry for the Orthodox, but a recognition that all good things have been given to humanity in order to participate in communion with the Giver.

The Eastern Orthodox show reverence for God's creation by bringing creation into the sacramental worship of the Lord. The created elements that are consecrated as the Holy Eucharist—the grain and the grape—are first made by human creativity into bread[52] and wine, and then brought by human action to the Liturgy as an offering of thanksgiving. In this way the inanimate grape and grain also participate in the communion in Christ's Body, through the Holy Spirit. In *Against Heresies*, St. Irenaeus describes the joy of an abundant harvest in Paradise, in which the grapes themselves call out to be chosen for the eternal Eucharist: "I am a better cluster, take me; bless the Lord through me."[53]

Another example of the mystery of all creation's renewal in Christ is the Orthodox Feast of the Baptism of the Lord. This Great Feast is called "Holy Theophany" (which means "manifestation or appearance of God") because the Holy Trinity was fully revealed, both visibly and audibly:

> When He had been baptized, Jesus came up immediately from the water; and behold, the heavens were opened to Him, and He saw the Spirit of God descending

51. Solrunn Nes, *The Mystical Language of Icons* (Grand Rapids: Eerdmans, 2005), 63.
52. The leavened bread that is offered and used in the Eucharist is called *Prosforo*, which means "offering." *Prosforo* is prepared and baked prayerfully by members of the congregation. It is a round loaf, stamped on top with a special seal before baking. The inscribed top part of the loaf is used for the Eucharist, and the rest is cut into small pieces to be distributed as *antidoron*, or "instead of the gifts." Although the antidoron is also blessed, it is not the Eucharist, so a non-Orthodox visitor to the Divine Liturgy may partake of the antidoron.
53. Irenaeus, *Against Heresies* 5.33.3.

like a dove and alighting upon Him. And suddenly a voice came from heaven, saying, "This is My beloved Son, in whom I am well pleased." (Matt. 3:16–17)

Theophany is celebrated annually in the Orthodox Church, twelve days after Christmas. Since Christ sanctified the waters of the Jordan River by stepping into them, on this day it is typical for water to be consecrated in the "Great Blessing of Water" and sprinkled on people and buildings as a sign of the healing of all creation. Also, on this day the Orthodox faithful around the world go out to oceans and rivers (even where the waters are frozen in winter!) to bless the waters by the power of the Holy Cross.

In the visual icons of this biblical feast day, the waters of the Jordan are always shown as being agitated, because they were stirred up when they recognized that their Creator had set foot in their midst. The hymns of the Blessing of Water on Theophany often reflect an active recognition and participation on the part of nonhuman creation as it, too, is being blessed by its Creator: "Today the nature of the waters is sanctified. The Jordan is parted in two; it holds back the flow of its waters as it beholds the washing of the Master."[54]

From the "Great Blessing of Water" on the Feast of Theophany

To the voice of one crying in the wilderness,
Prepare ye the way of the Lord,
You came, O Lord, taking the form of a servant,
Asking for baptism though you have no sin.
The waters saw You and were afraid. The Forerunner began to tremble
and cried out, saying:
How shall the lampstand illumine the Light?
How shall the servant lay hands upon the Master?
Sanctify both me and the waters, O Savior,
Who takes away the sins of the world.[a]

a. The Verses at the Great Blessing of Water on the Theophany of Our Lord, quoted in Thomas Hopko, *The Winter Pascha: Readings for the Christmas Epiphany Season* (Crestwood, NY: St. Vladimir's Seminary Press, 1984), 155. Used with permission.

54. This is a typological allusion to the Prophet Elijah at the Jordan River, which was parted so that Elijah could cross (2 Kings 2:8, 14) and also so that Joshua and Israel could cross with the ark of the covenant (Josh. 3:5–4:18).

Humanity, We Have a Problem

The first step in solving a problem is understanding the nature of the problem—this is not rocket science (as they say). This logic applies to all aspects of daily life, and it applies to theology as well. Creation has a problem, and the Good News of the Christian Gospel is that Jesus Christ is the solution. Yet a lot of human history has passed between the first big problem in Genesis 3 and the apocalyptic victory of the Lord of lords in Revelation 19. Within the pages of the Bible are stories about all kinds of problems: disobedience, paganism, murder, deceit, despair, evil, corruption, bondage, confusion of tongues, blindness, hunger, deafness, demonic possession, hardness of heart, imprisonment, stormy seas, illness, and death, just to name a few! Since the starting point for any solution must be in the problem statement, it is fair to ask, What is the true problem of humankind? What should be the focus of theological anthropology? In other words, which problem does a soteriological narrative purport to solve?

Western Problem Statements

For example, the experiences of a well-known Protestant scholar, Jürgen Moltmann, in a World War II prison camp made him aware that many people are suffering in despair for lack of hope. Moltmann subsequently outlined a theology of hope based on the suffering of Jesus on the Cross. In Moltmann's view, Jesus suffers in solidarity with all who suffer, especially with those who are oppressed, and He brought hope that God will be all in all in the eschaton.[55] Moltmann's solution is well aligned to his problem statement. Like Moltmann, many theological scholars have suggested various themes of salvation in Christ, all touching on different aspects of the problems we have either inherited or caused. Scholars may each describe Christ's work differently, but most of these differences stem from how the underlying theological problem is portrayed.

An earlier idea that is still affirmed by many Western Christians today is generally stated like this: "Jesus died on the Cross to pay the price for my sin." The theology of each individual owing a debt that Jesus satisfied on the Cross was famously emphasized by Anselm, a Roman Catholic bishop in the eleventh century who developed a solution to Augustine's idea of inherited

---

55. Jürgen Moltmann, *Theology of Hope: On the Ground and the Implications of a Christian Eschatology*, trans. James Leitch (New York: Harper & Row, 1967; repr., Minneapolis: Fortress, 1993).

guilt. In his *Cur Deus Homo*,[56] Anselm draws an analogy between the Father's honor and that of a medieval feudal overlord to whom serfs and knights owe a debt of honor. Anselm surmises that God is due much more than an earthly lord. God was rightly offended by the insult of Adam and Eve's sin and is justified in demanding satisfaction. Anselm penned a narrative that describes something like a negotiation. The payment to satisfy God's offended honor could not be made by a mere human, so the Son volunteered Himself to satisfy humanity's debt for its guilt. In doing so, the Son earned a particular kind of merit, which Anselm argues was made available to believers through the Roman Catholic sacraments.

This view worked well in its original medieval setting, where obedience and honor were so highly regarded. The idea of Christ satisfying humanity's debt has shaped much of Western Christian thought even into the present day. Anselm's view is often categorized as the "satisfaction" model of atonement. The influential Reformers Luther and Calvin also built their theologies on the Augustinian foundation of inherited guilt. The offense to God's honor was less important to them than the violation of God's justice, however. Since every human is guilty and deserves to die, Jesus was the guiltless victim who took the punishment due to every other individual human. Generally speaking, this view has been referred to as the "substitutionary" or "penal substitution" model of atonement.

Eastern Problem Statements

Neither Anselm's satisfaction model nor the Reformers' substitutionary model of Christ's atoning work has resonated within Eastern Orthodoxy. One simple reason for this is that both models offered solutions to what had not been identified as the primary problems of humanity in Orthodox thought. There are certainly elements of truth in both Western models—a cosmic problem occurred, and Jesus is the solution. Yet, from an Orthodox perspective, neither of these views provide a solution to an identified problem, and they are too narrowly limited in context to provide a universal remedy.

One Orthodox response to Anselm's idea of God demanding satisfaction is to point out that in the Bible, God forgives again and again without any request for payment. Psalm 103[57] is read at every Orthodox Matins service:

56. See the discussion in Alister E. McGrath, *Historical Theology: An Introduction to the History of Christian Thought* (Oxford: Wiley-Blackwell, 2012), 106. See also Jonathan Hill, *The History of Christian Thought* (Oxford: Lion Hudson, 2013), 127.
57. Psalm 103 in the Masoretic Hebrew text is numbered as 102 in the Septuagint (Greek) version of the Old Testament.

> The LORD is merciful and gracious,
> Slow to anger, and abounding in mercy.
> He will not always strive with us,
> Nor will He keep His anger forever.
> He has not dealt with us according to our sins,
> Nor punished us according to our iniquities.
> For as the heavens are high above the earth,
> So great is His mercy toward those who fear Him. (vv. 8–11)

A familiar New Testament demonstration of God's supreme and generous mercy comes from the parable Jesus Himself tells about the prodigal son in Luke 15:11–32. The loving father in the parable, who represents God the Father, reaches out to embrace his returned and penitent son even before the son can ask for forgiveness. Not only does the father not require payment for the son's grave offense to his honor, he gives the son far more, ordering that a ring be put on his son's finger, having him dressed in the finest apparel, and throwing a feast to celebrate his return. The Orthodox world sees the God of the Bible in this way: offering open arms to the penitent as a loving, long-suffering, and merciful Father. The main point I wish to make here is that the Orthodox problem statement does not include anything like an offense to God's honor, nor is payment needed in order for God to forgive, so there is no need to state the solution in Christ in terms of payment or satisfaction.

Vladimir Lossky critiques Anselm's satisfaction model from several perspectives: it is narrow and focuses nearly exclusively on Christ's death, it ignores the Holy Spirit, and it fails to do justice to Christ's Incarnation and Resurrection. Further, Anselm's limited proposition does not reflect any change in the human condition—no renewal of human nature—but only a change in God's attitude toward humanity.[58] In contrast, the main anthropological

The Sunday of the Prodigal Son

Matins Hymn

I squandered your riches, O Lord, and in my misery, I served the perverse demons. But in the tenderness of your heart, O Savior, have mercy on me a prodigal, wash away my sin, and give me the choice robe in your kingdom, O Lord.[a]

a. Sisters of the Order of St. Basil the Great, *Lenten Triodion* (Uniontown, PA, 1995), 19.

58. Vladimir Lossky, "Redemption and Deification," in *In the Image and Likeness of God*, ed. John H. Erickson and Thomas E. Bird (Crestwood, NY: St. Vladimir's Seminary Press, 1974), 97–110.

problem statement of Eastern Orthodoxy is that humanity has been separated from communion with God because of sin and we die. Salvation in Orthodoxy is therefore conceived in terms of reuniting the human and the divine to restore the communion lost by our primal ancestors. The Incarnation solves the problem, so stated, since in Jesus Christ the communion between human and divine nature has been restored.

Christ's Incarnation is not understood by the Orthodox as a preliminary step needed before the Cross, but as an essential event in the salvation of the world. The troparion (or hymn) of the Orthodox Great Feast of the **Annunciation**, celebrated on March 25 (exactly nine months before the Nativity of Christ), proclaims that our salvation begins in the Incarnation: "Today is the beginning of our salvation and the revelation of the pre-eternal mystery; the Son of God becomes the son of the Virgin."[59] "The Word became flesh and dwelt among us, and we beheld His glory, the glory as of the only begotten of the Father, full of grace and truth" (John 1:14).

Athanasius of Alexandria, in *On the Incarnation*, states the human problem in a variety of easily understood metaphors. In one of his examples, the human condition is likened to a portrait painted on a wood panel that has been "soiled by dirt from the outside." The panel will not be thrown away, but the outline of the portrait needs to be renewed. The one whose original "likeness" was painted needs to "come again, so that the image can be renewed on the same material." The soiled portrait of humanity was originally made after the likeness of the Son of God, and He returned to renew it:

> In the same way the all-holy Son of the Father, being the Image of the Father, came to our place to renew the human being made according to himself, and to find him, as one lost, through the forgiveness of sins, as he himself says in the Gospels, "I came to seek and to save that which was lost" (Luke 19:10).[60]

The Cross and Resurrection

Although Western Christianity is broadening its scholarly theology of atonement, it still typically presents the problem in terms of the individual, inherited guilt of original sin. Very simply stated, justice requires that if the law has been broken, a punishment needs to be executed. If a debt has been incurred, the debt needs to be repaid. In the Western view, Jesus solved both

59. Quoted in Ecumenical Patriarch Bartholomew, *Speaking the Truth in Love: Theological and Spiritual Exhortations of Ecumenical Patriarch Bartholomew*, ed. John Chryssavgis (New York: Fordham University Press, 2011), 85.
60. Athanasius, *On the Incarnation* 14 (trans. Behr, 63–64).

of these closely related problems of humanity by paying the debt and taking the punishment on behalf of guilty humanity. Calvin, for example, says that in order to satisfy God's anger and righteous judgement, "it was necessary that he [Jesus] should feel the weight of divine vengeance."[61] The resultant Western emphasis on the Cross and on Jesus as the innocent victim is understandable, as is the hope of Christians in the West to have their debt to God paid by His suffering. This is also why the emphasis during Passion Week in the West is on **Good Friday**, since Christ's work was finished in His suffering on the Cross.

In Orthodoxy, as we have seen, the theological problem of humanity is stated more in terms of enemies: evil and death. The solution to the problem stated in this way is that the enemies need to be defeated and what has been corrupted needs to be restored. The Orthodox see all of Christ's life and work, not just the Cross, as part of the solution. His Incarnation restored communion between the divine and the human. His voluntary crucifixion showed the depth of God's love for His creation and put in motion God's plan to destroy death itself: "I am the resurrection and the life. He who believes in Me, though he may die, he shall live" (John 11:25).

Although it is correct to say that the Orthodox emphasize the Resurrection more than their Western friends do, the Resurrection is not more important to the Orthodox than the Cross. They are both essential to salvation, and they are both part of the same saving action. St. Paul, for example, connects justification by the Cross directly to the Resurrection: "He was delivered over to death for our sins and was raised to life for our justification" (Rom. 4:25 NIV).

Nevertheless, Orthodoxy understands the Cross quite differently from how Western Christianity understands it. Metropolitan Ware sees the difference in terms of Orthodoxy not separating the human suffering of Christ from His divinity: "When Orthodox think of Christ Crucified, they think not only of His suffering and desolation; they think of Him as Christ the Victor, Christ the King, reigning in triumph from the Tree."[62] The somber, profound, and poetic Orthodox hymn from Good Friday illustrates that the one crucified was not just the man who suffered but the Creator Himself:

> Today is hanged upon the tree
>> He who hanged the earth in the midst of the waters.
> A crown of thorns crowns Him
>> Who is the king of the angels.

61. John Calvin, *Institutes* II.16.10, quoted in Georges Florovsky, "On the Tree of the Cross," *St. Vladimir's Seminary Quarterly* 1, nos. 3–4 (1953): 21.
62. Ware, *Orthodox Church*, 221.

> He is wrapped about with the purple of mockery
> Who wraps the heaven in clouds.[63]

The one who ascended the Cross in loving humility was also fully God. As St. Gregory of Nazianzus puts it, "He lays down His life, but He has power to take it again. . . . He dies but He gives life, and by His death destroys death."[64]

I mentioned in chapter 5 that the "hypostatic union" of Christ's divine and human natures also speaks to the Orthodox understanding of the Crucifixion. Fr. Florovsky repudiates Calvin's view that Christ was forsaken by God, or that Christ needed to satisfy God's anger, since this view does injustice to Christ's acceptance of death out of love for His creation. Moreover, the "hypostatic union" of Christ's two natures cannot be divided, broken, or destroyed—not even in death. Remember, the Incarnate Word is not a divine part next to a human part but an inseparable union of both natures. Although Christ suffered death, His was a unique death. Florovsky calls it "a resurrecting death" and an "incorrupt death" because corruption and death were both overcome by contact with the Incarnate Word. "The Lord's flesh does not suffer corruption, it remains incorruptible even in death itself, i.e., alive, as though it had never died, for it abides in the very bosom of the Life in the Hypostasis of the Word."[65] This is why, even when they see Christ hanging on the Cross, the Orthodox see the glory of God—the God of life. It is also why, in the midst of the solemnity of Good Friday, the Orthodox are already anticipating the joy of the Resurrection.

Easter in the Orthodox Church is the "Feast of Feasts" and is called "Pascha" (from the Jewish Passover). Before the tenth plague described in Exodus, the Israelites were instructed to kill one-year-old lambs and put their blood on the doors of their homes, so that the angel of death would pass them by (Exod. 12). The Orthodox consider the Passover event typologically: Jesus Christ is the pure Lamb of God, and it is through His blood on the Cross that we may pass from death to life. The Feast of Pascha begins near midnight on Holy Saturday night. The icons and the entire sanctuary are decorated with flowers; the clergy are vested in bright vestments, and the congregation is wearing their holiday best. The sanctuary is darkened, and everyone stands quietly and expectantly with an unlit candle. The Resurrection Service begins with a grand procession of the Cross, the Gospel book, banners, and icons, while this hymn is chanted a number of times: "Your resurrection, O Christ

---

63. Quoted in Ware, *Orthodox Church*, 221.
64. Gregory of Nazianzus, *Oration* 41, quoted in Florovsky, "Tree of the Cross," 18.
65. Florovsky, "Tree of the Cross," 19.

our Savior, the angels in heaven sing. Enable us on earth to glorify you in purity of heart."[66]

The priest or bishop emerges from the altar with one lit candle as he chants, "Come receive the Light from the Light, that is never overtaken by night. And glorify Christ, Who is risen from the dead." The chanters and congregation repeat the hymn while the Resurrection Light of Christ is passed from person to person. Following this is the Gospel reading of the Resurrection, and the proclamation (in many languages) of "Christ is Risen!" and the response "Truly He is Risen!" The Paschal Troparion (hymn) is sung dozens upon dozens of times on Pascha night and throughout all the services of the Church during the next forty days until Christ's Ascension: "Christ is Risen from the dead, trampling down Death by death, and upon those in the tomb bestowing life."[67]

Pascha is the "Feast of Feasts"—an exuberant and joyful liturgical celebration. The Cross is certainly necessary. As Fr. Florovsky writes, we make the sign of the Cross because "we belong to the Crucified." But "the Crucified is Risen indeed."[68] It is through the Cross and Resurrection that Christ's saving action has been accomplished: death has been destroyed, and all creation rejoices at being released from the bondage of death and decay into newness of life. The Lenten fast is broken after the Divine Liturgy on Holy Saturday night, at which time feasting begins. During the forty days between Pascha and Ascension, Orthodox Christians will enthusiastically greet one another, begin emails, send text messages, and even answer their phones with "Christ is Risen!" The joyful response is, "Truly He is Risen!"

▪ DISCUSSION QUESTIONS ▪

1. How would you describe the primary Orthodox understanding of "image" and "likeness" as they are used in Genesis 1:26–27?

2. What is the main Eastern Orthodox description of the "problem" of humanity after the Fall? How is the solution to that problem described?

66. *The Incarnate God: The Feasts of Jesus Christ and the Virgin Mary*, ed. Catherine Aslanoff, trans. Paul Meyendorff, 2 vols. (Crestwood, NY: St. Vladimir's Seminary Press, 2002), 2:147.

67. John Baggley, *Festival Icons for the Christian Year* (Crestwood, NY: St. Vladimir's Seminary Press, 2000), 117. The Paschal Troparion was originally written in Byzantine Greek in the sixth century. Baggley offers a robust description of the worship of Pascha in chap. 12, "Now Are All Things Filled with Light."

68. Florovsky, "Tree of the Cross," 11.

3. Discuss the Eastern Orthodox understanding of salvation as theosis, in contrast to typical Western views or the view of your tradition.

4. How is Good Friday understood differently in the Orthodox Church and in most Western Christian traditions?

7

The Holy Trinity

Go and make disciples of all nations, baptizing them in the name
of the Father and of the Son and of the Holy Spirit.

—Matthew 28:19 (NIV)

One will not find many writings by Orthodox Christians on certain topics,
such as speculation about the end times or **eschatology** in general, but one
can certainly find a great many writings on the doctrine of the Holy Trinity.
Metropolitan Ware writes that "Orthodoxy believes most passionately that
the doctrine of the Holy Trinity is not a piece of 'high theology' reserved for
the professional scholar, but something that has a living, *practical* importance
for every Christian."[1] The main and obvious point is that if God is indeed the
origin of all that exists, having a wrong idea of God means having a wrong
idea about the world.

Sometimes theological concepts can be exaggerated to enhance understanding, but it is not an exaggeration to suggest that the Orthodox Church
is "fully trinitarian," unlike any Western Christian tradition. Generally speaking, Pentecostal Christians tend to emphasize the Holy Spirit and Pentecost,
while Protestants and Roman Catholics tend to emphasize the work of Christ
and Good Friday. To this point, systematic theology professor and Lutheran
pastor Veli-Matti Kärkkäinen summarizes various Christian traditions in his

1. Timothy Ware, *The Orthodox Church: An Introduction to Eastern Christianity*, 3rd ed.
(London: Penguin, 2015), 202.

popular ecclesiology textbook and notes that "there is a genuine trinitarian outlook in the Eastern view" in ways not typical of the Christian West.[2]

An example to illustrate this point comes from the World Council of Churches (WCC), which until 1961 self-described as a "fellowship of churches which accept our Lord Jesus Christ as God and Saviour." This statement reflected well the Christological emphases of the majority of delegates from Protestant traditions, but it was the Eastern Orthodox delegates who reminded their colleagues that Jesus told His disciples to baptize "in the name of the Father and of the Son and of the Holy Spirit" (Matt. 28:19) and that salvation comes from the Father, through the Son, in the Holy Spirit.[3] The Eastern Orthodox delegates insisted that explicit references to the Holy Trinity be incorporated into the WCC's basis. The idea found majority agreement at the third assembly in New Delhi, and this clause was added to the end of the above-quoted original basis: ". . . according to the scriptures, and therefore seek to fulfill together their common calling to the glory of the one God, Father, Son and Holy Spirit."[4]

Orthodox Christians consider, encounter, and pray to the Holy Trinity constantly. The trinitarian balance that is manifest in all aspects of Orthodox Christianity is nowhere more apparent than in Orthodox prayer and worship, which are "in the Name of the Father, and of the Son, and of the Holy Spirit" (not only in Jesus's name).[5] Orthodox Christians proclaim in the Divine Liturgy, "Let us love one another, that with oneness of mind we may confess: Father, Son, and Holy Spirit: Trinity one in essence and undivided."[6] Orthodox Baptism takes place by a threefold immersion in the name of the Father, the Son, and the Holy Spirit. Orthodox Christians cross themselves three times, both as a faithful gesture of praise to the Trinity and for protection. Many hymns and prayers are repeated three times in honor of the Trinity, such as "Lord have mercy, Lord have mercy, Lord have mercy," or the **Thrice-Holy Hymn**: "Holy God, Holy Mighty, Holy Immortal, have mercy on us."

---

2. Veli-Matti Kärkkäinen, *An Introduction to Ecclesiology: Ecumenical, Historical, and Global Perspectives* (Downers Grove, IL: InterVarsity, 2002), 17.

3. This formula is implicit in Scripture. See Gregory of Nyssa, *On Not Three Gods: To Ablabius*.

4. "The Basis of the WCC," World Council of Churches, accessed July 1, 2020, https://www.oikoumene.org/en/about-us/self-understanding-vision/basis.

5. The one exception is the sole prayer in the Orthodox Tradition directed to the Holy Spirit: "O Heavenly King, Comforter, the Spirit of Truth . . ." See the section "The Holy Spirit" later in this chapter.

6. Greek Orthodox Archdiocese of America, *The Divine Liturgy of St. John Chrysostom* (Brookline, MA: Holy Cross Orthodox Press, 2015), 45.

The Revealed Trinity

The Trinity is the central and defining doctrine of Christianity. The doctrine of the Trinity developed as the Church reflected on the life and ministry of Christ in doing the Father's will, and on the sending of the Holy Spirit. The faithful recognized that God was not just one, but also three. Yet the word "Trinity" is not used anywhere in the Bible. Scripture says very little about the eternal mystery of the Trinity, but Scripture has definitely revealed the Father, the Son, and the Holy Spirit. Even the Scriptures of Israel revealed that God is never without His Word and Spirit.

It is the "mystery of all mysteries, the truth of all truths. God has a Son. God is Father by nature. And his Son, because he is God's Son, is divine with the Father's very own divinity."[7] This Son voluntarily came to earth to become one of us. John 3:16 repeats Jesus's own words: God the Father loved the world so much that He sent His only begotten Son. We have no "inside information" into how the Son could be eternally begotten of the Father, but it has been revealed to us by the Holy Spirit that "begotten" is the best way to talk about it. Similarly, for the Holy Spirit, the Evangelist John relates Jesus's words: "the Spirit of truth who *proceeds* from the Father" (John 15:26, emphasis added).

The doctrine of the Trinity that arose as a direct consequence of God's self-revelation to the Church was canonized in a Creed by the Fathers of the first two Ecumenical Councils:

> We believe in one God, the Father, almighty, Creator of heaven and earth, and of all things visible and invisible; and in one Lord, Jesus Christ, the only begotten Son of God, begotten of the Father before all ages. Light of Light, true God of true God, begotten, not created, of one essence with the Father, through whom all things were made. . . . And in the Holy Spirit, the Lord, the Giver of Life, who proceeds from the Father, who together with the Father and the Son is worshipped and glorified, who spoke through the prophets.[8]

Any field of inquiry demands clarity with regard to technical terms. The doctrine of the Trinity is no exception. It took decades and decades to clarify what everyone meant by using certain terms. Even though great care was taken, there was still confusion between the Latin words and the Greek words used to describe the same realities. But there was no doubt in the Church that

7. Thomas Hopko, "The Trinity in the Cappadocians," in *Christian Spirituality: Origins to the Twelfth Century*, ed. Bernard McGinn, John Meyendorff, and Jean Leclercq (New York: Crossroad, 1985), 264.

8. Nicene-Constantinopolitan Creed, AD 325 and 381.

there was a divine Trinity and that the three persons were unique, but that the three were also one.

"Hear, O Israel: The LORD our God, the LORD is one!" This is the foundational *Shema* of Judaism, taken from three passages in the Torah (Deut. 6:4–9; 11:13–21; Num. 15:37–41). One of the theological challenges the primitive Church faced was how to reconcile the divinity of the Son with Israel's rigid monotheism, without ending up with polytheism (many gods). If there is only one God, how can the Son also be God? Does that mean there are two (or more) Gods? This was the challenge taken up by the North African author Tertullian in the second century. In fact, it was Tertullian who contributed the language of "Trinity" that is so characteristic within Christianity today.[9] Tertullian took common Latin terms and applied them to God: The *trinitas* (threeness) consists of the Father, Son, and Spirit, each of whom is a *persona* (person). All together they share (or are) a single *substantia* (substance). Tertullian's formula for the Trinity was therefore *tres personae, una substantia*, or "three persons, one substance." Tertullian had some very good ideas that have survived the test of time these two-thousand-plus years, mainly because what he described about God was consistent with the consensus of the Church's experience.

Many of the earliest trinitarian heresies arose from good intentions to protect the monotheism of Israel against the problem of polytheism. Two versions of a category of heresy called Monarchianism ("sole sovereignty") arose as challenges to the Trinity. In "Dynamic" Monarchianism, the Father is divine, but Jesus is not. Instead, God's power (Greek: *dynamis*) made Jesus into a special human with power and insight. This heresy is also referred to as Adoptionism. Its main representative was Theodotus, who claimed that Jesus was born as a mortal man and was adopted into the Godhead at His Baptism.

The other form was "Modalist" Monarchianism, which held that any distinctions between the three persons of the Trinity are not real. Instead, the three are just "modes of being." Father, Son, and Spirit are just different names for the same reality. This heresy is also called Sabellianism after its main proponent, Sabellius, a late second-century Roman presbyter who made an analogy to the theater, where actors wear masks to portray different characters. Sabellius suggested that God figuratively puts on masks and acts

9. Tertullian was the first to use the Latin term *trinitas*, but Theophilos of Antioch had earlier used the term *trias* to refer to the Trinity. Tertullian, however, enlarged the idea. A robust discussion is found in M. C. Steenberg, *Of God and Man: Theology as Anthropology from Irenaeus to Athanasius* (London: Bloomsbury, 2009), 104.

as Father sometimes, as Son sometimes, and as Spirit at other times. So the Father became incarnate as the Son.[10]

Both ideas fail theologically since they compromise both the divinity of Christ and the "otherness" of the persons of the Trinity. They also fail with regard to the "rule of truth," since they do not describe the Trinity that the Church has known and experienced through its worship. Today's Dynamic Monarchianism is Unitarianism, in which there is one Creator who sent out an impersonal force into the world. According to this view, the mortal Jesus was particularly inspired by God through the Spirit and thus became a moral teacher and a savior. Today's Sabellianism is Oneness Pentecostalism, according to which there is only one God who acts in three ways. Neither of these views is considered to be classically Christian, by the simple fact that neither is trinitarian.

So, while it is not a bad idea at all to want to protect God's oneness, Scripture clearly supports the eternal "otherness" and divinity of the Son and the Spirit. Scripture also supports the Incarnation of the Son of God—His "taking flesh" from the Virgin Mary through the Holy Spirit. This is the essence of the Apostolic Christian Faith. Moreover, this is the truth that has been revealed to the faithful by the Holy Spirit and that has been guarded against error in the Orthodox Church.

Trinitarian *Taxis*

St. Justin Martyr was one of those very early Christian teachers who tried to protect the Church against error and paved the way toward a formal understanding of the Trinity. Writing in the second century, Justin was the first to speak of the Father as *Protos* (first), the Son as "second," and the Spirit as "third." Christ's Great Commission clearly supports this idea: ". . . baptizing them in the name of the Father and of the Son and of the Holy Spirit" (Matt. 28:19). The Greek word that Justin uses for the ordering of the Trinity is *taxis*. By suggesting a hierarchy or *taxis*, Justin is not asserting that there are greater and lesser degrees of divinity—that the Father is superior to the others, or that the Father is the "boss" of the Trinity. Instead, Justin is supporting the scriptural testimony that the Father is the eternal cause of the Son's begetting (John 3:16) and of the Spirit's procession (John 15:26). Consider this excerpt from Justin Martyr's *First Apology*:

10. "Monarchianism," in *New Dictionary of Theology*, ed. Sinclair B. Ferguson, David F. Wright, and J. I. Packer (Downers Grove, IL: InterVarsity, 1988), 440–41.

Our teacher of these things is Jesus Christ, who was born for this end, and who was crucified under Pontius Pilate, procurator of Judea, in the reign of Tiberius Caesar. We shall prove that we worship Him with reason, since we have learned that He is the Son of the living God Himself, and believe Him to be in the second place, and the Prophetic Spirit in the third. For this they accuse us of madness, saying that we attribute to a crucified man a place second to the unchanging and eternal God, the Creator of all things, but they are ignorant of the mystery which lies herein. To this mystery we entreat you to give your attention, while we explain it to you.[11]

You might have noticed here that by including the Son together with the Father, Justin was clearly defending the divinity of Jesus Christ against the heretical teachers of his day (such as those described in the previous section). It is not madness, he insisted, to give a "crucified man" a place second to the eternal God, because that man is also God. Those who teach otherwise are "ignorant of the mystery" of the Christian Faith.

The Cappadocian "Settlement": One Essence and Three Persons

The basics of the classical trinitarian doctrine articulated by Tertullian, Irenaeus, Justin Martyr, and others were taken up in the fourth century by St. Athanasius to defend against Arius, who placed Jesus in the category of created beings. As you may recall from the discussion in chapter 5, Athanasius said that the Father and the Son share the exact same divine nature (*homoousios*). Athanasius's defense of the Trinity was later adapted and refined by the Cappadocian Fathers St. Basil the Great (ca. 329–379), St. Gregory of Nazianzus (ca. 329–389), and St. Gregory of Nyssa, Basil's brother and youngest of the Cappadocian Fathers (ca. 335–394). While Athanasius especially needed to emphasize the unity of Christ and the Father, the Cappadocians emphasized the communion of the three persons and were successful in providing the right balance of unity and diversity.

Metropolitan Ware affirms the collective honor of these Fathers: "Never before or since has the Church possessed four theologians of such stature within a single generation."[12] Many volumes on the Trinity were written by the Cappadocian Fathers, and many more volumes have been written about their theologies. Here I will briefly summarize some of their more important ideas.

11. Justin Martyr, *First Apology* 13, trans. Thomas B. Falls, Fathers of the Church 6 (Washington, DC: Catholic University of America Press, 2010), 46.

12. Ware, *Orthodox Church*, 22. The Cappadocians were greatly influenced by Athanasius. He was the senior of the three Cappadocians by thirty to forty years, but his career still overlapped each of theirs.

Gregory of Nazianzus, who is one of only three designated "Theologians" of the Orthodox Church, summarizes the Orthodox view of the Trinity in *Oration* 21.35, written in honor of Athanasius: "We, in an orthodox sense, say one *ousia* and three *hypostases*, for the one denotes the nature of the Godhead, the other the properties of the three."[13] For the Cappadocians, *ousia* means the existence or essence of God, and *hypostasis* means the existence in a particular mode or manner of the three persons of the Trinity. In English, the shorthand for the Cappadocian language of the Trinity would be "three persons, one essence."

Basil is especially adamant in emphasizing that the identity of each person—Father, Son, and Holy Spirit—is unique: "For, if we do not consider the definite qualities of each, such as paternity and sonship and holiness, but confess God from the general idea of existence, it is impossible to give a sound account of our faith."[14] The Christian God is a personal and specific God, not a general concept: "There is one God and Father and one Only-begotten and one Holy Spirit. We proclaim each of the persons singly."[15] These terms were laid down at the Councils of Nicaea (AD 325) and Constantinople (381) and were ratified as dogma at the Second Constantinopolitan Council of 553 under Emperor Justinian, thus:

> If anyone does not confess that the Father, Son and holy Spirit have one nature or substance, that they have one power and authority, that there is a consubstantial Trinity, one Deity to be adored in three subsistences or persons: let him be anathema. There is only one God and Father, from whom all things come, and one Lord, Jesus Christ, through whom all things are, and one holy Spirit, in whom all things are.[16]

This statement was a product of nearly two centuries of potentially perilous challenges to Christian Orthodoxy, which eventually made it clear that the three divine persons were each constituted in their personhood by their distinctively different relations with each other. The variation of one from

13. Gregory of Nazianzus, *Oration* 21.35, "On the Great Athanasius, Bishop of Alexandria," in *A Select Library of Nicene and Post-Nicene Fathers*, 2nd series, ed. Philip Schaff and Henry Wace, 14 vols. (1890–1900; repr., Grand Rapids: Eerdmans, 1955), 7:279. See https://www.newadvent.org/fathers/310221.htm.

14. Basil the Great, "Letter 236: To Amphilochius," in *Letters*, vol. 2, *186–368*, trans. Agnes Clare Way, Fathers of the Church (Washington, DC: Catholic University of America Press, 1955), 171.

15. Basil the Great, *On the Holy Spirit* 18.44, trans. Stephen Hildebrand, Popular Patristics 42 (Yonkers, NY: St. Vladimir's Seminary Press, 2011), 59.

16. Norman P. Tanner, *Decrees of the Ecumenical Councils: Nicaea I to Lateran V* (Washington, DC: Georgetown University Press, 2016), 114.

another is not an "add-on" to their essence or substance—their differences constitute their personhood, and their personhood is the content of the divine nature. Basil continually asserts that the three divine persons are unique, but at the same time there is "the particularity of the persons and the inseparability of their communion."[17] Metropolitan Ware summarizes the Eastern Orthodox understanding of the Trinity, based on the writings of the Cappadocian Fathers:

> The distinctive characteristic of the second person is Sonship: although equal to the Father and coeternal with Him, He is not unbegotten or sourceless, but has His source and origin in the Father, from whom He is begotten or born from all eternity—"before all ages," as the Creed says. The distinctive characteristic of the third person is Procession: like the Son, He has His source and origin in the Father; but His relationship to the Father is different from that of the Son, since He is not begotten but from all eternity He *proceeds* from the Father.[18]

The Holy Spirit

> The true goal of our Christian life consists in the acquisition of the Holy Spirit of God. (St. Seraphim of Sarov)

In many ways, it seems contrary to an Orthodox ethos to devote a separate section to the Holy Spirit. This is because the entire life of the Orthodox Church (and of the Christian) is dependent upon the abiding presence of the Holy Spirit.[19] The Holy Spirit proclaims not Himself, but Christ (John 16:13–15), and "no one can say that Jesus is Lord except by the Holy Spirit" (1 Cor. 12:3). The nineteenth-century **starets** St. Seraphim of Sarov taught his spiritual children that the true goal of Christian life is to acquire the Holy Spirit. It is the Holy Spirit "Who acts within us and establishes within us the Kingdom of God." He taught that "fasts, and vigils, and prayer, and almsgiving, and every good deed done for Christ's sake, are only means of acquiring the Holy Spirit of God."[20]

The Holy Spirit inspires and guides every aspect of the Church: "He who has an ear, let him hear what the Spirit says to the churches" (Rev. 2:7). We do

17. See Basil the Great, *On the Holy Spirit* 25.59 (trans. Hildebrand, 74); Epistle 52.3; *Contra Eunomius* 2.12.
18. Ware, *Orthodox Church*, 205.
19. See the section "Holy Tradition" in chap. 3.
20. N. A. Motovilov, "St. Seraphim of Sarov's Talk with N. A. Motovilov: On the Goal of Christian Life," in *The True Goal of Our Christian Life Consists in the Acquisition of the Holy Spirit*, trans. Vladimir Djambov (N.p.: Amazon Digital Services, 2019), 5–6.

not even know how to pray, "but the Spirit Himself makes **intercession**" (Rom. 8:26). It is for this reason that the only Orthodox prayer directed exclusively to the Holy Spirit begins every worship service:

> O heavenly King, O Comforter, the Spirit of Truth, everywhere present and filling all things, the treasury of blessings and giver of life, come and abide in us. Cleanse us from all impurity, and of Your goodness save our souls.[21]

The Holy Spirit, present everywhere and filling all things, brings the faithful together as the Body of Christ and establishes the context of prayer and worship.

The communion (*koinōnia*) of the Holy Trinity is being revealed to the Church continually through the Holy Spirit as "an event of communion, which transforms everything the Spirit touches into a relational being."[22] Metropolitan Ware, commenting on the Descent of the Holy Spirit at Pentecost, notes that the Spirit brings the gift of diversity, but in unity: "Not only does the Holy Spirit make us all one, but he makes us each different. At Pentecost the multiplicity of tongues was not abolished, but it ceased to be a cause of separation; each spoke as before in his own tongue, but by the power of the Spirit each could understand the others."[23]

The Holy Spirit Is God

The fourth century also gave rise to a group called the Pneumatomachians ("Spirit fighters"), who denied that the Spirit is God. St. Gregory the Theologian begins his *Fifth Theological Oration* on the Holy Spirit with an amusing commentary on human nature in light of this challenge.[24] Gregory posits that some people had become exhausted by the debates about the Son and found the Spirit to be an easier target—but he also suggests that some simply "must have something to blaspheme or life would be unlivable." Even the Church, he says, became so worn down by so many issues that "we are in the same condition as men who lose their appetite for all food regardless of what it is, after being disgusted with some particular dish; we take an equal dislike to all

21. Ware, *Orthodox Church*, 224.
22. John D. Zizioulas, *Communion and Otherness: Further Studies in Personhood and the Church*, ed. Paul McPartlan (London: T&T Clark, 2006), 6.
23. Kallistos Ware, *The Orthodox Way* (Crestwood, NY: St. Vladimir's Seminary Press, 1979), 77.
24. Gregory of Nazianzus, *The Fifth Theological Oration* 31.1–2, in *On God and Christ: The Five Theological Orations and Two Letters to Cledonius*, trans. Lionel Wickham, Popular Patristics 23 (Yonkers, NY: St. Vladimir's Seminary Press, 2002), 83.

doctrinal discussion."[25] St. Gregory's fatigue is palpable, but he nonetheless calls on the Spirit's aid so that God will be glorified.

St. Basil also took on the cause, defending the Holy Spirit's divine credentials by Scripture, since throughout the Old and the New Testaments the Spirit is called both "Holy" and "Lord." Basil relies heavily on the *lex orandi, lex credendi* principle that worship establishes belief. Since the Church had always worshiped in the name of the Trinity, the Holy Spirit had always been considered equal to the Father and the Son. Basil refers to the hymn *Fos Ilaron* ("O Joyful Light")[26] and asserts that no one has ever accused the people of blasphemy for singing, "We glorify the Father and the Son and the Holy Spirit of God."[27]

The Fathers at the Second Ecumenical Council (381), held in Constantinople, would echo the Cappadocian teachings by adding a clause to the Creed of Nicaea to affirm the divinity of the Holy Spirit: "Who proceeds from the Father, Who together with the Father and the Son is worshiped and glorified, Who spoke through the prophets." This clause, of course, is compatible with the Orthodox view that the Holy Spirit is fully personal and fully divine, and that He reveals God's will to the faithful.

The Filioque Controversy

About the same time that the Second Ecumenical Council affirmed the proper language to speak about the divinity of the Holy Spirit, St. Augustine, bishop of Hippo, who was a creative thinker and a prolific Christian writer, was also thinking about the Spirit. By Augustine's day, the authority of the Cappadocian Fathers had been solidly established in the Church, and especially in the Christian East. Unfortunately, by Augustine's own admission, he was not very competent in Greek. Writing in the early fifth century about the Cappadocian reference to the Trinity in Greek as *tris hypostases, mia ousia* ("three persons, one essence"), Augustine remarks, "I do not know what distinction they wish to make."[28] Instead of building on the Cappadocian theology regarding the Trinity, Augustine developed some distinct ideas of his own. One of Augustine's ideas is that the Holy Spirit is the "bond of love" (*vinculum caritas*) between the Father and the Son. Many modern-day authors, including C. S. Lewis,

25. Gregory of Nazianzus, *Fifth Theological Oration* 31.1–2 (trans. Wickham, 83).
26. See the text of "The Hymn of the Evening" in chap. 5 in the section "Singing Theology."
27. Basil the Great, *On the Holy Spirit* 29.73 (trans. Hildebrand, 87).
28. Augustine of Hippo, *De Trinitate* 5.10. "When we look at Augustine's treatment of the topic, it becomes evident that he has scarcely if at all understood the central point. It is difficult for him to understand the meaning of the Greek *hypostasis* . . . : 'I do not know what distinction they wish to make.'" Colin Gunton, *The Promise of Trinitarian Theology*, 2nd ed. (Edinburgh: T&T Clark, 2004), 40.

have also used this phrase to refer to the Holy Spirit. It is indeed a lovely idea, but from an Orthodox point of view it is theologically problematic for a few reasons, not the least of which is that nothing like it appears in Scripture. Additionally, it triggers theological concern because of the suggestion that the Holy Spirit is not a full person, but rather an insentient force.[29]

Augustine expands this idea further, proposing that since the Spirit is the love between Father and Son, why not also consider the Spirit to proceed from both the Father and the Son? Augustine writes,

> Why, then, should we not believe that the Holy Spirit proceeds also from the Son, seeing that He is likewise the Spirit of the Son? For did He not so proceed, He could not, when showing Himself to His disciples after the resurrection, have breathed upon them, and said, "Receive the Holy Spirit." For what else was signified by such a breathing upon them, but that from Him also the Holy Spirit proceeds?[30]

In his writing, Augustine rightly presents this idea as a theologoumenon (a pious idea that may or may not be correct), but his reputation in the Latin West promoted it to an official teaching in Rome. Subsequently, one little Latin word, *Filioque* (which means "and the Son"), became the lightning rod that ultimately separated the Eastern Orthodox bishops and the bishop of Rome from one another in the so-called Great Schism of 1054.

A Theological Problem and an Administrative Problem

The Eastern Fathers believed that the *Filioque* was based on flawed theology. According to Metropolitan Ware, "what Orthodoxy does not teach, and what the Bible does not actually say, is that the Spirit proceeds from the Son."[31] Although Augustine was certainly correct that the Resurrected Lord sent the Holy Spirit from the Father to His disciples, Augustine conflated the terms "send" and "proceed" into one action. Jesus did send the Spirit into history to the disciples on earth, but Jesus also took care to clarify that this same Spirit proceeds eternally from the Father, and from the Father alone:

> But when the Helper comes, whom I shall send to you from the Father, the Spirit of truth who proceeds from the Father, He will testify of Me. (John 15:26)

29. "The Spirit 'is not just a divine blast' as I once heard someone describe him." Ware, *Orthodox Way*, 74.

30. Augustine of Hippo, *Homilies on John* 99.7, https://www.newadvent.org/fathers/1701099.htm.

31. Ware, *Orthodox Church*, 206.

Furthermore, the Cappadocian understanding of the Trinity was grounded in the unique internal relations between the Divine Persons. There is only one relationship of begetting, and it is between the Father and the Son. There is only one relationship of processing, and it is between the Father and the Spirit (John 3:16; 15:26). The "double procession" of the *Filioque* eliminates the eternal uniqueness of the Father-Spirit relationship, in addition to not being supported by Scripture.[32]

Though this theological disagreement was important, a far more vehement opposition to the *Filioque* by the Christian East occurred much later, after the West had unilaterally added the *Filioque* to the recitation of the Creed that had been established by the Councils of Nicaea and Constantinople. The Byzantine East believed that matters of doctrine could only be solved synodally with the Holy Spirit's guidance through an Ecumenical Council, and had affirmed that the Creed of Nicaea "is, above all else, to remain inviolate."[33]

In a noteworthy letter, Pope Nicholas I (ca. 800–867) declared that the one who holds the Chair of Peter (i.e., himself) has the final word on any theological issue and total authority over the Church: "The pope is endowed with authority 'over all the earth, that is, over *every* Church.'"[34] The East was scandalized by Pope Nicholas's assertion that he alone was the supreme earthly representative of Christ and by his claim that no council would be needed to solve the *Filioque* controversy. The Eastern Church believed that the Creed was the common possession of the whole Church, and that neither one person nor even a part of the Church had a right to tamper with it. Debates about the theology of the *Filioque* continued until 1014, when Pope Benedict VIII ordered the Creed with the *Filioque* to be sung at a papal Mass, thus establishing its papal endorsement in the West once and for all.

Church historians have reminded us that what resulted in the Great Schism of 1054 began as a gradual estrangement between East and West on a variety of issues of greater or lesser importance, such as the enforced celibacy of the clergy in the West. However, what might seem on the surface to be differences of opinion about words and practices in actuality indicates two differing perceptions of church authority that could not be harmonized: one conciliar and one papal. The papacy's claim of power continued into the contemporary era with the declaration of the Second Vatican Council in the mid-twentieth century that "the Roman Pontiff, by reason of his office as Vicar of Christ, and as pastor of the entire Church, has full, supreme and universal power

32. See Basil the Great, *On the Holy Spirit*, 71–75.
33. By declaration of the Ecumenical Council at Chalcedon in 451, "the creed of the 318 fathers is to remain inviolate."
34. Letter from Pope Nicholas I, quoted in Ware, *Orthodox Church*, 51.

over the whole Church."[35] The theological discussion surrounding whether the *Filioque* is a correct biblical understanding of the Trinity remains secondary, even today, to this far greater issue: the breach of conciliarity in the Holy Spirit that occurred because of the rise of the Roman papacy.

The Church as an Icon of the Trinity

Many Orthodox scholars have suggested that the Church is an icon of the Holy Trinity. At first glance, this identification might appear to be in conflict with the Church's identity as the Body of Christ. Yet the Creator Himself said, "Let Us make man in Our image" (Gen. 1:26)—and this image of plurality is also an image of unity, equality, and freedom. Since, as we have already discussed, an icon (*eikōn*) makes visible a reality that is already present,[36] the Trinity is more than a mere model of these ideal attributes. As an icon, the Church participates directly in the unity, diversity, equality, and freedom of the Holy Trinity that is the source of being of her members.

Even the institutional aspects of the Church are bound to the being of God as Trinity.[37] The notion of equality is especially important here, in light of the preceding discussion of the origins of papal authority. In the Orthodox conception of the Trinity, the Father is the *Protos* or "first among equals," but the Father is not superior to the Son and to the Holy Spirit. Metropolitan Ware, for example, states boldly that because each divine person in the Holy Trinity is autonomous and equal, "there is unity, but no totalitarianism" in the Church.[38] That is to say, every member of the Body of Christ is equal in dignity—and further, with regard to administration, this means that no bishop in the Church "can claim to wield an absolute power over all the rest."[39]

The same trinitarian principles of equality, freedom, and unity in diversity also explain the importance of the Ecumenical Councils in the Orthodox Church. When the many bishops who assembled at a council eventually reached an agreement through the Holy Spirit, their relationship was also an icon of the mystery of unity in diversity. Moreover, because each person of the Holy Trinity is autonomous, the Orthodox Church, likewise, is made up

35. *Lumen Gentium* 22, quoted in Peter Kreeft, *Catholic Christianity: A Complete Catechism of Catholic Beliefs Based on the Catechism of the Catholic Church* (San Francisco: Ignatius, 2011), 100–101.

36. See the section "The *Eikōn*" in chap. 3.

37. John D. Zizioulas, *Being as Communion: Studies in Personhood and the Church* (Crestwood, NY: St. Vladimir's Seminary Press, 1985), 15.

38. Ware, *Orthodox Church*, 233.

39. Ware, *Orthodox Church*, 234.

of many autocephalous (self-headed) local churches. Again, echoing Ware, there is unity in diversity, equality, and freedom, but there can be no totalitarianism in the Church.

Fr. Thomas Hopko explains that the many in the one Body of Christ should not be thought of as individuals in a relationship, but as a true union—or communion—as in the Holy Trinity:

> Like the God in whose image they are made, human beings are not intended to be separate individuals in relationship with one another in an external manner. Neither are they called to exist as a "collective" without personal "standing" or integrity. They are rather, like their Creator, made to be persons in community, distinct hypostases in an identity of nature, called to a perfect—and, according to Gregory of Nyssa, ever more perfect—union of being and action in fulfillment of all virtues, the greatest of which is love.[40]

Hypostases is the Greek term that the Cappadocian Fathers used to describe the threeness of the Trinity. Fr. Hopko means that, in their multiplicity, the diverse humans in the Church are also intended to share in a oneness of nature. But this one nature is not their common biological human nature. The biological human nature has been transformed by the Holy Spirit, so that human persons may genuinely, mystically, *become* the Body of Christ in order to worship the Father, through the Son, in the Holy Spirit.[41]

▪ DISCUSSION QUESTIONS ▪

1. Why it is so important for Orthodox trinitarian theology to maintain the scriptural language that the Holy Spirit "proceeds" from the Father alone (John 15:26)?
2. Discuss the issues surrounding the reasons why the Orthodox bishops believed that it was not proper for one person to make a change to the Creed of Nicaea (AD 325) and Constantinople (381). For example, how does the principle of conciliarity and the idea of "communion" relate to the *Filioque* controversy?
3. Discuss how a hierarchy of order, or *taxis*, in the Holy Trinity relates to the Orthodox form of synodal or conciliar leadership.

40. Hopko, "Trinity in the Cappadocians," 273.
41. Zizioulas, *Being as Communion*, 56–65.

4. Trinitarian heresies usually arose because of good intentions, to preserve either the unity or the diversity of the Trinity, but ended up leaning too far in one direction. Discuss how the Cappadocian language for the Trinity found a better balance between oneness and threeness.

8

Orthodox Worship

Liturgy

"Liturgy" is another of those terms that requires a context for clarity since it can be applied to almost any ceremonialized human gathering, sacred or secular. "Liturgy" (Greek: *leitourgia*) is a combination of the Greek words for people (*laos*) and work (*ergon*). In ancient Greece, a liturgy was a public work performed for the benefit of the city or state. English translations of the Bible do not use the terms "liturgy" or "liturgist" to describe worship or ministers, even though these terms are there in the Greek. In the New Testament, St. Paul speaks of the civic authorities as liturgists (*leitourgoi*) of God (Rom. 13:6) and refers to himself as a "minister [*leitourgon*] of Jesus Christ to the Gentiles" (Rom. 15:16). In Hebrews 8:1–2, Jesus Christ is described as the high priest of the heavenly liturgy: "We have such a High Priest, who is seated at the right hand of the throne of the Majesty in the heavens, a Minister [*leitourgos*] of the sanctuary and of the true tabernacle which the Lord erected, and not man." Acts 13:2 specifically refers to the liturgical worship of the Church on earth: "As they ministered [*leitourgounton*] to the Lord and fasted, the Holy Spirit said, 'Now separate to Me Barnabas and Saul for the work to which I have called them.'"

In an ecclesial setting, "liturgical" is often used in the Christian West to describe "high church" or very formal worship. In the Eastern Orthodox Church, however, "Liturgy" is the proper name of the Church's primary worship, the Divine Liturgy. True to the term's semantic origins, the whole community participates in the Divine Liturgy, which is the essential action

of the priesthood of all believers (1 Pet. 2:5). The two primary liturgies of
the Orthodox Church are the Divine Liturgy of St. John Chrysostom and the
Divine Liturgy of St. Basil the Great. Both liturgies were well established by
the late fourth or early fifth centuries and have been in continual use since
then. The ancient Liturgy of St. James is even older, but is celebrated only
a few times each year on feast days related to St. James. The opening words
of the Divine Liturgy, "Blessed is the Kingdom of the Father and of the Son
and of the Holy Spirit," attest to the understanding that earthly creation is
preparing to enter into the eternal and heavenly Kingdom of Jesus Christ.[1]

Ancient Liturgy

It might surprise some people to learn that before any of the books of the
Christian Bible had been written, Christian liturgy was already developing.
This fact *did* surprise a group of campus leaders in the Campus Crusade for
Christ organization in the 1970s. These leaders wanted to more closely align
their evangelical "house churches" to the early Church. Dr. Jack Sparks, who
was the campus leader at Penn State University, was responsible within the
group for researching early Christian worship. Sparks reported that "Christian
worship was liturgical from the start."[2] This was an unexpected revelation
for the other campus leaders, since they had all assumed that worship in the
primitive Church was spontaneous, informal, and without a consistent order.
One of the campus leaders, Peter Gillquist, reported that Sparks "introduced
us to three early and universally recognized sources outside the Scriptures that
tell us what early Christian worship was like."[3] These three sources were the
First Apology of St. Justin Martyr (ca. AD 150), the anonymous *Didache*
or *Teaching of the Twelve* (ca. AD 50), and the *Apostolic Tradition* of Hippolytus (ca. AD 200). Gillquist further reported:

> From the records of the early Church, it was clear to us that worship was
> liturgical and that the sacrament of holy communion was the centerpiece of
> the entire service. Honestly, it took some of us, including myself, awhile to get
> emotionally comfortable with liturgy and sacrament. I had become so attached
> to "winging it."[4]

1. "The church is an earthly heaven in which the supercelestial God dwells and walks about."
Germanos of Constantinople, *On the Divine Liturgy*, trans. Paul Meyendorff, Popular Patristics
(Crestwood, NY: St. Vladimir's Seminary Press, 1984), 42.
2. Peter E. Gillquist, *Becoming Orthodox: A Journey to the Ancient Christian Faith* (Brentwood, TN: Wolgemuth & Hyatt, 1989), 34.
3. Gillquist, *Becoming Orthodox*, 35.
4. Gillquist, *Becoming Orthodox*, 38–39.

The campus leaders learned that the primitive Christian Church had worshiped with hymns and formal prayers that were mainly based on the Psalms. In fact, within a few decades of Christ's Resurrection, there was already a well-established structure for prayer and worship. Fr. Alexander Schmemann, a leading authority on Orthodox liturgical theology in the twentieth century, argues convincingly in his *Introduction to Liturgical Theology* that this clear structure developed rather quickly in part because there was a "genetical link" between early Christian worship and the liturgical tradition of Judaism.[5] Among other similarities, the earliest Christian prayer followed the exact same structure as the prayer of the ancient Jewish synagogue, and in the same order. Schmemann calls the relationship between synagogue and early Christian worship "a dependency of order" and "identity of sequence" in that both began by blessing the name of God; moved on to praising God, confession of sins, and intercession; and concluded by glorifying God for His work in history.[6]

This structural dependence is not surprising given the heavily Jewish makeup of the earliest Christian communities. These communities simply continued in the form of worship most familiar to them. Schmemann's main point is that the evidence of early liturgy and dependence on the worship of the synagogue dispels any notion that early Christian worship lacked order (for example, as had been the assumption of Gillquist and his Campus Crusade colleagues). Early Christian worship was indeed charismatic, but it was also ordered and formal.

Fr. Schmemann also notes that an exclusively Christian and new form of worship developed alongside the traditional Hebrew worship. Early Christian rites included Baptism, participation in the eucharistic breaking of the bread, and common prayer. "Although in its outward forms this independent Christian worship clearly derives from specifically Hebrew 'Prototypes,' no one would deny its newness in relation to the cult of the Temple and the synagogue."[7] Schmemann refers to this bond as "liturgical dualism"—the old and the new together. Christianity is, therefore, "Hebrew in form and spirit,"[8] so its newness should not be thought of as a separation from Judaism. Rather, its newness is the accomplishment of that which had been long awaited by Judaism—the coming of the Messiah. In Jesus, all the promises and prophecies of the Old Testament have been fulfilled.

5. Alexander Schmemann, *Introduction to Liturgical Theology* (London: The Faith Press, 1966), 43.
6. Schmemann, *Introduction to Liturgical Theology*, 44.
7. Schmemann, *Introduction to Liturgical Theology*, 47.
8. Schmemann, *Introduction to Liturgical Theology*, 47.

The Divine Liturgy of today has retained many of the core elements of the Christian movement's Jewish roots at the time of the Apostles.[9] Following the ancient example, the entire Divine Liturgy is still chanted as a liturgical conversation of clergy and congregation with God. The prayers and readings are "intoned" rather than sung, although hymns are sung by the congregation, usually led by a chanter or choir and traditionally without accompaniment. Unlike much of contemporary Christian music, both the texts and the melodies have been handed down over many centuries.

Although all the liturgical rites of the Orthodox Church today share a common essence with the early Church, some of the outward expressions have developed depending on circumstance, time, and locale. For example, the Divine Liturgy celebrated in parts of Africa might include drums and tribal dancing, which makes it look strikingly different from the same Divine Liturgy celebrated in North America—yet it is the same Divine Liturgy. Since many Orthodox churches in the United States were planted by ethnic communities in the nineteenth and twentieth centuries, some still worship mainly, or partially, in the liturgical languages they brought with them, such as Church Slavonic or Byzantine Greek. When Christians who are not Orthodox encounter the Divine Liturgy for the first time, they often report that the experience feels quite foreign, even if the service is all (or mostly) in English!

First Impressions

After her first visit to an Orthodox liturgy, one of my graduate seminary students, Martha, said that the active participation of the congregation throughout the service was a notable change from her evangelical worship experience, where the service is structured around a sermon. Another student, Brendan, said that the "staggered arrivals and folks rising to light candles, kiss icons, etc. certainly takes some getting used to. The lack of a perceivable start time is also a bit jarring at first. However, once one is clued into the order of events, there is a calming effect to the chants of the priests and the freedom of quiet prayer and contemplation."

After her first visit, my student Janine said, "Although I had no idea what was being said and I couldn't see much of what was going on, I still felt like I was in the presence of God. The liturgy created a sort of sacred space for me to connect with God." And finally, Raphael commented on the absence of technology in the service:

9. See Benjamin D. Williams and Harold B. Anstall, *Orthodox Worship: A Living Continuity with the Synagogue, the Temple, and the Early Church* (Minneapolis: Light and Life Publishing, 1990; repr., Chesterton, IN: Ancient Faith Publishing, 2018).

Although I struggled with the rituals, the priest and congregation knew all the words by heart and were able to recite them without skipping a beat. This is very uncommon in modern nondenominational churches, who often have to include words on PowerPoint slides for the congregation to follow along. The lack of technology was also a reminder for the modern church that technology is not needed for a beautiful and worshipful service, although modern believers, especially millennial believers, may struggle with this.

What first-time observers of the Divine Liturgy usually miss, however, is that the actual text of each Divine Liturgy in the Orthodox Church is taken directly from the Bible. It has been estimated that 98 direct quotations from the Old Testament and 114 from the New Testament are woven together in the prayers, responses, and hymns of the Divine Liturgy.[10] In this way, Scripture forms the liturgical language that is celebrated communally as well as encountered individually. In reality, the Orthodox are praying Holy Scripture in the Liturgy.

As Raphael observed, many Orthodox believers do know the words and hymns of the liturgy by heart. My maternal grandmother, Paraskevè (we are both named after the second-century martyr Paraskevè of Rome), lived out her Christian faith daily in the fear of God, and knew the entire Divine Liturgy (in Greek). This meant that she also knew many, many Bible verses by memory, even though she probably could not recite chapter and verse. Since my grandmother had internalized the liturgy as part of her being, the Scriptures were also internalized and had become a part of her.

The Troparion of the Great Martyr Paraskevè (Paraskevi) of Rome (Commemorated on July 26)

Appropriate to your calling, O Champion Paraskevi, you worshipped with the readiness your name bears. For an abode you obtained faith, which is your namesake. Wherefore, you pour forth healing and intercede for our souls.[a]

a. English translation courtesy of Narthex Press, Northridge, CA, https://www.goarch.org/-/feast-of-the-holy-righteous-martyr-saint-paraskevi.

10. Timothy Ware, *The Orthodox Church: An Introduction to Eastern Christianity*, 3rd ed. (London: Penguin, 2015), 195.

An Earthly Heaven

> In the year that King Uzziah died, I saw the Lord sitting on a throne, high and lofty; and the hem of his robe filled the temple. Seraphs were in attendance above him; each had six wings: with two they covered their faces, and with two they covered their feet, and with two they flew. And one called to another and said:
>
> > "Holy, holy, holy is the LORD of hosts [*savaoth*];
> > the whole earth is full of his glory." (Isa. 6:1–3 NRSV)

One of the unique features of Orthodox worship is that the Divine Liturgy is not a solely human rite or action directed toward God, but is considered to be "heaven on earth"—since Emmanuel ("God is with us") comes to us.[11] The opening words of the Divine Liturgy, "Blessed is the Kingdom of the Father and of the Son and of the Holy Spirit," attest to the understanding that earthly humans are preparing to enter the eternal Kingdom of the Lord. In Orthodoxy, there is a cooperation, or synergy, between God and humanity in all of life, but especially in Orthodox worship. The Church is not understood as a merely human activity or construction, nor is it mainly a divine activity or construction—rather, the Church is a joining together of heavenly and earthly action.

I must stop here for a moment to anticipate a potential misunderstanding. The highly mystical worship of Eastern Orthodoxy should not be interpreted as an escape from earthly reality—as Fr. Schmemann writes, "from the dull world of 'action.'"[12] Rather, the Liturgy gives the earthbound a glimpse into true reality—a reality that is intended to infuse all of life. There is no division between the liturgical and the "real world" outside of the Liturgy. Both are facets of the one life in Christ. Fr. Alexander Schmemann speaks of the entrance to the liturgy as an entrance into a fourth dimension that enhances the perspective of actual reality, in much the same way as a three-dimensional photograph adds more than a two-dimensional photograph. That fourth dimension is not time but reality: "Our *entrance* into the presence of Christ is an entrance into a fourth dimension which allows us to see the ultimate reality of life."[13]

Inside the Liturgy

The Orthodox worship space is often referred to as a temple or sanctuary and is a consecrated space, blessed and set apart as holy (*agios*) for Ortho-

11. Alexander Schmemann, *The Eucharist: Sacrament of the Kingdom* (Crestwood, NY: St. Vladimir's Seminary Press, 1987), 20.

12. Alexander Schmemann, *For the Life of the World: Sacraments and Orthodoxy* (Crestwood, NY: St. Vladimir's Seminary Press, 1998), 21.

13. Schmemann, *For the Life of the World*, 26–27.

dox worship. Most Orthodox temples or sanctuaries have a dome, and in that dome is usually a painted or mosaic icon of Christ the Almighty God (*Pantocrator*) seated upon His heavenly throne. There are several important things to say about this. The first is that when Orthodox Christians enter the sanctuary under that dome, it is a reminder that they are not "doing" a new worship service, but rather "entering into" the heavenly worship always going on around the throne of Jesus Christ. The Gothic cathedrals of medieval Europe, with their steep spires, imply that worshipers are reaching up to heaven. But the Orthodox dome suggests that worshipers have entered a complete cosmos, a place where heaven and earth meet. The Church is not "reaching up"; rather, God is already present within. This is more than imagery, since the Orthodox believe that the heavenly descends and the earthly ascends in the Holy Eucharist. His All Holiness Patriarch Bartholomew states, "In liturgy, Orthodox Christians sense that they are a part not only of something larger than themselves. They are a part of a world that simultaneously transcends and contains this world; they are a part of no less than heaven."[14]

How can anyone know what heavenly worship looks like? The quotation from the Prophet Isaiah that opens this section tells of the Prophet's vision of the Lord sitting on a throne with the angels in attendance above Him. Isaiah writes that the Lord was so high and lofty that the hem of His robe filled the temple. Isaiah sees the angels in attendance around the Lord and even reports details of their appearance: "Each had six wings: with two they covered their faces, and with two they covered their feet, and with two they flew" (Isa. 6:2 NRSV). Isaiah also describes what he hears the angels saying to one another: "Holy, holy, holy is the LORD of hosts [*savaoth*]; the whole earth is full of his glory" (Isa. 6:3 NRSV). The Orthodox understand this to be a vision of the heavenly worship around the eternal throne of Jesus Christ. The words of a hymn common to both of Orthodoxy's primary Divine Liturgies are taken directly from what the Prophet Isaiah hears the angels singing: "Holy, Holy, Holy, Lord God of Savaoth, heaven and earth are full of your glory. Hosanna in the highest, blessed is He who comes in the Name of the Lord" (from Isa. 6:3 and Matt. 21:9).

This "Thrice-Holy Hymn" is also referenced in the "Hymn of the Cherubim," which was added to the Divine Liturgy sometime in the sixth century: "Let us, who mystically represent the Cherubim and sing the Thrice-Holy Hymn to the Life-giving Trinity, lay aside all earthly cares, that we may receive the King of all, invisibly escorted by the angelic hosts. *Alleluia, alleluia,*

---

14. His All Holiness Ecumenical Patriarch Bartholomew, *Encountering the Mystery: Understanding Orthodox Christianity Today* (New York: Doubleday, 2008), 35.

alleluia." The Greek word for "mystically represent" in the "Hymn of the Cherubim" is *eikonizontes*, which means something like "icon" used as a verb instead of a noun. The profound theology of that word in the hymn is that when the congregation chants "Holy, holy, holy" in praise of the Lord during the Divine Liturgy, the congregation is an icon of the heavenly angels (the cherubim) who are always chanting hymns of praise before Christ's heavenly throne. It is not that there are two parallel Thrice-Holy Hymns—one being sung on earth by humans, and one being sung in heaven by angels—but that those who are singing it on earth are doing so simultaneously with the angels in heaven, as Isaiah heard. Similarly, there are not two instances of the liturgy; rather, the heavenly liturgy is present in the earthly liturgy and vice versa. This is why the Orthodox believe they are "entering into" heavenly worship, not merely "doing" a new worship service. Chrysostom writes, "We enter heaven when we enter the church; not in place, I mean, but in disposition. . . . For it is possible for one who is actually on earth to stand in heaven, and to see the things there, and to hear words from there."[15]

Three Stages, Three Sections

It is common for Orthodox architecture to be cruciform in style—in the shape of a cross. The building is separated into three sections, intentionally hearkening back to the Jerusalem Temple, which was separated into the outer court, the holy place, and the most holy place.[16] The three sections of the Orthodox sanctuary together also represent three distinct stages of spiritual development in the Christian life: (1) turning away from the world and toward God; (2) being guided by the Holy Spirit to knowledge of God; and (3) communing with God. The Church Fathers spoke about these three stages as purification, illumination, and theosis (union with God).[17] Since there is a continual need for Christians to turn away from the world, to be illumined by God's grace, and to participate in the divine life, this cycle repeats again and again, and in that same order, throughout one's life.

The Orthodox narthex is the small vestibule at the entrance (usually nearest the west side of the building) where an Orthodox Christian will make an intentional effort to turn away from the world outside and prepare to turn toward Christ to be illumined and purified by the Holy Spirit. As Orthodox Christians prepare to enter into worship, they light candles in the narthex

15. Quoted in David Rylaarsdam, *John Chrysostom on Divine Pedagogy: The Coherence of His Theology and Preaching* (Oxford: Oxford University Press, 2014), 200.
16. See Exod. 26:30–37; 27:9–19; 1 Kings 6:14–36; 2 Chron. 3–4.
17. See the section "Theosis" in chap. 6.

as a physical expression of prayer, and venerate (bow in front of, or kiss) the Holy Icons of Christ and His saintly friends.

The middle section of an Orthodox Church is where the congregants are together being illumined by the Holy Spirit during worship that also includes the reading of Scripture. This is the section where there might be pews or seats. Most Orthodox temples, however, do not have pews, allowing freedom of movement during the service. Some people stand in place, and others move around to venerate the icons or light candles.

The holy altar is at the front of the sanctuary and is typically on the east side of the building. The congregation and clergy always face east—the direction of the rising sun—since Jesus Christ brought light to a darkened world as the "Sun of Righteousness" (Mal. 4:2) and the "light of the world" (John 8:12). The ancient authors Origen, Tertullian, and Cyprian all indicated that Christians should pray standing up, with hands raised, and facing east.[18] The altar is the place of communion between heaven and earth, where the Orthodox priest or bishop calls down the Holy Spirit to sanctify the congregation and to make the bread and wine into the Body and Blood of Jesus Christ. The cycle of turning away from the world, being illumined by the Holy Spirit, and communing in the Holy Eucharist is repeated every time Orthodox Christians enter the sanctuary for worship.

It bears repeating here that worship is primary in Eastern Orthodoxy. It is through worship that the Holy Spirit guides the faithful to understand the nature of God. Theological reflection, while important, requires the primary activity of worship since, in the Orthodox Church, *theologia* cannot be separated from prayer and contemplation. In Protestant worship today, the sermon or message is often the focus, with worship in a supporting role. When a new Protestant congregation or denomination is planted, the leaders will often first determine the group's core beliefs and how these beliefs can best be communicated to their intended demographic. This priority was evident at the beginning of the "seeker-sensitive" movement in the late 1970s, which arose out of a specific theological stance to present a Christianity and worship style that was welcoming to unchurched Americans.

I mentioned previously an example from my hometown, where a senior pastor refused to soften his fire-and-brimstone sermons and ultimately left to start a new congregation. The group he left behind subsequently built a three-thousand-seat, stadium-style worship center to support its new seeker-friendly

18. Andrew Louth, "The Body in Western Catholic Christianity," in *Religion and the Body*, ed. Sarah Coakley (Cambridge: Cambridge University Press, 1997), 113. Early Christians also expected the Messiah to return from the east, as in Matt. 24:27: "For as the lightning comes from the east and flashes to the west, so also will the coming of the Son of Man be."

emphasis, with rock-concert-quality music, enormous video screens, and padded, theater-style seats with cup holders. The contrast with the "smells and bells" of Orthodox Christian worship is obvious. What I hope to convey by this illustration is not the contrast in worship style, but rather that this group's new worship style developed as an outgrowth of its new theology and mission statement.

Relevant and Ancient

Change is not a bad thing, and the Orthodox do not fear change. Because the Holy Spirit is dynamically guiding the Holy Tradition of the Church, there must always be fresh expressions of truth. There have been liturgical developments in the Orthodox Church over many centuries, and there is diversity of expression in each Orthodox culture in which the Church has been planted. Orthodoxy has never equated its unity with the imposition of uniformity. As Archbishop Anastasios of Albania states, "Unity is not impaired by the existence of a variety of outlooks, languages, customs, or political states."[19]

Change for the sake of following today's trends, however, is not at all consistent with the Orthodox ethos. Unchanging divine truths and the Apostolic Tradition must not be compromised. As Patriarch Bartholomew states, "It has always been crucial to preserve the invaluable treasure of the faith with care and respect, 'neither adding anything, nor taking anything away.'"[20]

A humorous story about change in Christian circles emerged a few years ago after a well-known Baptist preacher, Rev. Dwight A. Moody, visited an Orthodox Divine Liturgy for the first time. As the dean of the Georgetown College chapel, Moody was free on Sundays to visit other churches. On one particular Sunday, Moody visited St. Andrew Antiochian Orthodox Church near his home in Lexington, Kentucky, and found himself "in a cloud of **incense**, trying to figure out what the worshipers were chanting, why they rarely sat down, and when the 9 a.m. service was going to end so that the 10 a.m. service could begin." Speaking to a reporter about his visit, Moody said, "It was the most in-your-face, retrograde old stuff you could imagine. What fascinated me was that this was the *total* antithesis of everything that is happening in the contemporary church."[21] Having experienced several megachurches during his Sunday visits, many of which had been formed by church-growth consultants,

---

19. Archbishop Anastasios (Yannoulatos), *Facing the World: Orthodox Christian Essays on Global Concerns* (Crestwood, NY: St. Vladimir's Seminary Press, 2003), 90.

20. Bartholomew, *Encountering the Mystery*, 6.

21. Terry Mattingly, "Edgy Orthodoxy 4 Seekers," Patheos, https://www.patheos.com/blogs/tmatt/2003/02/edgy-orthodoxy-4-seekers/, accessed July 1, 2020.

Moody wondered how the Orthodox Church would fare if it were critiqued by such a consultant. So he penned a satirical "Survival Guide" for the Orthodox Church, which was published in several local newspapers. It was later featured in *Christian Century* and included in his book *On the Other Side of Oddville*. Here are a few excerpts from Moody's "Survival Guide" for the Orthodox Church:

> Food: I recommend that you secure a Starbucks franchise; locate it in what is now the prayer room just off the foyer. If a communion service is absolutely necessary, develop techniques to make it move a little quicker; research indicates that videos shown during the lag time are well received.
>
> Furnishings: I took pictures of your interior: hardwood floors, unpadded pews, plain windows and walls, and—how shall I describe them?—painted panels of old people. It needs a complete makeover. Down with the panels and up with video screens; two will do fine. Theater chairs are a must.
>
> Music: Choirs, especially acappella types, were fine for the last century, but no more. I liked the male quartet, but surely you have people slimmer and more sophisticated, and at least one female. Modern, younger people—those you must seek to appease, I mean, attract—are drawn toward drum sets and speakers; make them very visible, even if you actually use sound tracks (sample enclosed).
>
> WARNING: Do not assume that because you have thrived for two millennia and even now include 250 million members, your church can survive the fickle and ferocious religious market of modern America. Act soon, before it is too late![22]

In the version printed in his book, Moody adds, "Fortunately the Orthodox people found it funny."[23] I agree that it was all very funny. Moody wanted to make sure that the Orthodox people knew he was not making fun of them for being "retrograde." His critique was directed to the ever-changing contemporary evangelical world. As he explained to the reporter, "There are people in all kinds of traditional churches who are being told, 'If you don't change, you're going to die. If you don't buy into the latest fads, you're history.' Ministers are under incredible pressure to strip away anything that's connected to the past. Well, some people have had enough."[24]

One of the most well-respected Lutheran Church historians of the twentieth century, Jaroslav Pelikan, was reported to have said, "When the Lutheran Church–Missouri Synod (LCMS) has become Baptist, and the Evangelical Lutheran Church in America (ELCA) has become Methodist, I'll be

22. Dwight Allan Moody, *On the Other Side of Oddville* (Macon, GA: Mercer University Press, 2006), 164–65.
23. Moody, *On the Other Side of Oddville*, 165.
24. Mattingly, "Edgy Orthodoxy 4 Seekers."

Orthodox."[25] What he meant was that these two Lutheran denominations had been swept along with the tide and had changed too much. The Orthodox Church is intact today because unchanging divine truths have not changed, will not change, and must not change. This was the main consideration of the Holy Fathers of Orthodoxy when they faced similar challenges, and it was the point of Moody's satire: change for the sake of change is not always a good thing.

The more important detail to consider, with regard to the concept of change, is that Orthodox prayer and worship did not arise either out of a focus group on church growth or from the desire to attract a particular demographic. It did not even develop as an expression of a particular set of beliefs. As Fr. Steven Tsichlis often tells his congregation, "I didn't make this stuff up!" Eastern Orthodox worship continues to be relevant today, even in its ancient forms, because it is reflective (an "icon") of heavenly worship. Orthodoxy believes that the desire to worship God purely and authentically is not limited to a specific demographic.

Parts of Isaiah, Daniel, and Ezekiel offer a glimpse into heavenly worship.[26] When Orthodox Christians read Revelation 4 and 5 and the marriage supper of the Lamb in Revelation 19, they recognize the timeless Eucharist over which Christ Himself presides as the high priest (Heb. 2:17; 4:14). The Orthodox believe that the *timebound* liturgy of the Church on earth participates in the *timeless* liturgy of the Church in eternity. It is this understanding of liturgy as an icon of heavenly worship that informs the Orthodox belief that the liturgy will always be relevant in all places and at all times.

The Holy Mysteries

It was Tertullian in the second century who first used the term *sacramentum* to refer to the rites of the Christian Church. A *sacramentum* in the Roman Empire was the oath of allegiance to the emperor taken by a soldier. Its ecclesial use, therefore, suggests something like a vow or promise between the believer and God. Although Orthodox Christians do use the term "sacraments," the proper term is **Holy Mysteries** (Greek: *Agia Mysteria*). The English understanding of "mystery" can be misleading, though. *Mysterion* refers not to something hidden (as in a mystery novel) but to the ways of God that are being fully revealed and yet transcend human reason. Jesus told His disciples

---

25. Mickey L. Mattox and A. G. Roeber, *Changing Churches: An Orthodox, Catholic, and Lutheran Theological Conversation* (Grand Rapids: Eerdmans, 2012), 8.
    26. See Isa. 6; Ezek. 1; Dan. 7.

that they had been given to know "the mystery [*mysterion*] of the kingdom of God" while others must depend on parables (Mark 4:11). St. Paul refers to the coming of Christ as the *mysterion*, the "hidden wisdom" of God that has been revealed fully by the Spirit of God to those who love God (1 Cor. 2:7–10).

The Orthodox Church does not officially limit the number of sacraments (as did the Roman Catholic Council of Trent),[27] since the grace and power of God is communicated to believers in many ways. There are at least seven Holy Mysteries that fall into two categories: necessary and optional. The necessary Holy Mysteries are Baptism, Chrismation, Eucharist, **Confession**, and **Unction** (anointing for healing). The optional sacraments are Holy Matrimony (marriage) and Holy Orders (ordination). Other liturgical rites that convey divine strength and grace, and could be considered Holy Mysteries, include monastic tonsure, the commissioning of missionaries, and even possibly the Orthodox funeral service. Space does not allow more than an introduction to the specific Holy Mysteries. I will focus briefly on four of the necessary Mysteries: Baptism, Chrismation, Eucharist, and Confession.

Baptism

Baptism is the Holy Mystery by which a person enters the Church and becomes a member of the Body of Christ. It is also called **Holy Illumination**, since the Light of Christ is bestowed on the one who is baptized. St. Paul teaches that Baptism is an unrepeatable act: "There is one body and one Spirit . . . ; one Lord, one faith, one baptism; one God and Father of all" (Eph. 4:4–6). The First Council of Nicaea affirmed the same understanding in its Creed: "I believe in one Baptism for the remission of sins." This was affirmed once again at the Sixth Ecumenical Council (in Trullo, AD 692).

Baptism in the Orthodox Church signifies the beginning of the Christian life. It is understood in Orthodoxy as a dying with Jesus Christ and rising with Him to new life as a new creation into a new world—the Kingdom of God. In Baptism, whatever has been lost or tarnished in the ancestral sin is renewed, and all personal guilt and sin is washed away. Baptism is a free gift that cannot be earned. St. Gregory the Theologian wrote that as Christ has many names, so the gift of His Baptism also has many names:

> We call it a Gift, Grace, Baptism, Anointing, Illumination, the Garment of Immortality, the Bath of New Birth, the Seal—in short, all that is excellent.

27. "If any one saith, that the sacraments of the New Law were not all instituted by Jesus Christ, our Lord; or, that they are more, or less, than seven, . . . let him be anathema" (seventh session, March 3, 1547). See *Sacraments and Worship: The Sources of Christian Theology*, ed. Maxwell E. Johnson (Louisville: Westminster John Knox, 2012), 20–21.

We call it a Gift because it is given without any previous contribution; Grace because it is granted even to those who are in debt; Baptism because sin is buried with it in the water; Anointing because it is priestly and royal since priests and kings were the ones who were anointed; Illumination because of its splendor; Clothing since it covers our shame; Bath because it washes us; Seal because it preserves us.[28]

By at least the second century, new Christians were baptized at Pascha in acknowledgment that it is in dying to self with Christ that one is resurrected with Christ. The adult **catechumens** who would be baptized at Pascha would prepare for Baptism with a period of prayer, fasting, and intensive instruction. By the early fourth century, this practice had developed into what is now the forty-day period of **Great Lent,** in which the entire congregation together prepares for Christ's Crucifixion and Resurrection in solidarity with the catechumens who will join them at Pascha.[29]

Whether for infants or adults, Baptism in the Orthodox Church has always taken place by threefold full immersion in the name of the Holy Trinity (Matt. 28:19). The three immersions signify the three days Christ spent in the tomb before His Resurrection. Pastoral exceptions are made in special cases, such as for infirmity or where there is no basin or body of water.

Chrismation

Chrismation is the Holy Mystery of anointing to receive "the Seal of the Gift of the Holy Spirit" following Baptism. As Baptism is participation in Christ's Cross and Resurrection, Chrismation is understood as participation in Christ's sending of the Spirit at Pentecost. Pentecost followed the Resurrection, so Chrismation follows Baptism, and together they conform one to Christ and make one a Christian. In the Holy Mystery of Chrismation, "human nature purified by Baptism is made ready to receive the manifold gifts of the Holy Spirit."[30] The main prerequisite for receiving Chrismation in the Orthodox Church is Baptism, and a trinitarian Baptism in another Christian tradition is usually deemed acceptable in pastoral practice, since Baptism is not repeatable.

28. Gregory of Nazianzus, *Oration 40 on Baptism* 4, in *Worship in the Early Church,* by Lawrence J. Johnson, vol. 2, *An Anthology of Historical Sources* (Collegeville, MN: Liturgical Press, 2017), 147.

29. Maxwell E. Johnson, *The Rites of Christian Initiation: Their Evolution and Interpretation* (Collegeville, MN: Liturgical Press, 2007), 214.

30. Anthony M. Coniaris, *These Are the Sacraments: The Life-Giving Mysteries of the Orthodox Church* (Minneapolis: Light and Life Publishing, 1981), 37.

Orthodox Chrismation is sometimes called "Confirmation," but it is not actually a confirmation of Baptism. Chrismation is a separate rite, but together with Baptism it is understood to be an ordination into the royal priesthood of Christ (1 Pet. 2:9)—an anointing that offers the gifts of the Holy Spirit needed throughout one's life in order to follow Christ as a disciple. Fr. Schmemann calls Chrismation a "personal Pentecost" and the "entrance into the new life in the Holy Spirit which is the true life of the Church."[31]

During the time of the Apostles, the newly baptized would immediately receive the Holy Spirit by the laying on of hands of one of the Apostles (Acts 8:14–19). As the Church grew, the successor bishops to the Apostles could not be present at all Baptisms. Because of the high priority on the gifts of the Holy Spirit in the life of each baptized Christian, the method of the rite in the Christian East changed from laying on of hands to anointing with holy oil or Chrism.[32] The Holy Chrism is prepared from pure olive oil and dozens of aromatic herbs that symbolize the variety of gifts of the Holy Spirit that the chrismated Christian receives, and it is blessed annually by a bishop (usually a Patriarch). In this way, the rite of Chrismation can still be administered with Chrism by a priest in the absence of the bishop, thus keeping the three sacraments of Baptism, Chrismation, and Eucharist together. Chrismation is thus the "indissoluble bond between Baptism and Eucharist," according to Fr. George Dragas.[33] After being united to the Body of Christ in Baptism and receiving the Gifts of the Holy Spirit in Chrismation, the newly illumined joins the congregation in the Eucharist, or Holy Communion in the Body and Blood of Christ.

Children Are Also Baptized and Chrismated

The Orthodox Church also baptizes and chrismates infants and children who are being raised in Orthodox Christian families. St. Paul says that Baptism fulfills circumcision (Col. 2:11–12), which would take place on the eighth day after birth, according to the Jewish law (Lev. 12:3). St. Peter instructs his hearers at Pentecost to repent and be baptized for the remission of sins, "and you shall receive the gift of the Holy Spirit. For the promise is to you and your children" (Acts 2:38–39). Numerous biblical passages also suggest that entire households were baptized.[34] Although the oral tradition suggests that infant

31. Schmemann, *For the Life of the World*, 75.
32. See Exod. 30:22–25 for the instructions given to Moses to make fragrant anointing oil.
33. George Dion Dragas, "The Seal of the Gift of the Holy Spirit: The Sacrament of Chrismation," *Greek Orthodox Theological Review* 56, nos. 1–4 (2011): 144.
34. These include the households of Lydia (Acts 16:15), the Philippian jailor (Acts 16:33–34), and Stephanas (1 Cor. 1:16).

Baptism has been practiced throughout the history of the Church, the clearest early written evidence comes from Hippolytus, who wrote in about AD 200 that "they shall baptize the little children first. And if they can answer for themselves, let them answer. But if they cannot, let their parents or someone from their family [answer for them]."[35] With regard to Chrismation, in the fourth century, Gregory of Nazianzus wrote, "Do not allow sin to gain any opportunity, but let the infant be sanctified from childhood. Let the infant be consecrated by the Spirit from the very tenderest of age."[36]

The Orthodox Church understands both Baptism and Chrismation to be undeserved gifts that are not dependent on works or intellect or academic achievement. Therefore, it is believed that neither of these spiritual gifts should be withheld from children because of their age, especially since Jesus tells His followers to become like little children to enter the Kingdom of Heaven (Matt. 18:3). Anyone who has been baptized and chrismated into the Orthodox Church, regardless of age, is considered to be a full member of the Body of Christ, and therefore may also participate in the Holy Eucharist.

The Eucharist

"Eucharist" literally means "thanksgiving" in Greek (*evcharistia*), but it is much more. Embedded linguistically in the Greek word for Eucharist are also the ideas of grace (*charis*) and joy (*chara*). The Eucharist is a joyful offering of thanksgiving in return for the abundant gifts of grace given by God, as in the offering prayer of the Divine Liturgy: "We offer to You these gifts from Your own gifts in all and for all." The Eucharist is not merely a symbol of the Lord's Supper or a memorial meal, as it is in some Protestant traditions, but is considered by the Orthodox to be an actual communion of the earthly with the heavenly. Most Orthodox Christians refer to the Eucharist as Holy Communion or just Communion, as did St. Paul: "The cup of blessing which we bless, is it not the communion of the blood of Christ? The bread which we break, is it not the communion of the body of Christ?" (1 Cor. 10:16). As Fr. Emmanuel Hatzidakis affirms, "Communion is not our 'invention.' It was instituted by the Lord as a means to be in direct communion with us. He found the perfect way to unite us with Him."[37]

---

35. Hippolytus, *The Apostolic Tradition*, in *The Treatise on the "Apostolic Tradition" of St. Hippolytus of Rome*, ed. Gregory Dix and Henry Chadwick, 2nd ed. (1968; repr., London: Routledge, 1992), 33.

36. Gregory of Nazianzus, *Oration 40 on Baptism* 17 (trans. Johnson, 147).

37. Emmanuel Hatzidakis, *The Heavenly Banquet: Understanding the Divine Liturgy* (Clearwater, FL: Orthodox Witness, 2013), 325.

A careful study of St. Paul's teaching on the Eucharist in 1 Corinthians 11:18 ("when you come together as a Church") suggests that only when the Church celebrates the Eucharist at the Divine Liturgy is it fully Church. In this sense, the Eucharist is not only something the Church *does*, but rather what the Church *is*—or, rather, what it is always in the process of becoming. Metropolitan Zizioulas asserts that it is not actually correct to call the Eucharist a sacrament, since it makes the Eucharist an object. Rather, the Eucharist is *the* mode of life of the congregation. What the Church receives in Holy Communion at the Divine Liturgy is not just holy things, or even the words or deeds of Christ, but rather the "person of Christ in its totality."[38]

In imitation of Jesus's example at His Last Supper (Luke 22:7–20), the elements offered and consecrated for the Eucharist are typically bread and wine.[39] The offering is brought to the sanctuary by members of the congregation, to be prepared by the officiant priest or bishop as he prays for the entire Church of the living and those departed from this life. During the Divine Liturgy, the Holy Spirit is called upon to first descend upon the assembled congregation to make the individual imperfect members of the congregation into the perfect Body of Christ, and also to transform the offered bread and wine into the Body and Blood of Jesus Christ. All aspects of the rite are carried out with solemn reverence. Only those who have prepared through self-examination (1 Cor. 11:27–29), prayer, fasting, and repentance will approach the common chalice "with fear of God, faith and love," recognizing that it contains the true Body and Blood of Jesus Christ for the forgiveness of sins and eternal life (Matt. 26:28; John 6:53–54).

Unlike Roman Catholic Scholasticism, Eastern Christianity has made no attempt to explain how what is perceived as bread and wine is truly the physical Body and Blood of Christ. The Eucharist is a mystery to be received as food and drink, yet not to be "seen" through physical eyes.[40] St. Cyril of Jerusalem offers this advice on dealing with the enigma:

> Do not think of the elements as merely bread and wine. According to the Lord's declaration, they are Christ's body and blood. Although sense suggests the opposite, let faith hold you firm. Instead of judging the matter by taste, let faith

---

38. John D. Zizioulas, *The Eucharistic Communion and the World*, ed. Luke Ben Tallon (London: T&T Clark, 2011), 26.

39. In extraordinary circumstances, such as liturgies that were conducted by prisoner priests in the Soviet gulags of the twentieth century, other elements may be consecrated instead of bread and wine.

40. John Meyendorff, *Byzantine Theology: Historical Trends and Doctrinal Themes*, 2nd ed. (New York: Fordham University Press, 1983), 204.

give you an unshakeable confidence that you have been privileged to receive the body and blood of Christ.[41]

The Orthodox understanding of the Eucharist also takes seriously Christ's own words: "He who eats My flesh and drinks My blood abides in Me, and I in him" (John 6:56). As the Body and Blood of Jesus Christ, the Holy Eucharist is considered so sacred that Orthodox Christians will not consume any food or drink for many hours before receiving the Eucharist, and great care is taken so that not even one drop is spilled. These practices may seem exaggerated to some, but the Eucharist is treated by the Orthodox as that which it is believed to be: the true Body and Blood of the crucified and risen Savior.

The Orthodox Eucharist is also not understood as a "means toward unity," as it is in some non-Orthodox Christian traditions that practice "open communion." Rather, it is an expression and sign of the genuine unity of faith that already exists by reason of a common Baptism and Chrismation into the Orthodox Church, as well as a shared belief with the historical Church across all ages and in every place, and especially the shared belief that the Holy Eucharist is truly the Body and Blood of Jesus Christ. The idea of "closed communion" was described by St. Justin Martyr in the second century:

> This food we call the Eucharist, of which no one is allowed to partake except one who believes that the things we teach are true, and has received the washing for forgiveness of sins and for rebirth, and who lives as Christ handed down to us.[42]

Even in the primitive Church, the Eucharist required a common belief, a common sacramental Baptism into Christ's death and Resurrection, and a life in the process of being conformed to the likeness of Christ.

Divine and Human Communion in Christ

St. Gregory of Nyssa states that since the purpose of Christ's coming was to bring human nature into closeness with the divine nature, then "through his flesh, constituted by bread and wine, he implants himself in all believers."[43] Another word picture of the close physical communion of believers in Christ

41. Cyril of Jerusalem, *Mystagogical Lectures* 4.6, quoted in James Payton, *Light from the Christian East: An Introduction to the Orthodox Tradition* (Downers Grove, IL: IVP Academic, 2007), 149.

42. Justin Martyr, *First Apology* 66, quoted in James F. White, *Documents of Christian Worship: Descriptive and Interpretive Sources* (Louisville: Westminster John Knox, 1992), 184.

43. Gregory of Nyssa, *Catechetical Orations*, quoted in Payton, *Light from the Christian East*, 148.

through the Eucharist was provided by St. Cyril of Alexandria in the fifth century. He writes, "Just as if someone were to entwine two pieces of wax together and melt them with a fire, so that both are made one, so too through participation in the Body of Christ and His Precious Blood, He is united in us and we too in Him."[44]

The Eucharist is where all the dimensions of communion are found: God communicates Himself in the Eucharist, where human persons enter into communion with Him; the participants of the sacrament enter into communion with one another; and creation as a whole (in the bread and the wine) enters through humanity into communion with God.[45] Simply put, the Eucharist of Orthodox Christianity is not a symbolic human gesture. It is the locus of the most intimate (physical and spiritual) communion possible of the members of the Church with Jesus Christ Himself. Furthermore, it is the intimate, spiritual communion of the faithful with one another, brought together by the Holy Spirit in Christ as the Body of Christ.

Sin, Confession, and Reconciliation

There is a common anecdote told in Orthodox circles about a monk who was asked, "What do you do in that monastery?" He answered, "We fall down and we get up. We fall down and we get up." It is a popular story because it resonates with the struggle of every Christian life, not only lives lived within a monastery. St. John the Evangelist and Theologian reminds his readers that "if we say that we have no sin, we deceive ourselves, and the truth is not in us" (1 John 1:8). The Greek word for sin is *amartia* and literally means "miss the mark." Sin occurs when we miss the target. Whether the target has been missed by a little or by a lot, the result is still sin in the Orthodox understanding.

This is why, in the prayers before Holy Communion in the Orthodox Church, the believer confesses, "I am the first [among sinners]" (1 Tim. 1:15):

I believe, Lord, and confess, that You are truly the Christ, the Son of the living God, Who came into the world to save sinners, of whom I am the first. . . . Therefore, I pray to You, have mercy on me, and forgive my transgressions, whether voluntary or involuntary, committed in word or deed, knowingly or unwittingly; and make me worthy, without condemnation, to partake in Your pure Mysteries, for remission of sins and for everlasting life. Amen.

44. Cyril of Alexandria, *Commentary on John*, in *The Faith of the Early Fathers*, ed. and trans. William A. Jurgens (Collegeville, MN: Liturgical Press, 1979), 3:220.

45. John D. Zizioulas, *Being as Communion: Studies in Personhood and the Church* (Crestwood, NY: St. Vladimir's Seminary Press, 1985), 81.

The Orthodox Church does not expect sinless perfection of Christians, since God does not expect perfection. The anonymous author of *The Didache* advises Christians, "For if you are able to bear all the yoke of the Lord, you will be perfect; but if you are not able, what you are able that do."[46]

The most common personal prayer of Orthodox Christians is the **Jesus Prayer**. In its longer form, it is "Lord Jesus Christ, Son of God, have mercy on me, a sinner." Fr. Tsichlis calls attention to the fact that since the prayer begins by addressing Jesus as "Lord," "Christ," and "Son of God," it is a prayer of the Spirit, since—as St. Paul writes—"no one can say that Jesus is Lord except by the Holy Spirit" (1 Cor. 12:3). The Jesus Prayer also allows believers to share in the cry of the tax collector in Luke 18:13: "God, be merciful to me a sinner." Fr. Tsichlis sees this prayer as "the first step of the spiritual journey . . . : the recognition of our own sinfulness, our essential estrangement from God and the people around us. The Jesus Prayer is a prayer in which we admit our desperate need of a Saviour."[47]

In his comparison of the Christian East with the Christian West, James Payton recognizes that in "much of Western Christian teaching, sin ends up being presented as the infraction of a set of rules."[48] Eastern Orthodoxy, by contrast, generally does not take a legalistic approach to sin. There are no categories of sin in the Orthodox Church (such as "venial" versus "mortal" sins in Roman Catholicism). While some acts are always sinful (adultery, for example), a sinful act or thought by one person may not be sinful for another. Of course, the Ten Commandments are foundational for the Christian life, but even if no commandment has been broken, sin (in the Orthodox understanding) is not always the doing of wrong. Sin can also be *not* doing what we know to be right: "To him who knows to do good and does not do it, to him it is sin" (James 4:17). Since the purpose of Christian life in Orthodoxy is to grow closer to God, sin is whatever results in greater distance from God.

In Eastern Christianity, sin is less about the breaking of rules and more about the violation of one's personal relationship with God by intentional rebellion against God and turning away from God. "In the Orthodox understanding of what it means to sin, God remains in focus, and human responsibility is therefore all the more crushing."[49] The Eastern Orthodox focus is, therefore, not on the guilt inherited because of the sin of another, but rather on the willful separation from God caused by one's own sin.

46. See full text in the appendix.
47. Fr. Steven Peter Tsichlis, *The Jesus Prayer*, Greek Orthodox Archdiocese of America, 1985, available at https://www.goarch.org/-/the-jesus-prayer.
48. Payton, *Light from the Christian East*, 119.
49. Payton, *Light from the Christian East*, 119.

The Sacrament of Confession and Reconciliation

The prescription for sin is not the same for every person in the Christian East. This is why Orthodox Christians are encouraged to have a spiritual guide, usually (but not always) their parish priest, who is also referred to as a "spiritual father." The spiritual father helps the Orthodox Christian to navigate the struggles of life and helps interpret the root cause of a specific spiritual problem. If he is also a priest, the spiritual father hears the confessions of his spiritual children through the sacrament (or Holy Mystery) of Confession.

The sacrament of Confession is also often called the sacrament of Reconciliation, since it is "a formal act of reconciliation with God in the Church when sin has severed us from the Church's life."[50] According to monastic scholar Mother Melania (Salem), the two main reasons for the sacrament of Confession are "1) reconciliation with God and the church; and 2) help in *staying* reconciled."[51] The second reason is equally important. Just as one who is physically ill often requires expert medical attention, one who is separated from God is spiritually ill and will also require help from an experienced practitioner to seek the remedy.

Orthodox Confession is always face-to-face, typically while standing together in front of the icon of Jesus Christ. Orthodox Christians do not confess *to* the priest, though. Confession is to God in the presence of the priest, who has been given the grace from the Lord to forgive sins: "He breathed on them, and said to them, 'Receive the Holy Spirit. If you forgive the sins of any, they are forgiven them'" (John 20:22–23). The priest will first say something like this example from the Russian Orthodox practice:

> Behold, my child, *Christ stands here invisibly and receives your confession.* Therefore do not be ashamed or afraid; conceal nothing from me, but tell me without hesitation everything that you have done, and so you shall have pardon from Our Lord Jesus Christ. See, His holy icon is before us: and *I am merely a witness*, bearing testimony before Him of all the things which you have to say to me.[52]

The priest will listen to the Confession and may ask questions or offer advice. After confessing, the penitent will kneel or bow the head, and the priest will

---

50. Thomas Hopko, quoted in Mother Melania (Salem), "Why Must I Confess My Sins to a Priest?," in *Re-Introducing Christianity: An Eastern Apologia for a Western Audience*, ed. Amir Azarvan (Eugene, OR: Wipf & Stock, 2016), 157.

51. Mother Melania, "Why Must I Confess My Sins to a Priest?," 156.

52. Quoted in Ware, *Orthodox Church*, 282.

place his stole on the penitent's head. Laying his hand on the stole, the priest reads the prayer of absolution, such as this prayer from the Greek Orthodox practice:

> May God who pardoned David through the prophet Nathan when he confessed his sins, and also Peter when he wept bitterly for his denial, and also the sinful woman weeping at his feet, and the publican as well as the prodigal son, may this same God, through me a sinner, forgive you all things both in this world and in the world to come, and cause you to stand uncondemned before his awesome Judgement Seat. Have no further care for the sins which you have confessed. Depart in peace. May Christ our true God through the prayers of his most holy Mother, and of all the saints, have mercy on us and save us, for he is gracious and loves mankind.[53]

The Orthodox priest is not himself forgiving the sin, but rather acknowledging that it is only God who forgives. The priest is there to bear witness to repentance, forgiveness, and reconciliation on behalf of the community. A Russian priest who is the spiritual father to many once told of the joy he felt at hearing confessions:

> It is not that I am glad anyone has sins to confess but when you come to confession it means these sins are in your past, not your future. Confession marks a turning point and I am the lucky one who gets to watch people making that turn.[54]

Another anecdote is from an Orthodox Christian who wrote out a list of personal sins and brought the list to Confession: "The priest saw the paper in my hand, took it, looked through the list, tore it up, and gave it back to me. That was my confession even though I never said a word! But I felt truly my sins had been torn up and that I was free of them."[55] The feeling of freedom expressed here is a common experience of Orthodox Christians after participating in the sacrament of Reconciliation.

---

53. Quoted in John Anthony McGuckin, *The Orthodox Church: An Introduction to Its History, Doctrine, and Spiritual Culture* (Oxford: Blackwell, 2008), 305.
54. Jim Forest, *Confession: Doorway to Forgiveness* (Maryknoll, NY: Orbis Books, 2012), 120.
55. Forest, *Confession*, 136.

▪ DISCUSSION QUESTIONS ▪

1. What characteristic of Orthodox worship described in this chapter caught your attention?
2. Do you think a fourth-century worship service is able to engage twenty-first-century Christians? Why or why not?
3. How do you understand the Orthodox view that the Eucharist is the "sign of unity" and not the "means to unity"? How is the Eucharist or Lord's Supper understood in your congregation?
4. Discuss the three stages of the spiritual life, in the context of the three sections of the Orthodox sanctuary.

Epilogue

Thus says the LORD:
  "Stand in the ways and see,
  And ask for the old paths, where the good way is,
  And walk in it;
  Then you will find rest for your souls."
                        —Jeremiah 6:16

There is certainly much more to be said about Eastern Orthodox beliefs and practices. For example, very little has been written here about the great cloud of witnesses (Heb. 12:1)—the departed saints whom the Orthodox consider to be very much alive in Christ. Very little has been presented about the personal piety of an Orthodox Christian—daily prayers, meditation, fasting, almsgiving, and so forth. I have intentionally focused on major Eastern Orthodox themes and basic theological ideas, connecting the present-day beliefs of the Orthodox Church to their Apostolic origins through the witness of the early Church Fathers. I believe that many of the Eastern Christian perspectives presented in this book (especially on Christology, Salvation, and the Trinity, as discussed in chaps. 5–7) can be assimilated into the worldview of Western Christians. I pray that this humble and brief opportunity to walk in the "good way" of the "old paths" (Jer. 6:16) of Eastern Orthodox Christianity will indeed offer the reader new insights. While the path may be old, the Holy Spirit always brings fresh perspectives to the Good News of Jesus Christ.

One of the assignments in the Orthodox theology course that inspired this book is to visit an Orthodox Church during the Divine Liturgy and write a reflection. (I have shared a few of my students' actual observations in chap. 8.)

Most of my students have found the Divine Liturgy to be quite different from their own Christian tradition's worship, yet nonetheless fascinating and even countercultural, since many North American Orthodox churches were planted by immigrant communities and still retain their ethnic flavor to some degree. To anyone who is intrigued by the ideas presented in these pages, I recommend visiting an Orthodox Church during worship, so that the ideas can blossom within the liturgical reality from which they originally took root. Despite the Orthodox Church's unbroken historical and eucharistic identity with the Church of the Apostles and its biblically sound apophatic theology, one will be disappointed if one thinks that there is something like an ideal or perfect Orthodox parish. Each congregation has its own unique flaws and experiences all the usual struggles and joys of doing Christian ministry in a fallen, pluralistic world. There is nevertheless something to be said for the beauty of Orthodox liturgical worship and the stability of its teachings.

> May the Lord of peace Himself give you peace always in every way.
> The Lord be with you all. (2 Thess. 3:16)

Appendix

Excerpts from Selected Apostolic and Patristic Writings

Excerpts from the *Epistle of St. Ignatius to the Philadelphians*[1]

Chapter 3. Avoid Schismatics

Keep yourselves from those evil plants which Jesus Christ does not tend, because they are not the planting of the Father. Not that I have found any division among you, but exceeding purity. For as many as are of God and of Jesus Christ are also with the bishop. And as many as shall, in the exercise of repentance, return into the unity of the Church, these, too, shall belong to God, that they may live according to Jesus Christ. Do not err, my brethren. If any man follows him that makes a schism in the Church, he shall not inherit the kingdom of God. If any one walks according to a strange opinion, he agrees not with the passion [of Christ].

Chapter 4. Have but One Eucharist

Take heed, then, to have but one Eucharist. For there is one flesh of our Lord Jesus Christ, and one cup to [show forth] the unity of His blood; one altar; as there is one bishop, along with the presbytery and deacons, my fellow-servants: that so, whatsoever you do, you may do it according to [the will of] God.

---

1. *The Ante-Nicene Fathers*, ed. Alexander Roberts and James Donaldson, 10 vols. (1885–1896; repr., Grand Rapids: Eerdmans, 1950–1951), 1:80–82. See also https://www.newadvent.org/fathers/0108.htm.

Chapter 5. Pray for Me

My brethren, I am greatly enlarged in loving you; and rejoicing exceedingly [over you], I seek to secure your safety. Yet it is not I, but Jesus Christ, for whose sake being bound I fear the more, inasmuch as I am not yet perfect. But your prayer to God shall make me perfect, that I may attain to that portion which through mercy has been allotted me, while I flee to the Gospel as to the flesh of Jesus, and to the apostles as to the presbytery of the Church. And let us also love the prophets, because they too have proclaimed the Gospel, and placed their hope in Him, and waited for Him; in whom also believing, they were saved, through union to Jesus Christ, being holy men, worthy of love and admiration, having had witness borne to them by Jesus Christ, and being reckoned along with [us] in the Gospel of the common hope.

Excerpts from the *Epistle of St. Ignatius to the Smyrnaeans*[2]

Chapter 4. Beware of These Heretics

I give you these instructions, beloved, assured that you also hold the same opinions [as I do]. But I guard you beforehand from those beasts in the shape of men, whom you must not only not receive, but, if it be possible, not even meet with; only you must pray to God for them, if by any means they may be brought to repentance, which, however, will be very difficult. Yet Jesus Christ, who is our true life, has the power of [effecting] this. But if these things were done by our Lord only in appearance, then am I also only in appearance bound. And why have I also surrendered myself to death, to fire, to the sword, to the wild beasts? But, [in fact,] he who is near to the sword is near to God; he that is among the wild beasts is in company with God; provided only he be so in the name of Jesus Christ. I undergo all these things that I may suffer together with Him, He who became a perfect man inwardly strengthening me.

Chapter 5. Their Dangerous Errors

Some ignorantly deny Him, or rather have been denied by Him, being the advocates of death rather than of the truth. These persons neither have the prophets persuaded, nor the law of Moses, nor the Gospel even to this day, nor the sufferings we have individually endured. For they think also the same thing regarding us. For what does any one profit me, if he commends me,

2. *The Ante-Nicene Fathers*, ed. Alexander Roberts and James Donaldson, 10 vols. (1885–1896; repr., Grand Rapids: Eerdmans, 1950–1951), 1:87–90. See also https://www.newadvent.org/fathers/0109.htm.

but blasphemes my Lord, not confessing that He was [truly] possessed of a body? But he who does not acknowledge this, has in fact altogether denied Him, being enveloped in death. I have not, however, thought good to write the names of such persons, inasmuch as they are unbelievers. Yea, far be it from me to make any mention of them, until they repent and return to [a true belief in] Christ's passion, which is our resurrection.

Chapter 6. Unbelievers in the Blood of Christ Shall Be Condemned

Let no man deceive himself. Both the things which are in heaven, and the glorious angels, and rulers, both visible and invisible, if they believe not in the blood of Christ, shall, in consequence, incur condemnation. He that is able to receive it, let him receive it. Let not [high] place puff any one up: for that which is worth all is faith and love, to which nothing is to be preferred. But consider those who are of a different opinion with respect to the grace of Christ which has come unto us, how opposed they are to the will of God. They have no regard for love; no care for the widow, or the orphan, or the oppressed; of the bond, or of the free; of the hungry, or of the thirsty.

Chapter 8. Let Nothing Be Done without the Bishop

See that you all follow the bishop, even as Jesus Christ does the Father, and the presbytery as you would the apostles; and reverence the deacons, as being the institution of God. Let no man do anything connected with the Church without the bishop. Let that be deemed a proper Eucharist, which is [administered] either by the bishop, or by one to whom he has entrusted it. Wherever the bishop shall appear, there let the multitude [of the people] also be; even as, wherever Jesus Christ is, there is the Catholic Church. It is not lawful without the bishop either to baptize or to celebrate a love-feast; but whatsoever he shall approve of, that is also pleasing to God, so that everything that is done may be secure and valid.

Chapter 9. Honor the Bishop

Moreover, it is in accordance with reason that we should return to soberness [of conduct], and, while yet we have opportunity, exercise repentance towards God. It is well to reverence both God and the bishop. He who honors the bishop has been honored by God; he who does anything without the knowledge of the bishop, does [in reality] serve the devil. Let all things, then, abound to you through grace, for you are worthy. You have refreshed me in all things, and Jesus Christ [shall refresh] you. You have loved me when absent as well as when present. May God recompense you, for whose sake, while you endure all things, you shall attain unto Him.

Excerpts from *Against Heresies* 3.3 by St. Irenaeus, Bishop of Lyons[3]

A Refutation of the Heretics, from the Fact That, in the Various Churches, a Perpetual Succession of Bishops Was Kept Up

1. It is within the power of all, therefore, in every Church, who may wish to see the truth, to contemplate clearly the tradition of the apostles manifested throughout the whole world; and we are in a position to reckon up those who were by the apostles instituted bishops in the Churches, and [to demonstrate] the succession of these men to our own times; those who neither taught nor knew of anything like what these [heretics] rave about. For if the apostles had known hidden mysteries, which they were in the habit of imparting to the perfect apart and privily from the rest, they would have delivered them especially to those to whom they were also committing the Churches themselves. For they were desirous that these men should be very perfect and blameless in all things, whom also they were leaving behind as their successors, delivering up their own place of government to these men; which men, if they discharged their functions honestly, would be a great boon [to the Church], but if they should fall away, the direst calamity.

2. Since, however, it would be very tedious, in such a volume as this, to reckon up the successions of all the Churches, we do put to confusion all those who, in whatever manner, whether by an evil self-pleasing, by vainglory, or by blindness and perverse opinion, assemble in unauthorized meetings; [we do this, I say,] by indicating that tradition derived from the apostles, of the very great, the very ancient, and universally known Church founded and organized at Rome by the two most glorious apostles, Peter and Paul; as also [by pointing out] the faith preached to men, which comes down to our time by means of the successions of the bishops. For it is a matter of necessity that every Church should agree with this Church, on account of its preeminent authority, that is, the faithful everywhere, inasmuch as the apostolical tradition has been preserved continuously by those [faithful men] who exist everywhere.

3. The blessed apostles, then, having founded and built up the Church, committed into the hands of Linus the office of the **episcopate**. Of this Linus, Paul makes mention in the Epistles to Timothy. To him succeeded Anacletus; and after him, in the third place from the apostles, Clement was allotted the bishopric. This man, as he had seen the blessed apostles, and had been conversant with them, might be said to have the preaching of the apostles still echoing [in his ears], and their traditions before his eyes. Nor was he alone

3. *The Ante-Nicene Fathers*, ed. Alexander Roberts and James Donaldson, 10 vols. (1885–1896; repr., Grand Rapids: Eerdmans, 1950–1951), 1:415–16. See also https://www.newadvent.org/fathers/0103303.htm.

[in this], for there were many still remaining who had received instructions from the apostles. In the time of this Clement, no small dissension having occurred among the brethren at Corinth, the Church in Rome dispatched a most powerful letter to the Corinthians, exhorting them to peace, renewing their faith, and declaring the tradition which it had lately received from the apostles, proclaiming the one God, omnipotent, the Maker of heaven and earth, the Creator of man, who brought on the deluge, and called Abraham, who led the people from the land of Egypt, spoke with Moses, set forth the law, sent the prophets, and who has prepared fire for the devil and his angels. From this document, whosoever chooses to do so, may learn that He, the Father of our Lord Jesus Christ, was preached by the Churches, and may also understand the apostolic tradition of the Church, since this Epistle is of older date than these men who are now propagating falsehood, and who conjure into existence another god beyond the Creator and the Maker of all existing things. To this Clement there succeeded Evaristus. Alexander followed Evaristus; then, sixth from the apostles, Sixtus was appointed; after him, Telephorus, who was gloriously martyred; then Hyginus; after him, Pius; then after him, Anicetus. Soter having succeeded Anicetus, Eleutherius does now, in the twelfth place from the apostles, hold the inheritance of the episcopate. In this order, and by this succession, the ecclesiastical tradition from the apostles, and the preaching of the truth, have come down to us. And this is most abundant proof that there is one and the same vivifying faith, which has been preserved in the Church from the apostles until now, and handed down in truth.

Full Text of *The Didache: The Lord's Teaching through the Twelve Apostles to the Nations*[4]

Chapter 1. The Two Ways; The First Commandment
There are two ways, one of life and one of death; but a great difference between the two ways. The way of life, then, is this: First, you shall love God who made you; second, your neighbor as yourself; and all things whatsoever you would should not occur to you, do not also do to another. And of these sayings the teaching is this: Bless those who curse you, and pray for your enemies, and fast for those who persecute you. For what reward is there, if you love those who love you? Do not also the Gentiles do the same? But love those who hate you, and you shall not have an enemy. Abstain from fleshly

4. *The Ante-Nicene Fathers*, ed. Alexander Roberts and James Donaldson, 10 vols. (1885–1896; repr., Grand Rapids: Eerdmans, 1950–1951), 7:377–82. See also https://www.newadvent.org/fathers/0714.htm.

and worldly lusts. If someone gives you a blow upon your right cheek, turn to him the other also, and you shall be perfect. If someone impresses you for one mile, go with him two. If someone takes away your cloak, give him also your coat. If someone takes from you what is yours, ask it not back, for indeed you are not able. Give to every one that asks you, and ask it not back; for the Father wills that to all should be given of our own blessings (free gifts). Happy is he that gives according to the commandment; for he is guiltless. Woe to him that receives; for if one having need receives, he is guiltless; but he that receives not having need, shall pay the penalty, why he received and for what, and, coming into straits (confinement), he shall be examined concerning the things which he has done, and he shall not escape thence until he pay back the last farthing. But also now concerning this, it has been said, Let your alms sweat in your hands, until you know to whom you should give.

Chapter 2. The Second Commandment: Gross Sin Forbidden
And the second commandment of the Teaching; You shall not commit murder, you shall not commit adultery, you shall not commit pederasty, you shall not commit fornication, you shall not steal, you shall not practice magic, you shall not practice witchcraft, you shall not murder a child by abortion nor kill that which is begotten. You shall not covet the things of your neighbor, you shall not forswear yourself, you shall not bear false witness, you shall not speak evil, you shall bear no grudge. You shall not be double-minded nor double-tongued; for to be double-tongued is a snare of death. Your speech shall not be false, nor empty, but fulfilled by deed. You shall not be covetous, nor rapacious, nor a hypocrite, nor evil disposed, nor haughty. You shall not take evil counsel against your neighbor. You shall not hate any man; but some you shall reprove, and concerning some you shall pray, and some you shall love more than your own life.

Chapter 3. Other Sins Forbidden
My child, flee from every evil thing, and from every likeness of it. Be not prone to anger, for anger leads the way to murder; neither jealous, nor quarrelsome, nor of hot temper; for out of all these murders are engendered. My child, be not a lustful one; for lust leads the way to fornication; neither a filthy talker, nor of lofty eye; for out of all these adulteries are engendered. My child, be not an observer of omens, since it leads the way to idolatry; neither an enchanter, nor an astrologer, nor a purifier, nor be willing to look at these things; for out of all these idolatry is engendered. My child, be not a liar, since a lie leads the way to theft; neither money-loving, nor vainglorious, for out of all these thefts are engendered. My child, be not a murmurer, since

it leads the way to blasphemy; neither self-willed nor evil-minded, for out of all these blasphemies are engendered. But be meek, since the meek shall inherit the earth. Be long-suffering and pitiful and guileless and gentle and good and always trembling at the words which you have heard. You shall not exalt yourself, nor give over-confidence to your soul. Your soul shall not be joined with lofty ones, but with just and lowly ones shall it have its intercourse. The workings that befall you receive as good, knowing that apart from God nothing comes to pass.

Chapter 4. Various Precepts

My child, him that speaks to you the word of God remember night and day; and you shall honor him as the Lord; for in the place whence lordly rule is uttered, there is the Lord. And you shall seek out day by day the faces of the saints, in order that you may rest upon their words. You shall not long for division, but shall bring those who contend to peace. You shall judge righteously, you shall not respect persons in reproving for transgressions. You shall not be undecided whether it shall be or no. Be not a stretcher forth of the hands to receive and a drawer of them back to give. If you have anything, through your hands you shall give ransom for your sins. You shall not hesitate to give, nor murmur when you give; for you shall know who is the good repayer of the hire. You shall not turn away from him that is in want, but you shall share all things with your brother, and shall not say that they are your own; for if you are partakers in that which is immortal, how much more in things which are mortal? You shall not remove your hand from your son or from your daughter, but from their youth shall teach them the fear of God. You shall not enjoin anything in your bitterness upon your bondman or maidservant, who hope in the same God, lest ever they shall fear not God who is over both; for he comes not to call according to the outward appearance, but unto them whom the Spirit has prepared. And you bondmen shall be subject to your masters as to a type of God, in modesty and fear. You shall hate all hypocrisy and everything which is not pleasing to the Lord. Forsake in no way the commandments of the Lord; but you shall keep what you have received, neither adding thereto nor taking away therefrom. In the church you shall acknowledge your transgressions, and you shall not come near for your prayer with an evil conscience. This is the way of life.

Chapter 5. The Way of Death

And the way of death is this: First of all it is evil and full of curse: murders, adulteries, lusts, fornications, thefts, idolatries, magic arts, witchcrafts, rapines, false witnessings, hypocrisies, double-heartedness, deceit, haughtiness, depravity, self-will, greediness, filthy talking, jealousy, over-confidence, lofti-ness, boastfulness; persecutors of the good, hating truth, loving a lie, not knowing a reward for righteousness, not cleaving to good nor to righteous judgment, watching not for that which is good, but for that which is evil; from whom meekness and endurance are far, loving vanities, pursuing re-quital, not pitying a poor man, not laboring for the afflicted, not knowing Him that made them, murderers of children, destroyers of the handiwork of God, turning away from him that is in want, afflicting him that is distressed, advocates of the rich, lawless judges of the poor, utter sinners. Be delivered, children, from all these.

Chapter 6. Against False Teachers, and Food Offered to Idols
See that no one cause you to err from this way of the Teaching, since apart from God it teaches you. For if you are able to bear all the yoke of the Lord, you will be perfect; but if you are not able, what you are able that do. And concerning food, bear what you are able; but against that which is sacrificed to idols be exceedingly on your guard; for it is the service of dead gods.

Chapter 7. Concerning Baptism
And concerning baptism, baptize this way: Having first said all these things, baptize into the name of the Father, and of the Son, and of the Holy Spirit, in living water. But if you have not living water, baptize into other water; and if you can not in cold, in warm. But if you have not either, pour out water thrice upon the head into the name of Father and Son and Holy Spirit. But before the baptism let the baptizer fast, and the baptized, and whatever others can; but you shall order the baptized to fast one or two days before.

Chapter 8. Concerning Fasting and Prayer (the Lord's Prayer)
But let not your fasts be with the hypocrites; for they fast on the second and fifth day of the week; but fast on the fourth day and the Preparation (Friday). Neither pray as the hypocrites; but as the Lord commanded in His Gospel, thus pray: Our Father who art in heaven, hallowed be Your name. Your king-dom come. Your will be done, as in heaven, so on earth. Give us today our daily (needful) bread, and forgive us our debt as we also forgive our debtors. And bring us not into temptation, but deliver us from the evil one (or, evil); for Yours is the power and the glory forever. Thrice in the day thus pray.

Chapter 9. The Thanksgiving (Eucharist)
Now concerning the Thanksgiving (Eucharist), thus give thanks. First, con-cerning the cup: We thank you, our Father, for the holy vine of David Your

servant, which You made known to us through Jesus Your Servant; to You be the glory forever. And concerning the broken bread: We thank You, our Father, for the life and knowledge which You made known to us through Jesus Your Servant; to You be the glory forever. Even as this broken bread was scattered over the hills, and was gathered together and became one, so let Your Church be gathered together from the ends of the earth into Your kingdom; for Yours is the glory and the power through Jesus Christ forever. But let no one eat or drink of your Thanksgiving (Eucharist), but they who have been baptized into the name of the Lord; for concerning this also the Lord has said, Give not that which is holy to the dogs.

Chapter 10. Prayer after Communion

But after you are filled, thus give thanks: We thank You, holy Father, for Your holy name which You caused to tabernacle in our hearts, and for the knowledge and faith and immortality, which You made known to us through Jesus Your Servant; to You be the glory forever. You, Master almighty, created all things for Your name's sake; You gave food and drink to men for enjoyment, that they might give thanks to You; but to us You freely gave spiritual food and drink and life eternal through Your Servant. Before all things we thank You that You are mighty; to You be the glory forever. Remember, Lord, Your Church, to deliver it from all evil and to make it perfect in Your love, and gather it from the four winds, sanctified for Your kingdom which You have prepared for it; for Yours is the power and the glory forever. Let grace come, and let this world pass away. Hosanna to the God (Son) of David! If anyone is holy, let him come; if anyone is not so, let him repent. Maran atha. Amen. But permit the prophets to make Thanksgiving as much as they desire.

Chapter 11. Concerning Teachers, Apostles, and Prophets

Whosoever, therefore, comes and teaches you all these things that have been said before, receive him. But if the teacher himself turn and teach another doctrine to the destruction of this, hear him not; but if he teach so as to increase righteousness and the knowledge of the Lord, receive him as the Lord. But concerning the apostles and prophets, according to the decree of the Gospel, thus do. Let every apostle that comes to you be received as the Lord. But he shall not remain except one day; but if there be need, also the next; but if he remain three days, he is a false prophet. And when the apostle goes away, let him take nothing but bread until he lodges; but if he ask money, he is a false prophet. And every prophet that speaks in the Spirit you shall neither try nor judge; for every sin shall be forgiven, but this sin shall not be forgiven. But not everyone that speaks in the Spirit is a prophet; but only if he hold the ways of the Lord. Therefore from their ways shall the false prophet and the prophet be known. And every prophet who orders a meal in the Spirit eats not from it, except indeed he be a false prophet; and every prophet who teaches the truth, if he do not what he teaches, is a false prophet. And every prophet, proved true, working unto the mystery of the Church in the world, yet not teaching others to do what he himself does, shall not be judged among you, for with God he has his judgment; for so did also the ancient prophets. But whoever says in the Spirit, Give me money, or something else, you shall not listen to him; but if he says to you to give for others' sake who are in need, let no one judge him.

Chapter 12. Reception of Christians

But let everyone that comes in the name of the Lord be received, and afterward you shall prove and know him; for you shall have understanding right and left. If he who comes is a wayfarer, assist him as far as you are able; but he shall not remain with you, except for two or three days, if need be. But if he wills to abide with you, being an artisan, let him work and eat; but if he has no trade, according to your understanding see to it that, as a Christian, he shall not live with you idle. But if he wills not to do, he is a Christ-monger. Watch that you keep aloof from such.

Chapter 13. Support of Prophets

But every true prophet that wills to abide among you is worthy of his support. So also a true teacher is himself worthy, as the workman, of his support. Every first-fruit, therefore, of the products of wine-press and threshing-floor, of oxen and of sheep, you shall take and give to the prophets, for they are your high priests. But if you have not a prophet, give it to the poor. If you make a batch of dough, take the first-fruit and give according to the commandment. So also when you open a jar of wine or of oil, take the first-fruit and give it to the prophets; and of money (silver) and clothing and every possession, take the first-fruit, as it may seem good to you, and give according to the commandment.

Chapter 14. Christian Assembly on the Lord's Day

But every Lord's day gather yourselves together, and break bread, and give thanksgiving after having confessed your transgressions, that your sacrifice may be pure. But let no one that is at variance with his fellow come together with you, until they be reconciled, that your sacrifice may not be profaned. For this is that which was spoken by the Lord: In every place and time offer to me a pure sacrifice; for I am a great King, says the Lord, and my name is wonderful among the nations.

Chapter 15. Bishops and Deacons; Christian Reproof
Therefore, appoint for yourselves bishops and deacons worthy of the Lord, men meek, and not lovers of money, and truthful and proven; for they also render to you the service of prophets and teachers. Despise them not therefore, for they are your honored ones, together with the prophets and teachers. And reprove one another, not in anger, but in peace, as you have it in the Gospel but to every one that acts amiss against another, let no one speak, nor let him hear anything from you until he repents. But your prayers and alms and all your deeds so do, as you have it in the Gospel of our Lord.

Chapter 16. Watchfulness; The Coming of the Lord
Watch for your life's sake. Let not your lamps be quenched, nor your loins unloosed; but be ready, for you know not the hour in which our Lord comes. But often shall you come together, seeking the things which are befitting to your souls: for the whole time of your faith will not profit you, if you be not made perfect in the last time. For in the last days false prophets and corrupters shall be multiplied, and the sheep shall be turned into wolves, and love shall be turned into hate; for when lawlessness increases, they shall hate and persecute and betray one another, and then shall appear the world-deceiver as the Son of God, and shall do signs and wonders, and the earth shall be delivered into his hands, and he shall do iniquitous things which have never yet come to pass since the beginning. Then shall the creation of men come into the fire of trial, and many shall be made to stumble and shall perish; but they that endure in their faith shall be saved from under the curse itself. And then shall appear the signs of the truth; first, the sign of an outspreading in heaven; then the sign of the sound of the trumpet; and the third, the resurrection of the dead; yet not of all, but as it is said: The Lord shall come and all His saints with Him. Then shall the world see the Lord coming upon the clouds of heaven.

Glossary of Orthodox Terms

Adoptionism: The **heresy** that Jesus was born human but was somehow thereafter adopted into the divine Godhead—for example, at His Baptism, Resurrection, or Ascension.

altar: The area in the front of the physical Orthodox sanctuary or **temple**, most often on the east end, separated from the congregation by the icon screen. The term also refers specifically to the altar table, on which is contained the Holy Gospel Book and other articles blessed for exclusive use in liturgical worship.

anathema: A biblical Greek word that refers to a curse or an exclusion, such as for teaching **heresy** or denying the truths of the Christian Faith (Rom. 9:3; 1 Cor. 12:3; 16:22; Gal. 1:8–9).

ancestral sin: The falling away from God described in Genesis 3, which separated humankind from communion with God and resulted in an unnatural condition that led to our mortality. Other terms (such as "primal curse") are also used in Orthodox writings to refer to "the Fall." Jesus Christ has reversed the primal curse of humanity by His death and Resurrection, and Christians can be liberated from the curse through **Baptism** and the **Holy Mysteries** of the Church.

Annunciation: The "announcement" by the Archangel Gabriel to the Virgin Mary that she had been chosen to be the Mother of God (Luke 1:26–33). The Orthodox Great Feast of the Annunciation is celebrated on March 25, exactly nine months before Christmas.

antichrist (Greek: "opposed to Christ" or "instead of Christ"): Anyone who willfully worships something "instead of Christ"—instead of the true God. The word "antichrist" is found in the Bible in two of the letters of

St. John the Evangelist (1 John 2:18, 22; 4:3; 2 John 1:7). John refers to false teachers, spirits of deception, and anyone who "does not confess that Jesus Christ has come in the flesh" (1 John 4:3) as "antichrist" or "antichrists." John says that many antichrists have come (1 John 2:18) leading people astray to follow that which is not the true God.

apocrypha (Greek: "hidden" or "secret"): Writings that may not be authoritative because, for example, they arose from unknown or questionable sources. Some English Bible translations published by Protestants refer to ten books of the **Septuagint** Old Testament as the "Apocrypha," mainly because they were not present in the Hebrew text that the Reformers chose for their canon. However, these ten Old Testament writings have long been considered by the Orthodox Church to be canonical Scripture. They include 2 Ezra (Esdras), Tobit, Judith, Wisdom of Solomon, Wisdom of Sirach, Baruch, Epistle of Jeremiah, and 1–3 Maccabees.

apophatic theology (Greek: *apo*, "away, from," and *phasis*, "statement"): The theological attitude of the Eastern Orthodox that is always mindful of the limits of finite human reasoning and language to understand or describe the infinite God. Also referred to as "the way of unknowing," apophatic theology maintains a mystical approach to theology, avoiding propositional statements about God in order to avoid limiting God by human concepts.

Arianism: The false teaching of a fourth-century presbyter, Arius, that Jesus was not divine, since human logic suggests that a father must precede his son. The First **Ecumenical Council** held at Nicaea in 325 was called explicitly to discuss this challenge to Orthodox teachings about Christ. The 318 **bishops** who attended the council declared Arianism to be **heresy** and proclaimed that Christ shares the same divine essence as His Father and that Christ is coeternal with His Father.

ascetic (Greek: *askēsis*, "athlete"): Having to do with spiritual exercises such as fasting, meditation, prayer, and self-denial, which are motivated by the love of God and undertaken in order to fight temptation and grow spiritually. As a noun, "ascetic" refers to anyone who has committed himself or herself to a life of ascetic practices. Monks and nuns, especially, have committed themselves to a monastic life of asceticism that includes celibacy.

autocephalous (Greek: "self-headed"): Describes an Orthodox church in a particular locale (a country or continent, for example) that is self-governed and enjoys administrative independence, including the election or appointment of its presiding hierarch.

Baptism (Greek: *baptizō*, "to be submerged"): The **Holy Mystery** (sacrament) of initiation by which one is born again by water and the spirit (John 3:5) and joined to Jesus Christ and to His Church. Baptism in the Orthodox Church is by threefold immersion in the name of the Father and of the Son and of the Holy Spirit (Matt. 28:19) and precedes **Chrismation**. Baptism is also called **Holy Illumination**.

Beatitude (Latin: *beati*, "supreme blessedness"): One of the nine blessings Christ offers in His Sermon on the Mount (Matt. 5:3–12).

bishop (Greek: *episkopos*, "overseer"): A leader whose primary role is to oversee the celebration of the **Eucharist** and to guard the Faith and preserve unity and community within the geographical area that he oversees. Since the sixth century, bishops in the Orthodox Church have been either single men or widowers and have been admitted to the **monastic** ranks.

Byzantine Empire: The Eastern Roman Empire, whose capital was established in Constantinople (now Istanbul) by Constantine the Great in AD 331. The Byzantine Empire was one of the greatest civilizations in history and one of the earliest Christian states. It was a dynamic center of culture and religious thought until 1453, when it was invaded and conquered by the army of the Ottoman Turks.

canon (Greek: *kanōn*, "rule" or "straight"): A biblical word mentioned in Philippians 3:16 and Galatians 6:16. "Canon" is most commonly associated with the books that the Church has determined to be the written Word of God. The term also describes the rules and decrees issued by the early Church (Acts 15:23–29) and by the **Ecumenical Councils** and some local councils, as well as the teaching of individual **Church Fathers**, such as St. Basil the Great. "Canon" also refers to a set of hymns that make up a part of Orthodox worship, such as the Canon of Orthros (Matins).

cataphatic: A positive conception about God that uses words, symbols, or ideas. A cataphatic expression focuses on what we can definitely know about God, such as "God is good" or "God is almighty."

catechumen: One who is preparing by prayer, fasting, and instruction over a period of time to receive **Holy Illumination** (**Baptism**). In the early Church, the catechumenate period could last from one to three years.

catholic (Greek: *katholou*, "according to the whole"): For the Orthodox, "catholic" describes both the universality of the Gospel message and the fullness of Christ in His Body, the Church.

Chrismation: The **Holy Mystery** (sacrament) of anointing, which usually follows **Baptism**. Chrismation imparts to the candidate the "seal of the gift of the Holy Spirit," enabling the candidate to follow Christ throughout his or her life as a disciple. The counterpart in the New Testament is the "laying on of hands" by one of the Apostles after Baptism (Acts 8:14–19). The nearest counterpart in Western Christian traditions is Confirmation, which often follows a course of catechetical instruction. Unlike in the practice of Confirmation in the West, there is no academic component in the practice of Orthodox Chrismation, since it is considered to be a free gift of the Holy Spirit and is normally bestowed in conjunction with Baptism.

Christ (Greek: *christos*, "the anointed one"): The Messiah (which is Hebrew for "the anointed one"). Jesus Christ is the anointed one of God, anointed by the Holy Spirit by the will of the Father. This term indicates that both the Father and the Spirit actively participate in the ministry of Jesus. Christians are named *Christians* because those who are "in Christ" participate through Christ in the divine life of the **Trinity**, and are also anointed by the Holy Spirit in **Baptism** and **Chrismation**.

Church Father: A formal title given to a **bishop** or teacher in the ancient Christian world who not only exhibited wise and correct (orthodox) teaching but also a holiness of life. Not every ancient Christian author is a Church Father. The designation "Church Father" also means that the bishop's writings are trustworthy and beneficial.

communion (Greek: *koinōnia*): The combination of English "common" and "union," suggesting an intimate closeness. Christians enjoy communion with God and with each other in the Church, especially through the Holy **Eucharist** (see John 6:56; 1 Cor. 10:16–17), which is called "Holy Communion." The Church is also an **icon** of the communion of the Holy **Trinity**—the mystery of unity in diversity.

conciliar: "Conciliar" means that decisions on doctrinal, moral, and liturgical questions are made in a council or synod under the guidance of the Holy Spirit. The Jerusalem Council of Acts 15 is an example of conciliar decision-making, specifically because the Apostles, the elders, and all the faithful gathered in "one accord" and called on the Holy Spirit to guide them to agreement. The seven **Ecumenical Councils** are held in high regard in the Orthodox Holy **Tradition** because of the conciliar nature of their proceedings in the Holy Spirit, and because their decisions and doctrinal statements have been recognized by the entire Church as being authoritative.

Confession: The **Holy Mystery** (or sacrament) of repentance, forgiveness, and reconciliation. Jesus Christ breathed on the Apostles to receive the Holy Spirit in order for them to forgive and retain sins (John 20:22–23).

creed (Latin: *credo*, "I believe"): A confession of faith or a statement of belief. The New Testament records early statements of faith used by the Apostolic Church (1 Cor. 15:3–8; Eph. 5:14; 1 Tim. 3:16; 2 Tim. 2:11–13). The **bishops** of the First and Second **Ecumenical Councils** (at Nicaea in AD 325 and Constantinople in 381) developed the Creed that has been proclaimed by Orthodox Christians in liturgical worship and in personal prayers since the fourth century.

deacon (Greek: *diakonos*, "server"): A person who serves in one of the three orders of ordained ministry in the Orthodox Church (deacon, **presbyter**, and **bishop**). The diaconate was established in the first generation of Christianity, as expressed in Acts 6:1–5. Deacons may offer the consecrated **Eucharist** to the congregation but may not themselves celebrate the **Holy Mysteries** (sacraments). The Orthodox Church has also maintained a long history of female deacons following the first-century deacon Phoebe, mentioned by St. Paul in his letter to the Romans. Although ordaining women to the diaconate is not prohibited for any theological reason, it has fallen out of contemporary practice in the Orthodox Church.

deify, deification: *See* **theosis.**

Divine Liturgy (Greek: *leitourgia*, "the work of the people"): The main worship service of the Orthodox Church at which the **Eucharist** is celebrated.

Docetism (Greek: *dokein*, "to seem/appear"): The collective term for false teachings (such as Eutychianism) asserting that Jesus Christ only appeared to be human, having only a divine nature. The **Ecumenical Councils** at Ephesus (AD 431) and Chalcedon (451) declared Docetism to be a **heresy**.

doctrine: A scriptural teaching or principle, such as the teaching of Christ (2 John 9) or the teaching of the Apostles (Acts 2:42). A doctrine is not merely an idea—it is a way of life. The life of the Christian believer is governed by a set of beliefs and foundational teachings of the Christian Faith.

dogma: A teaching or **doctrine** with ecumenical or **conciliar** status. Dogmas are essential beliefs of the Christian Faith that have been received and accepted by the entire Church, such as the dogmatic declarations of the seven **Ecumenical Councils.** For example, the Holy **Trinity** and the Incarnation of the Son of God are dogmas of the Orthodox Church. Like "doctrine," "dogma" does not refer merely to ideology or abstract concepts. The Christian life is a life lived in Christ, Who is "the way, the truth, and the life" (John 14:6). Dogma reveals truth and communicates how life in Christ to be lived out in the Church.

doxology (Greek: *doxa*, "glory," and *logoi*, "words"): The act of giving glory to God. A doxology is also a type of liturgical hymn directed to the **Trinity**, beginning with the words "Glory to . . ."

ecclesial (Greek: *ekklēsia*, "church" or "assembly"): Referring to a church setting.

Ecumenical Council: A worldwide assembly of **bishops**, convened under the guidance of the Holy Spirit in order to settle administrative or doctrinal disputes, and subsequently recognized as having declared authoritative dogma for the entire Church. The main intention of the Seven Ecumenical Councils was to avoid theological error, not to establish a criterion of truth external to the Spirit of truth (John 15:26; 16:13). A council must be accepted by the entire Church to be considered "ecumenical" by the Orthodox Church. The seven councils accepted as ecumenical by the Orthodox Church are Nicaea I (AD 325), Constantinople I (381), Ephesus (431), Chalcedon (451), Constantinople II (553), Constantinople III (680–681), and Nicaea II (787).

episcopacy/episcopate: The order of **bishops** in the Church, the successors of the Apostles.

eschatology: The theology pertaining to the last things (Greek: *eschaton*), such as the Second Coming of Christ, the Final Judgment, the revelation of the eternal Kingdom of God, and the renewal of creation.

Eucharist (Greek: *evcharistia*, "thanksgiving"): The principal **Holy Mystery** of the Orthodox Church and the center and goal of the Church's life. The Eucharist (also called Holy **Communion**) is celebrated at the Divine Liturgy, in which the Church gathers to celebrate the mystery of Christ's life, death, and Resurrection and to receive the true Body and Blood of Jesus Christ for the remission of sins and unto eternal life.

Filioque (Latin: "and the Son"): A phrase added unilaterally to the Niceno-Constantinopolitan **Creed** by the churches under Roman governance in order to state that the Holy Spirit proceeds both from the Father and from the Son. The Orthodox consider the theology of this belief to be in error on the basis of Jesus's statement that the Holy Spirit proceeds from the Father (John 15:26). It has also been opposed by the Orthodox on the basis of the breach of conciliarity, since neither a local council nor a **bishop** can supersede the declarations of an **Ecumenical Council**.

free will: The capacity to make one's own choices—specifically, to choose between good and evil—and the freedom to turn toward (or away from) God. According to Orthodox teaching, free will is active in human beings since the **image of God** has not been destroyed.

Gnosticism (Greek: *gnōsis*, "knowledge"): A broad category of heretical teachings holding that Jesus gave secret knowledge to only a select few who handed down their secret knowledge to a select few in the next generation. Gnostics also usually believe that all matter is corrupt, thus denying the scriptural witness that God became human, died, and resurrected bodily. The Church has always taught that matter is good, because God created it and said that it was good (Gen. 1:31), and that Jesus Christ is not only fully God but also fully human (John 1; 1 John 1).

Good Friday: Also known in the Orthodox Church as "Great and Holy Friday," the day on which the death and burial of Jesus Christ is commemorated in the Orthodox Church.

Gospel: Literally "good news" (Greek: *evangelion*). For example, "Repent, and believe in the gospel" (Mark 1:15). The life of the Church is centered in the Good News that Jesus Christ is God incarnate, Who dwells among His people, the Church, through the power of the Holy Spirit. The Book of the Gospels is enthroned upon the altar table in all Orthodox temples, representing that the centrality of the Orthodox Christian Faith is the Gospel of Jesus Christ.

grace: A gift of the uncreated glory of God, according to the Orthodox understanding. Grace is the life and power that flows from God eternally and cannot be earned. An experience of the grace of God is a direct experience of God—a **communion** in the divine nature (2 Pet. 1:4).

Great Lent: The forty days of preparation before **Holy Week**.

Hades: The Greek equivalent to the Hebrew *Sheol*, which in Scripture is the place of the dead. The Orthodox **icon** of the Resurrection shows Christ liberating the dead imprisoned in Hades, having bound the Evil One in chains (1 Pet. 3:18–20).

heresy (Greek: *airesis*, "to choose"): An intentional decision to deviate from a core **dogma** of the Christian Faith in favor of one's own insights, even when faced with a preponderance of evidence that the resulting belief is a false teaching (Matt. 7:15; 2 Pet. 2:1).

Holy Illumination: A term in Orthodoxy, as in the early Church, for the **Holy Mystery** of **Baptism**. In Baptism, the Light (Illumination) of Christ is received through the Holy Spirit. The image of God is restored and renewed, and the believer is freed from the darkness of sin.

Holy Mysteries (Greek: *agia mysteria*): In Scripture, *mysterion* refers to the ways of God that are being fully revealed and yet transcend human reason (Mark 4:11). Therefore, in that sense, everything in the Church is a "mystery." The Orthodox use the term "Holy Mysteries" to refer to the sacraments of the Church. There is no official number of sacraments in the Orthodox Church, since the entire Christian life is to be lived mystically and sacramentally; yet there are seven main Holy Mysteries: **Holy Illumination** (**Baptism**), **Chrismation** (Confirmation), Holy **Eucharist** (Holy **Communion**), **Confession** (Reconciliation), **Holy Orders** (ordination), Holy Matrimony (marriage), and Holy **Unction** (healing of soul and body). Other rites of the Orthodox Church that may be considered sacramental include the Blessing of Waters on Theophany, monastic tonsure, and the funeral service.

Holy Orders: The sacrament or **Holy Mystery** of ordination into the ranks of clergy in the Orthodox Church. The three orders of clerical ministry are **deacon, presbyter** (priest), and **bishop.**

Holy Week: The week in which the Church liturgically commemorates the passion of Christ before His glorious Resurrection on **Pascha** Sunday.

icon (Greek: *eikōn*, "true image"): A visual portrayal of Jesus Christ or a saint, or of a biblical event in the life of Christ. Icons are usually created with egg tempera paint on wood or with glass mosaic. Orthodox Christians venerate the Holy Icons but do not worship them, since worship is offered only to God. The Seventh **Ecumenical Council** declared that Holy Icons should be honored in the same way as the four Gospels, since both are witnesses to the truth of the Gospel message and there is a complete correspondence between the verbal message of the Gospels and the visual image of the Holy Icons.

idol: A statue or other image of a nonexistent deity; a false god. An idol is actually anything that is worshiped instead of, or more than, the true God.

image of God (Greek: *eikōn tou theou*, "**icon** of God"): The designation ascribed only to human creation that asserts a potential similitude to, and participation in, the divine life. According to Genesis 1:26–27, human beings were created in the image of God according to the likeness of God. The Orthodox Church teaches that although the image of God has become tarnished by sin, it has not been destroyed. By His Incarnation, Jesus Christ restored the image of God, thus enabling human nature to be returned to its original beauty. The image of God is renewed through **Baptism** by the grace of the Holy Spirit (2 Cor. 3:18).

incarnate (Latin: to be "en-fleshed" or "in-fleshed"): Having taken on flesh. In the Incarnation, the Son of God took on flesh and became fully human, yet remained fully God.

incense: An aromatic plant substance, dried and burned in honor of God. God commanded Moses to make incense from myrrh, frankincense, and other aromatics and to burn it as an offering to the Lord in the holy of holies (Exod. 30:34–38). Malachi the prophet declares that even the Gentiles will offer incense in God's name (Mal. 1:11). Incense accompanies the prayers of the saints being lifted up (Ps. 141:2 [140:2 **Septuagint**]; Rev. 5:8; 8:4). It is still used in the context of Orthodox worship today.

intercession: Praying to God on behalf of another person. Jesus prays to His Father for us (Rom. 8:34). Christians often intercede in prayer for one another. Orthodox Christians believe that the departed righteous saints are still alive in Christ (John 11:25–26) and thus may intercede in prayer to Christ for the faithful on earth.

Jesus Prayer: A short, simple prayer repeated often by Orthodox Christians to focus the mind on Christ and as a way of praying without ceasing (1 Thess. 5:17). The text of the Jesus Prayer is "Lord Jesus Christ, Son of God, have mercy on me [a sinner]."

Kingdom of God: The coming of Jesus **Christ** inaugurated God's Kingdom on earth, which is now present to the faithful through His Church. The Orthodox **Divine Liturgy** opens with "Blessed is the Kingdom of the Father and of the Son and of the Holy Spirit, both now and forever and to the ages of ages. Amen," testifying to the Orthodox understanding of eucharistic worship as a participation in the eternal Kingdom of God. Jesus Christ will return again to usher in the fullness of God's Kingdom (Rev. 12:10).

koinōnia: *See* **communion.**

laity: Believers who are not clergy (i.e., who have not been ordained into **Holy Orders**). All Orthodox Christians are ordained by **Baptism** into the royal priesthood of all believers, however (1 Pet. 2:5).

Magnificat (Latin: "it magnifies"): The biblical hymn sung in honor of the Virgin Mary—for example, during **Matins**. The word is taken from the first words exclaimed by Mary (in Latin) when she visited St. Elizabeth, the mother of John the Baptist, after Mary had been visited by the Archangel Gabriel (Luke 1:46–55): "My soul magnifies the Lord."

martyr (Greek: *martyria,* "witness"): A person who has voluntarily suffered death as a witness to Jesus Christ.

Matins: The morning prayer service of the Orthodox Church that usually precedes the **Divine Liturgy.**

monk/monastic (Greek: *monachos;* fem. *monachi*): The root of "monk/monastic" is the Greek word *monos,* which means "solitary" or "alone." Monastics, whether monks (male) or nuns (female), are those who have committed themselves to a life of prayer, fasting, poverty, celibacy, and obedience. Monastics may live in isolation or in monastic communities.

ontology: The philosophical study that deals with being itself, or "being *qua* being." "Ontological" is a term applied to divine and human personhood. An ontological category would not include "added" attributes such as gender, vocation, title, or status.

paradox: That which is true but does not make sense in the realm of human logic. Examples include how God can be one and three, and how a virgin could give birth.

Pascha (Greek for "Passover"): The Orthodox term for Easter, the Resurrection of Christ. Pascha is the "Feast of Feasts" and the focus of the Orthodox Christian life. The Jews who were enslaved in Egypt were told to mark their doors with the blood of the Passover lamb, and were thus delivered from death (Exod. 12:12–13). Jesus Christ is the pure Lamb of God whose blood on the Cross allows us to pass from death to life (1 Cor. 5:7–8). Orthodox Christians celebrate Pascha after the Jewish Passover has begun, and thus Pascha can be one or more weeks after the Roman Catholic and Protestant Easter.

patristics (Greek: *patēr*, "father"): The study of the theological teachings and witness of the early **Church Fathers**.

Pentecost: The Orthodox Christian Great Feast that commemorates the descent of the Holy Spirit on the Apostles fifty days after the Resurrection of Christ (Acts 2). The event of Pentecost is considered to be the formal inauguration of the Church by the Holy Spirit.

pneumatological: From the Greek for "spirit" (*pneuma*), "pneumatological" refers to a theological emphasis upon the Holy Spirit.

presbyter (Greek: *presvyteros*, "elder"): One who participates in one of the three orders of the ordained ministry of the Church: **deacon**, presbyter, and **bishop**. A presbyter is usually called a "priest" in English. Every presbyter serves under the supervision of a bishop.

priest: *See* **presbyter**.

primal curse: *See* **ancestral sin**.

repentance (Greek: *metanoia*, "change of mind" or "change of attitude"): A sorrowful recognition of one's sinful behavior that results in a turning away from that behavior and toward a life of righteousness in Christ.

Resurrection: Rising from the dead. Jesus Christ conquered death by His own death and Resurrection, and made the Resurrection to new and eternal life possible for all.

sacramental: The Orthodox Church is sacramental, not only because it celebrates certain sacraments but also because the life of an Orthodox Christian is defined and nourished by participation in the sacraments, or **Holy Mysteries.** Thus, "sacramental" defines what the Orthodox Church *is*, not only what the Church does.

sacraments: *See* **Holy Mysteries.**

saint(s): Scripture refers to all faithful believers as "saints" (e.g., Eph 4:12), and thus, in one sense, all members of the Church are saints. The term is also used in the Orthodox Church to refer to particular persons who have exemplified in their lives what it means to follow Christ with complete devotion. The Orthodox Church does not create saints, however; rather, it acknowledges those whom God has already set apart as being worthy of honor.

schism (Greek: *schisma*, "to tear"): A formal separation from the one Church. Many early **Church Fathers** (such as Cyprian of Carthage) believed that schism was worse than **heresy**, since the Body of Christ cannot be divided or torn in two. The "Great Schism" of 1054 separated the Christian East from the Christian West.

Septuagint: An ancient Greek translation of the Hebrew Bible from between the third and first centuries BC. The Septuagint is the primary Old Testament text cited by the writers of the New Testament.

starets: A spiritual guide—a spiritual father or mother.

synergy: Human and divine cooperation in the process of salvation.

temple: The physical Orthodox building (also referred to as a "sanctuary") where the faithful gather for worship.

theologoumenon: A pious teaching or idea that may or may not be accurate, and thus should not be taught as a **dogma** or official **doctrine**.

Theophany (Greek: *theofaneia*, "appearance or manifestation of God"): A manifestation or appearance of God. The Bible is filled with theophanies, including Exodus 3:1–4:17 and Isaiah 6:1–8. The Great Feast of Theophany in the Orthodox Church (also called "Epiphany") commemorates the appearance of the Holy Trinity at the Baptism of Jesus Christ in the river Jordan (Mark 1:9–11; Luke 3:21–22). The Orthodox Church celebrates the Baptism of Christ twelve days after Christmas.

theosis (Greek: "union with God"): The term used by the Orthodox to describe salvation as the transformative process of sharing in the divine nature (2 Pet. 1:4). Theosis is the lifelong process of **synergistic** cooperation between the Christian and God, in order to conform the Christian's life to the likeness of Christ.

Theotokos (Greek: "God-bearer"): A term used by the Orthodox to refer to Mary, the Mother of God. The term "Theotokos" became a point of debate during the Christological controversies of the fifth century about the two natures of Christ. It was concluded at the Council of Ephesus (AD 431) that since Mary's son is fully human and fully God, it is proper to refer to her as the bearer of God, or Theotokos.

Thrice-Holy Hymn (Greek: *trisagion*): A hymn and prayers based on the hymn of the angels heard by Isaiah the Prophet ("Holy, holy, holy is the LORD of hosts," Isa. 6:3) and John the Evangelist and Theologian (Rev. 4:8) at the heavenly throne of Christ. The threefold use of "holy" refers to the Holy **Trinity**.

Tradition: In one important sense, Tradition is the handing down or transmission of the Apostolic teaching from one person to the next, or from one generation to the next (2 Thess. 2:15; 3:6; 1 Cor. 11:2). However, the Orthodox understanding of Holy Tradition concerns not only the content—the teaching that was handed down—but also the context: the Church being guided "into all truth" (John 16:13) by the Holy Spirit throughout the ages.

Trinity: The Holy Trinity was revealed at the **Baptism** of Jesus Christ in the river Jordan (Matt. 3:13–17) when the Father spoke and the Spirit alighted on the Son. Jesus Christ instructed His disciples to baptize in the name "of the Father and of the Son and of the Holy Spirit" (Matt. 28:19). Orthodox Christians believe that God is a **communion** of persons, a Trinity in unity: one essence, three persons, undivided and inseparable.

troparion: A hymn that summarizes succinctly a feast or the life of a saint of the Church being commemorated.

Unction: One of the **Holy Mysteries** of the Orthodox Church. Holy Unction is the anointing with blessed oil for spiritual and physical healing (Mark 6:13; James 5:14–15). The sacrament of Holy Unction is offered to the Orthodox at a special service during **Holy Week**, and may be offered to one who is ill at any time during the year.

venerate: To venerate is to offer honor or deep respect. Veneration is not the same as worship, which is offered only to God. The Orthodox venerate Holy Icons and the Book of the Gospels (usually with a bow or a kiss) for the Truth of Christ that they convey, and venerate with praise and honor the Virgin Mary and other saints, with a sense of delight for what God has done in and through them.

Vespers: The evening prayer service in the Orthodox Church.

Index

Adam, 100, 103–7
Adoptionism, 81, 114, 128, 179
Against Heresies (Irenaeus), 74,
    83–84, 115, 170–71
agios ("not of the world"), 38, 146
Alexandria, 92–93
Anastasios of Albania (archbishop),
    150
anathema, 87, 91–92, 131, 153n27,
    179
ancestral sin, 103, 105, 179
Andrew (apostle), 71
Annunciation, 120, 179
Anselm, 14, 117–19
antichrist, 78, 81, 179–80
antidoron, 115n52
Antioch, 92–93
Apocrypha, 55–56, 79, 180
Apollinarianism, 93
Apollinaris, 93
apophatic theology, 24–25, 166, 180
Apostles. *See* Andrew; James; John
    "the Theologian" and Evangelist;
    Paul; Peter; Thomas
apostolicity, 10, 39–40, 74

Apostolic succession, 35, 71–75
Apostolic Tradition, 10, 34, 74, 150,
    171
Apostolic Tradition (Hippolytus),
    142, 156n35
Aquinas, Thomas, 15, 24n36
Arian controversy, 82, 88–92
Arianism, 4, 89, 91–92, 180
Arius, 88, 89, 130
Armenian Genocide, 4n2
ascetic/asceticism, 23, 58, 180
Athanasius of Alexandria, 43, 54,
    89–90, 92–93, 114, 120, 130
atonement, Western models of, 121
  penal substitution, 118
  satisfaction, 14, 118
Augsburg Confession, 12
Augustine, 103, 103n14, 104, 111,
    134, 135

"Ballad of East and West, The"
    (Kipling), 13
Baptism. *See* Holy Mysteries: Bap-
    tism (Holy Illumination)
Barnabas, 45, 141

Bartholomew, Patriarch, 62, 66, 147, 150
Basil the Great, 57, 69, 130–32, 134, 142
Beatitudes, 51, 181
Behr, John, 87–88
Bellah, Robert, 79
Benedict VIII (pope), 136
Bible
  Divine Liturgy text from, 53, 145
  "icons" can never contradict, 50
  as many reflections of the Word, 57
  preeminence belonging to, 49
  read in all Orthodox worship services, 52
  regarded as an image, 57
bishop. See *episkopos*
Body of Christ, 30–31, 33, 35, 38, 64, 72–73, 85, 91, 97, 101, 133, 137–38, 153, 155–57, 159
"branch theory" (Palmer), 32n6
Brown, Dan, 92
Brüning, Alfons, 100
Bruno, Giordano, 26n43
Bultmann, Rudolf, 16–17
Byzantine Empire, 89, 92, 181

Calvin, John, 32, 104, 118, 121
Campus Crusade for Christ, 7, 142–43
canon (*kanōn*), 55, 181
Cappadocian Fathers. See Basil the Great; Gregory of Nazianzus (the Theologian); Gregory of Nyssa
Carlton, Clark, 47
cataphatic theology, 25, 181
catechumens, 154, 181

celibacy
  of a bishop, 69n28
  Rome's introduction of celibate priesthood, 10
Chrismation (Confirmation). See Holy Mysteries: Chrismation
Christology, 77, 80–83, 88–96, 98
Christotokos ("Christ-bearer"), 94
Chrysostom, John, 37, 52–53, 69, 93, 142, 148
Church, the
  as Christ's Body on earth, 34
  constituted by people called out from the world, 31
  constituted by the celebration of the Eucharist, 73
  as an earthly heaven, 142n1
  established by Jesus upon the Faith of the Apostles, 53
  as an icon of the Trinity, 137–38
  identifying features of, 38
  Jesus Christ as the "chief cornerstone" of, 36
  in the New Testament, 30–33
  Orthodox view of, 35
church authority, differing perceptions of, 136
Church Fathers. See *individual names*
Clapsis, Fr. Emmanuel, 100
Clement of Alexandria, 114n46
Clement of Rome, 54, 171
communion (*koinōnia*), 20, 42, 133, 182
  communion with God, 64, 105
  in the Eucharist, 156, 159
  "of the Holy Spirit," 45
  Scripture as an event of, 53
conciliarity, 44–46, 66, 91, 137

Confession (Reconciliation). *See* Holy Mysteries: Confession (Reconciliation)

Confirmation. *See* Holy Mysteries: Chrismation

Coniaris, Fr. Anthony, 58

Constantine (emperor), 69n30, 88–89, 181

Copernicus, 26

Council of Chalcedon. *See* Ecumenical Councils: Fourth (Chalcedon)

Council of Ephesus. *See* Ecumenical Councils: Third (Ephesus)

Council of Trent, 104, 153

Cur Deus Homo (Anselm), 118

Cyril of Alexandria, 93, 94, 114, 159

Cyril of Jerusalem, 65, 157–58

Da Vinci Code, The (Brown), 92

deacon, 67, 69, 183, 186, 188

deification, 114. See also *Theosis*

De perfectione (Gregory of Nyssa), 112

Diadochos of Photiki, 101

diakonos. *See* deacon

Didache, The, 67, 142, 160, 171–77

Divine Liturgy
defined, 183
as different from other Christian traditions' worship, 166
"entering into" the eternal heavenly worship, 42
"heaven on earth," 42, 146
Matins preceding, 187
opening of, 142, 187
as retaining elements of Christianity's Jewish roots, 144
text taken directly from the Bible, 53, 145
whole community participating in, 141–42

Docetism/Docetists, 80–81, 183

doxa ("belief, glory"), 1, 184

doxology, 96, 184

Dragas, Fr. George, 155

East and West, dichotomies between, 13–17

Ebionites, 81

Ecumenical Councils
First (Nicaea I), 4n3, 27, 37–38, 91–92, 180
Second (Constantinople I), 4n3, 134, 183
Third (Ephesus), 4n3, 94–96, 183, 184, 190
Fourth (Chalcedon), 4n3, 95, 96, 136n33, 183, 184
Fifth (Constantinople II), 4n3, 97, 184
Sixth (Constantinople III), 4n3, 184
Seventh (Nicaea II), 4n3, 57–59, 184

Ecumenical Patriarch, role of, 66

Educating Icon, The (Vrame), 57

eikōn, 51–52, 56, 59, 137, 186

ekklēsia ("assembly, church"), 30–31

Ekklēsia tou Theou ("the Church of God"), 31, 35

elder. See *presvyteros*

Eleutherius, 74

Elijah (prophet), 116n54

Enlightenment, 16, 17, 82

Ephrem the Syrian, 56

episcopacy/episcopate, 170, 184
episkopos ("bishop, overseer"),
  67–68, 181
*Epistle of St. Ignatius to the Phila-
  delphians*, 167–68
*Epistle of St. Ignatius to the Smyr-
  naeans*, 39, 68, 73, 168–70
Eucharist. *See* Holy Mysteries:
  Holy Eucharist
Eutyches, 93, 97
Eutychianism, 93, 95
Evagrius of Ponticus, 22
evcharistia ("thanksgiving"), 156,
  184
Evdokimov, Paul, 105
Eve, 103, 105, 106
Expulsion from Paradise, 106–7

Fairbairn, Donald, 63
"Fall, the," 12, 103–6, 179
Farley, Fr. Lawrence, 28
feasts
  Annunciation, 120, 179
  Pascha (Easter), 19, 122–23, 154,
    186, 188
  Pentecost (Descent of the Holy
    Spirit), 19
  Theophany (Baptism of the Lord),
    115–16, 186, 189
Festal Letter (Athanasius), 43
Filioque ("and the Son"), 10, 134–
  37, 184
Fifth Theological Oration (Gregory
  of Nazianzus), 133
First Apology (Justin Martyr),
  129–30, 142
Florovsky, Fr. Georges, 48, 77,
  122–23
Francis (pope), 11n9

Galileo, 26
Gillquist, Peter, 7, 142–43
gnōsis ("knowledge"), 81, 83, 185
Gnosticism/Gnostics, 4, 27, 74,
  80–85, 87, 185
Good Friday. *See* Great and Holy
  Friday
Great and Holy Friday, 121–22, 125,
  185
"Great Blessing of Water," 116
Great Commission, of Christ, 39,
  129
Great Lent, 111n37, 154, 185
Great Schism of 1054, 10, 44, 135–
  36, 189
Greek Old Testament. *See*
  Septuagint
Gregory I, 15
Gregory of Nazianzus (the Theolo-
  gian), 23, 93–94, 114, 122, 130,
  131, 133, 153–54, 156
Gregory of Nyssa, 24–25, 89, 102,
  105, 112, 130, 138, 158
Gregory Palamas, 101–2

Habits of the Heart (Bellah), 79
Hades, 106, 185
Hagia Sophia, 4n2, 10, 21
Hanegraaff, Hank, 9
Harrison, Sister Nonna, 56
Hatzidakis, Fr. Emmanuel, 156
Helen (mother of Constantine),
  69n30
heresy, 87. *See also* Adoptionism;
  Apollinarianism; Arianism;
  Docetism/Docetists; Ebionites;
  Eutychianism; Gnosticism/Gnos-
  tics; Monarchianism; Monophy-
  sitism; Nestorianism; Pneuma-
  tomachians; Sabellianism

Hippolytus, 114n46, 142, 156
holy
    as *agios* in Greek, 38
    Church as, 38
Holy Communion. *See* Holy Mysteries: Holy Eucharist
Holy Icons, 57–59, 149, 186. See also *eikōn*
Holy Mysteries (sacraments)
    Baptism (Holy Illumination), 21, 38n21, 45, 67, 72, 81, 84, 109, 113, 126, 128, 143, 153–56, 158
    Chrismation, 153–56, 158, 181–82, 186
    Confession (Reconciliation), 153, 159–62, 182, 186
    Holy Eucharist, 10–11, 18, 30, 35, 38, 40, 68, 70–73, 115, 115n52, 147, 149, 152–53, 155–59
    Holy Matrimony, 14, 153, 186
    Holy Orders, 67, 72, 153, 186, 187
    Holy Unction, 153, 186, 190
Holy Spirit
    Filioque controversy and double procession of, 134–36
    life of in the Church, 48–49
    prayer to, 133
Holy Tradition, 46–52, 59, 63, 74, 150, 190
Holy Week, 109–10, 185, 186, 190
homoousios ("same essence"), 95, 130
Hopko, Fr. Thomas, 34, 138
Household of God, The (Newbigin), 5–6, 10
Humbert of Rome (cardinal), 10
hymns, 96, 97, 107, 126, 144
    "Akathist Hymn, The," 111
    Fos Ilaron ("O Joyful Light"), 134
    "Giver of Life," 106

"Great Blessing of Water," 116
    for the Great Feast of Pentecost, 19
"Hymn of the Cherubim," 147–48
"Hymn of the Evening, The," 96, 97
"Hymn of Justinian," 97
"Magnificat," 110, 187
Matins Hymn (Sunday of the Prodigal Son), 119
Orthodox Resurrectional Hymn, 78
Paschal Troparion, 123
Thrice-Holy Hymn, 126, 147, 190
Troparion of the Great Martyr Paraskevè (Paraskevi) of Rome, 145
Troparion of St. Phoebe the Deacon, 70
Troparion of St. Vladimir, 21
hypostasis/hypostases, 92, 95, 131, 134n28, 138
"hypostatic union," 94, 95, 122

icon. See *eikōn*
iconographer, 58–59
Ignatius of Antioch, 39, 54, 67, 68, 73–74, 167–70
    Epistle of St. Ignatius to the Philadelphians, 167–68
    Epistle of St. Ignatius to the Smyrnaeans, 39, 68, 73, 168–70
    Letter to the Trallians, 73
image of God, 51, 90, 100, 102, 104n17, 184, 186
Incarnation
    of Christ as essential, 120
    defined, 186
    of the eternal Word, the Logos, 78

as key to understanding Orthodox
Holy Icons, 58
Scripture supporting, 129
indulgences, 11, 11n9
Introduction to Liturgical Theology
(Schmemann), 143
Irenaeus of Lyons, 54, 74, 77n2,
81n8, 83–85, 87, 101, 105, 108,
114–15, 130, 170–71
Isaac the Syrian, 20
Isaiah (prophet), 24, 108, 147–48

James (apostle), 45, 71, 142
Jehovah's Witnesses, 82
Jeremiah (prophet), 64, 165
Jeremias II (patriarch), 12
Jerome, 77n2
Jerusalem Council, 44–46, 182
Jesus Prayer, 160, 187
John of Damascus, 4–5, 24, 56, 101,
114–15
John "the Theologian" and Evange-
list, 23, 78, 81, 87, 127, 159
Justinian (emperor), 4n2, 97, 131
Justin Martyr, 38n21, 129–30, 142,
158

Kariatlis, Philip, 37
Kärkkäinen, Veli-Matti, 125–26
Kavanagh, Fr. Aidan, 22
Kelly, J. N. D., 39
Khomiakov, Alexei, 33, 63, 64
Kipling, Rudyard, 13
Knight, Christopher, 27
koinōnia. See communion

Latin Vulgate translation, 103n14
Lent. *See* Great Lent

Letter to the Smyrnaeans (Ignatius),
39, 73
Letter to the Trallians (Ignatius), 73
Lewis, C. S., 134–35
lex orandi, lex credendi ("worship
establishes belief"), 22, 134
Light from the Christian East (Pay-
ton), 8
Light from the East (Nesteruk), 28
liturgy (*leitourgia*), 62, 141
Logos (Christ as "Word"), 22, 54,
59, 77–79, 77n2, 81, 93–95, 97–98
"Logos theology," 77–78
Lord's Prayer, 174
Lossky, Vladimir, 25, 27–28, 34,
48–50, 83, 119
Luther, Martin, 10–11, 15, 47n7,
104, 110, 113, 118

Marcian (emperor), 95
marks of the Church, 2
Mary Magdalene, 69n30
Masoretic Text, 55, 118n57
Matins (*Orthros*), 54, 106, 118–19,
181, 187
Maximus the Confessor, 66, 101
Meyendorff, Fr. John, 49, 102,
103n14, 106
Mitchell, Joni, 106
Moltmann, Jürgen, 117
Monarchianism
"Dynamic," 128–29
"Modalist," 128
Monophysitism, 93, 95
Moody, Rev. Dwight A., 150–51
Moses, 20, 22, 25, 51–52, 59, 79,
155n32
Mother Melania (Salem), 161
mysterion ("mystery"), 152–53, 185

Nektarios, 70
Nesteruk, Alexei, 28
Nestorianism, 93, 95
Nestorius, 93–94, 97–98
Newbigin, Lesslie, 5–6
New Earth, A (Tolle), 85
Nicene Council/Fathers, 39, 91–92.
　See also Ecumenical Councils:
　First (Nicaea I)
Nicene Creed, 2, 38, 107, 127
Niceno-Constantinopolitan Creed,
　49, 184
Nicholas I (pope), 136

Olympia (deacon), 69
On the Incarnation (Athanasius),
　90, 120
On the Other Side of Oddville
　(Moody), 151
open hermeneutic of the Orthodox
　Church, 27
ordained ministry, orders of, 183
ordination, 69–72
orthodoxia ("proper belief/wor-
　ship"), 1
Orthros. See Matins
ousia (existence or essence of God),
　131, 134
Ouspensky, Leonid, 58

Palmer, William, 32n6, 63
Pantocrator (icon), 147
paradosis ("tradition"), 47–48
Paraskevè of Rome, 145
Pascha, 19, 122–23, 154, 186, 188
Paul (apostle), 10, 24, 31, 45, 52–53,
　69, 80, 87–88, 102, 112, 115, 121,
　141, 153, 155–56, 160
Payton, James, 8–9, 13, 29–30, 48,
　50, 57, 64, 79, 88, 95, 160

Pelikan, Jaroslav, 9, 11, 15, 50, 151
Pentecost, 9, 15, 18–20, 125, 133,
　154–55, 188
Peter (apostle), 18–19, 31–32,
　35–37, 45, 53, 62, 65, 71, 73–74,
　87–88, 155
Petros ("rock"), 36
Philostorgius, 89
Phoebe, 69–70, 183
Photini, 69n30
Pius IX (pope), 62, 111
Pius X (pope), 62n3
Plato, 81
Pneumatomachians ("Spirit fight-
　ers"), 98, 133
Polycarp of Smyrna, 54
presvyteros ("elder"), 67–68, 188
Prosforo ("offering"), 115n52
Protestant Reformation/Reformers,
　5, 9, 11–12, 17, 44, 47, 56, 63,
　104, 118
Protos (God the Father), 129, 137
Pulcheria (empress), 95
purgatory, 11, 11nn9–10, 14

Reimarus, H. S., 16
Roman Catholic Catechism, 104
Roman Catholic Church, 9–10,
　11n9, 26, 34, 73
Roman Catholicism, 9–10, 12–15,
　17, 20, 26, 35, 41, 61, 63, 160
Roman Inquisition, 26
Roman See, 65
royal priesthood of Christ, ordina-
　tion into, 155
royal vocation of all people,
　62–65
rule of truth, 83–85, 88, 129
Russia, Christianization of, 20–22

Sabellianism, 128–29
Sabellius, 128
sacraments. *See* Holy Mysteries
sacramentum (oath of allegiance), 152
Saliba, Metropolitan Philip, 7
salvation
  beginning in the Incarnation, 120
  being saved, 112–13
  as a cooperative effort between the human person and God, 110
  as a free gift, 108
  as a healing and renewal of human nature, 106
  as a process, 101, 108
  themes, 117
sanctuary, 148, 179. *See also* temple
Schmemann, Fr. Alexander, 8, 103, 143, 146, 155
Scholasticism, 17, 26, 157
Schweitzer, Albert, 16
Second Vatican Council, 61, 136
Sees
  in the one, undivided Church, 10
  original five ancient, 10
Septuagint, 51, 55–56, 59, 100, 118n57, 180, 187, 189
Seraphim of Sarov, 132
"Sheilaism," 79, 83
Shema, 128
Shepherd of Hermas, The, 67
Silouan of Mount Athos, 23
sola Scriptura, 61, 63
Sparks, Jack, 142
Spirit of Eastern Christendom, The (Pelikan), 11
Stăniloae, Dumitru, 25
starets, 132, 189
Stavropoulos, Fr. Christoforos, 102

Stylianopoulos, Fr. Theodore, 36, 55
Summa Theologiae (Aquinas), 15
Swinburne, Richard, 102
Symeon the New Theologian, 23
synergy, 59, 110–12, 146, 189

taxis (hierarchy) and ordering of the Trinity, 129
temple, 54, 179, 189
Ten Commandments, 160
Tertullian, 128, 128n9, 130, 149, 152
Tetragrammaton, 59
theandric mystery, 33–34, 36
Thekla, 69n30
Theodotus, 128
theologia ("theology"), 1, 15, 22–24, 149
theologoumena/theologoumenon, 2, 13, 17, 135, 189
Theophilos of Antioch, 128n9
Theos (God), 22, 33
Theosis, 114, 189
Theotokos. *See* Virgin Mary: as Theotokos
Thomas (apostle), 71
Thomas Aquinas, 15, 24n36
Tolle, Eckhart, 85
Tradition. *See* Holy Tradition
trinitas ("threeness"), 128, 128n9
Tsagalakis, Fr. Tom, 59
Tsichlis, Fr. Steven, 65, 152, 160
Tyson, Neil deGrasse, 86

Ugolnik, Fr. Anthony, 56–57
Unction. *See* Holy Mysteries: Holy Unction

Unitarianism, 129
United States Catholic Catechism for Adults, 36
"The Unity of the Church as Koinonia: Gift and Calling" (World Council of Churches), 42

Vespers, 96–97, 107, 190
Virgin Mary, 65, 81, 129
  Immaculate Conception of (Roman Catholic doctrine), 111
  as Mother of God, 95, 110
  as Theotokos ("God-bearer"), 92, 94–95, 97–98, 110–11
Vladimir (prince of Kiev), 20–22
Vrame, Fr. Anton, 57, 109

Ware, Metropolitan Kallistos, 13, 15, 32, 49, 53, 65, 69, 102, 108, 114, 121, 125, 130, 132–33, 135, 137–38
Way, The (Carlton), 47
Winfrey, Oprah, 85
Word of God (*Logos*), 22, 54, 77–78, 90, 95
World Council of Churches (WCC), 8, 42, 126

Young, Frances, 95–96
Young Earth creationism, 17, 26

Zernov, Nicholas, 43
Zizioulas, Metropolitan John, 18, 42, 66, 72, 86, 100, 157